ENERGY AUTONOMY

ENERGY AUTONOMY

The economic, social and technological case for renewable energy

Hermann Scheer

EARTHSCAN

London • Sterling, VA

First published by Earthscan in the UK and USA in 2007

Copyright © Verlag Antje Kuntsmann GmbH, München, 2005

Originally published in German as *Energieautonomie: Eine Neue Politik für Erneuerbare Energien*

Translated by Jeremiah M. Riemer

ISBN-13:   978-1-84407-355-9
ISBN-10:   1-84407-355-6

Typeset by MapSet Ltd, Gateshead, UK
Printed and bound in the UK by Bath Press
Cover design by Andrew Corbett

For a full list of publications please contact:

Earthscan
8–12 Camden High Street
London, NW1 0JH, UK
Tel: +44 (0)20 7387 8558
Fax: +44 (0)20 7387 8998
Email: earthinfo@earthscan.co.uk
Web: www.earthscan.co.uk

22883 Quicksilver Drive, Sterling, VA 20166-2012, USA

Earthscan is an imprint of James and James (Science Publishers) Ltd and publishes in association with the International Institute for Environment and Development

A catalogue record for this book is available from the British Library

Library of Congress Cataloging-in-Publication Data

Scheer, Hermann, 1944-
  Energy autonomy : the economic, social and technological case for renewable energy / Hermann Scheer.
      p. cm.
  ISBN-13: 978-1-84407-355-9 (hardback)
  ISBN-10: 1-84407-355-6 (hardback)
  1. Renewable energy sources. 2. Energy policy. 3. Energy industries—Political aspects. I. Title.
  TJ163.2.S33 2007
  333.79'4—dc22
                                                                     2006021877

Mixed Sources
Product group from well-managed forests and other controlled sources
www.fsc.org Cert no. SGS-COC-2121
© 1996 Forest Stewardship Council

FSC

Contents

List of Tables

List of Acronyms and Abbreviations

ACORE	American Council on Renewable Energy
BDI	Bundesverband der Deutschen Industrie (Federation of German Industries)
CDM	Clean Development Mechanism
CFC	chlorofluorocarbon
CHP	combined heat and power
CSD	Commission on Sustainable Development
CSP	concentrating solar power
DOE	Designated Operational Entity
ECOSOC	Economic and Social Council of the UN
EdF	Electricité de France
EEG	Erneuerbare-Energien-Gesetz (Renewable Energy Sources Act)
ESA	European Space Agency
EURATOM	European Atomic Energy Community
FAO	Food and Agriculture Organization of the United Nations
FAZ	*Frankfurter Allgemeine Zeitung*
GATT	General Agreement on Tariffs and Trade
GNP	gross national product
HTR	high temperature reactor
IAEA	International Atomic Energy Agency
IEA	International Energy Agency
IMF	International Monetary Fund
IPCC	Intergovernmental Panel on Climate Change
IPHE	International Partnership for the Hydrogen Economy
IRENA	International Renewable Energy Agency
ISO	International Organization for Standardization
JI	Joint Implementation
JREC	Johannesburg Renewable Energy Coalition

LNG	liquid natural gas
NGO	non-governmental organization
NICE	Nuclear Information Committee Europe
NPT	Nuclear Non-Proliferation Treaty
OECD	Organisation for Economic Co-operation and Development
OPEC	Organization of the Petroleum Exporting Countries
OPURE	Open University for Renewable Energies
PV	photovoltaic
PV-GAP	Photovoltaic Global Accreditation Programme
R&D	research and development
RECS	Renewable Energy Certification System
RFF	Resources for the Future
ROC	Renewable Obligation Certificate
RPS	Renewable Energy Portfolio Standard
SEI	Strategic Environment Initiative
START	Strategic Arms Reduction Treaty
TEHG	Treibhausgas-Emissionshandelsgesetz (Greenhouse Gas Emissions Trading Law)
toe	tons of oil equivalent
UN	United Nations
UNDP	United Nations Development Programme
UNEP	United Nations Environment Programme
UNESCO	United Nations Education, Scientific and Cultural Organization
UNIDO	United Nations Industrial Development Organization
VDMA	Verband der deutschen Maschinen- und Anlagenindustrie (German Engineering Federation)
WCRE	World Council for Renewable Energy
WEC	World Energy Conference
WHO	World Health Organization
WSSD	World Summit on Sustainable Development
WTO	World Trade Organization
WWF	World Wide Fund for Nature

Introduction

Renewable Energy: The Deceptive Global Consensus

The method of physics is only of concern to physicists, its impact concerns everyone. What concerns everyone is something only all of us can solve.
                    Friedrich Dürrenmatt, *The Physicists*[1]

It seemed as if the new global consensus on renewable energy had been sealed. Early in June 2004, delegates from 154 national governments to the international conference, Renewables 2004, had converged on the city of Bonn, where they passed a 'Political Declaration' and an 'Action Program'. They had been invited there by Gerhard Schroeder in 2002, when the German Chancellor delivered his speech to the UN World Summit on Sustainable Development in Johannesburg. The fact that one of the three largest industrial countries in the world economy had seized this initiative seemed to signal a long-overdue recognition of renewable energy as a grand political theme. A sense of euphoria suffused and enveloped the more than 4000 participants in this cluster of meetings: now nobody can stop the global onset of renewable energy. Germany's Environment Minister Juergen Trittin declared: 'The age of renewable energy has begun'.

Optimism is a psychological drive conducive to motivating oneself and others. Yet it all too easily tempts people into auto-suggestion, clouds their view of contrary developments, and lulls them into a false sense of security. In fact, current growth rates for fossil energy usage remain significantly higher than growth rates for renewable energy resources in active use. In 1990, according to the International Energy Agency,[2] global consumption of fossil energy resources (petroleum, coal, natural gas) came to 5.63 billion (5,630,000,000) metric 'tons of oil equivalents' (the metric 'toe' is the conventional international unit of measurement for all forms of energy); in 2002 it was already 8.13 billion tons, which corresponds to an increase of 44 per cent in just 12 years. In 2003 and 2004, two years for which global statistics are still incomplete, we can expect the figures to show additional growth in the consumption of fossil fuels. Ten global conferences on the politics of climate protection that took place between 1995 and 2002 have not been able to change a single thing about this development; the world's fossil energy consumption grew more rapidly than ever before. In the same period, the share of renewable energy increased from 1.04 to 1.38 billion metric toe, in other words, by 33 per cent. The difference between the use of fossil and renewable energy expanded in just 12 years from 4.59 to 6.74 billion tons. Only when the employment of both fossil and atomic energy actually and irreversibly shrinks in favour of renewable energy will the age of renewable energy have commenced.

Even now that the internationally celebrated Kyoto Protocol on global climate protection has come into force (on 16 February 2005), this disastrous trend is not being reversed. Although the Intergovernmental Panel on Climate Change (IPCC), the official circle of scientific experts advising global climate conferences, regards a 60 per cent reduction of greenhouse gases by 2050 against the base year of 1990 as urgent, the Protocol obligates the industrial countries who are signatories to reduce no more than 5 per cent annually until 2012. But since the US, whose 5 per cent of the world's population consumes 25 per cent of the fossil energy supply, rejects this obligation, and since the developing countries are exempt (including the major growth societies of China and India, who jointly make up a third of the world's population), greenhouse gas emissions are still going to rise sharply even if the Kyoto Protocol were to be implemented (which remains a dubious prospect).

These numbers reveal how the world is heading at breakneck speed towards a debacle. But they also reveal how badly the 'fire brigade' of renewable energy is limping behind this alarming development – because it is so poorly equipped, with trucks that are too slow and a shortage of fire-fighting personnel and hoses. Initiatives for renewable energy lack the radical dynamism needed to match actual dangers. If an immediate and comprehensive shift towards renewable energy is going to take place, additional time is too precious to be squandered.

The clock for the traditional energy system keeps ticking louder. Yet the influence of the established energy corporations has actually grown, and their profound disregard for renewable energy has barely changed. Currently they are mobilizing on an international scale for a 'renaissance' in nuclear energy and for exhausting fossil energy reserves down to their last dregs. The energy corporations seem to be acting in line with that sarcastic remark made by the Polish satirist Stanislav Lec: 'It's true that we're on the wrong track, but we're compensating for this shortcoming by accelerating'. Even Renewables 2004 has not produced any change in the trend. In order to avoid jeopardizing the semblance of a new global consensus, nobody wanted to acknowledge that, in spite of all the rhetorical lip service, there has only been fragmentary progress in overcoming resistance to renewable energy. For the most part, the resistance persists, and to some extent it is even on the rise.

That resistance was signalled in exemplary fashion by two international conferences that took place after Renewables 2004 and that attracted considerably more attention in the international media. Both conferences aimed at a massive 'roll-on' for nuclear and fossil energy and a roll-back of renewable energy. Early in the summer of 2004, the international nuclear community convened in Moscow under the slogan 'Fifty Years of Nuclear Power – the Next Fifty Years'. At this conference the International Atomic Energy Agency declared that there would be twice as many nuclear power plants by 2030 – and four times as many by 2050 – as today. Later that summer, the World Energy Conference (WEC – which represents nuclear and fossil fuel power business internationally) convened in Sydney, Australia. It conveyed the message that there was no way to avoid increasing fossil energy consumption by 85 per cent by 2050, and that nuclear energy would have to be ranked higher in the future than any variety of renewable energy, which by the same date would only be able to contribute at most 10 per cent of world energy supplies (in other words, less than today). The Sydney Conference based its predictions on the *World Energy Outlook 2004*[3] of the International Energy Agency (IEA), an organization of the OECD countries. The IEA mentions US$16 trillion of essential energy investments between 2001 and 2030, in other words, US$550 billion annually, which would have to flow overwhelmingly into the provision of fossil energy.

In the international discussion about energy, there is a greater tendency for the year 2004 to symbolize a worldwide attempt at giving nuclear energy the chance to make a comeback than for that year to signal a breakthrough to renewable energy. To be sure, UK Prime Minister Tony Blair broadcast a video at the Renewables 2004 conference in which he waxed enthusiastic about renewable energy and displayed a determination to lower energy emissions in his country 60 per cent by the year 2050. Environmental organizations worldwide rewarded him with applause but overlooked that Blair was banking more on the expansion of nuclear energy than on renewable energy. Meanwhile, even the internationally renowned ecologist James Lovelock – in a spectacular article in the UK newspaper *The Independent*[4] headlined 'Nuclear energy is the only green solution' – has become a prominent witness for the prosecution advocating a massive expansion of nuclear energy, ostensibly because this would be the only way to avert the threat of global climate change. Although the Commission of the European Union is also not lacking in rhetoric favourable to renewable energy, in practice it has intensively renewed its nuclear orientation. According to a proposal of the EU Commission, the budget for the EURATOM authority, which is under the Commission's purview, is meant to be nearly tripled, and in December 2004 the EU concluded a comprehensive nuclear treaty with China. The Turkish government has promised France that it will order three nuclear reactors with a total capacity of 4500 megawatts; rumour has it that this was done in return for French support of Turkish EU membership. Even at the level of the G8 (the club of the major Western economic powers plus Russia, which was added to this circle in the 1990s), coordinated action on behalf of nuclear energy is on the agenda. This is something President Bush announced in a speech at the National Small Business Conference on 27 April 2005.[5] That the Bush initiative has a good prospect of success within the circle of the G8 can be seen not only by Blair's vote, but also on the basis of the pro-nuclear priorities of the French, Russian and Japanese governments. The parties in opposition to Chancellor Schroeder's ruling coalition in Germany likewise announced that, if there is a change of government in Berlin, they would cancel the 2001 decision to phase out nuclear energy and attempt to end the so-called 'overstrain' of renewable energy.

Every action provokes a counteraction, yet many advocates of renewable energy are unable either to perceive or take seriously how the forces opposing renewable energy within the established energy system have been fortifying their international line-up. By no means have those decades-long conflicts over energy become pointless all of a sudden. For the stakes in the shift to renewable energy involve nothing less than the most thorough and far-reaching structural change since the beginning of the Industrial Revolution. Only the naive can believe that this change can be achieved without friction and in agreement with the institutions responsible for traditional energy supplies, or even on the basis of common values. The 'energy business' complex is, after all, the largest and politically most influential sector in the world economy. Its resistance to renewable energy will grow to the same degree as the mobilization of the latter has progressed, to the point where renewable energy can not only supplement the supply of nuclear and fossil energy but actually start replacing non-renewable energy.

Unstoppable onset or danger of relapse?

In every discussion about energy, displaying sympathy for renewable energy has become a matter of good form. But this says nothing about the value actually placed on renewable energy: is it in first, second or third place, or is this just a hypocritical priority? For with every increase in the number of those seriously advocating renewable energy, there is a parallel rise in the amount of lip service and excuses, which is why, all too frequently, words are not followed by deeds. At the same time, never before has there been such a persuasive case justifying a new energy option. Never has a new energy technology been illuminated down to the last detail, so that sceptical questions can be answered and notoriously dissipated disinformation be countered. Never before has there been a perspective on energy with so many advantages for society, well beyond the immediate concerns of energy supplies and environmental protection. By this standard, strategic priorities should long ago have been initiated in order to help renewable energy achieve a broad-based breakthrough and take action against the forces opposing it – whether in politics, private business or science.

But only recently have efforts been initiated taking this urgent requirement into account. Germany, facilitated by the Renewable Energy Sources Act (the Act on the Priority of Renewable Energy or Gesetz für den Vorrang erneuerbarer Energien – best known in Germany as the Erneuerbare-Energien-Gesetz or EEG), now has the world's largest growth rate for electricity production from renewable energy – not counting traditional hydropower from dams – of 3000 megawatts in new capacity annually. In no time at all, numerous new businesses were established, like the wind power facility producer Enercon, Solar World AG or the Solarfabrik Freiburg. This was a break-through that recalled the era of great industrial start-ups in the 19th century, when handicraft operations were turned into global enterprises. In 2002 the EU decided – in an admittedly non-binding recommendation – that renewable energy in its member states should account for a share of 12.5 per cent of energy supplies by 2010. By 2020, California wants to cover a third of its energy needs with renewable energy. In China, in just a few years, over 50 million square metres of solar collectives have been installed, with annual growth rates at present of 12 million square metres, and early in 2005 China passed a Renewable Energy Sources Act that, like Germany's EEG, contains a provision for electricity input at guaranteed prices. Spain is on the verge of making solar installations legally binding for all new buildings. Japan is the world market leader in solar cell production and is developing a variety of new application technologies. Brazil is activating its programme for bio-fuels and is about to make the flex-fuel vehicle – which can use up to 85 per cent bio-alcohol in fuel – standard. Swedish cities have converted their bus operations completely to bio-fuels. Austria has increased its share of biomass in energy supplies since the start of the 1970s from 10 per cent to over 20 per cent. Cities like Los Angeles, New York, Chicago and San Francisco have started ambitious solar programmes. A growing number of small cities and counties have introduced initiatives to supply themselves completely with renewable energy. The new World Trade Center in New York will draw a major portion of its electrical consumption from wind rotors integrated into the building. The Reichstag in Berlin, the parliamentary building for the German Bundestag, is already being supplied up to 85 per cent with renewable energy from facilities inside the building. The number of 'solar home' systems in rural areas of developing countries has jumped up sharply. Within just five years, the Indian organization, West Bengal Renewable Energy Development, has outfitted complete villages, populated by a total of over 300,000 inhabitants, with solar energy facilities that are going to be financed by the villagers themselves, who will also be paying for the total electricity supply. These examples illustrate that nuclear and fossil energy supplies need no longer be swallowed as something that is 'unfortunately unavoidable'. They illuminate quite concretely the prospects for getting along without nuclear and fossil energy.

Even the economic interest is constantly growing. The number of conferences on renewable energy has become vast. Environmental and development organizations are emphasizing the value of renewable energy. There has been a jump in student interest. Development banks are elaborating financing concepts. In the agricultural sector there is a growing recognition of the prospects offered by the production of bio-energy. In 2002 the World Congress of Architecture convened in Berlin under the slogan 'Resource Architecture' in order to draw attention to solar building. Along with the founding of new firms, major companies are also reporting their entry into the business of renewable energy. Energy and technology corporations like Shell and BP, General Electric and Siemens have become active in the production of wind power installations. Car companies like Daimler-Chrysler, Ford and Volkswagen profess their faith in bio-fuels as an alternative to fossil fuels. Daimler-Chrysler devoted its 2003 environmental report exclusively to renewable energy.

Yet the practical onset of renewable energy remains confined to just a few nations and regions. 86 per cent of wind power facilities installed throughout the world are located in just five countries: Germany, Denmark, the US, Spain and India. 70 per cent of photovoltaic facilities installed worldwide are located in Japan and Germany. In most countries, with the exception of traditionally used biomass and hydroelectric power plants from dams, the active use of renewable energy has barely gone beyond initial baby steps. And the commitment of global corporations comes in for undue praise. In fiscal year 2003 BP had sales of US$233 billion. The sales share of BP Solar, however, was only 0.14 per cent (at US$330 million). Shell had total sales of US$269 billion, but the sales share of Shell Solar was just 0.11 per cent (at US$292 million). In their main business field of fuel sales, both businesses are arbitrarily restraining the intro-duction of bio-fuels.

And yet, most protagonists of renewable energy can no longer imagine that they might experience another setback. It also seemed inconceivable to those in the US who, roused by the oil crisis that started in 1973, set out on the path to renew-able energy. In 1974 the widely regarded report *A Time to Choose*, written by David Freeman for the Ford Foundation, opened a view towards the advantages of renewable energy and the practi-cal opportunities available for energy saving through technological productivity increases. The report showed that, by comparison, the nuclear path was full of technological obstacles and paved with immense risks.[6] The climate problem was not yet the issue; instead, the goals were things like clean air and overcoming the political and economic risks arising from depen-dence on imported energy. At the time, US oil import dependence was less than 30 per cent. President Nixon declared that the US had to become independent of energy imports by the year 2000, and so he started the Independence Energy

System project. In 1977 President Carter stated: 'If we fail to act soon, we will face an economic, social and political crisis that will threaten our free institutions.'[7] At that time the US undertook the largest research and development programme to date on behalf of renewable energy. Thousands of new businesses and grass-roots initiatives mushroomed. Numerous publications proclaimed the dawning of the Solar Age: *Self Reliant Cities* by David Morris,[8] *Reaching Up, Reaching Out: A Guide to Organizing Local Solar Events* by Rebecca Vories,[9] *Rays of Hope: The Transition to a Post Petroleum World*[10] and *Blueprint for a Solar America* by Denis Hayes.[11] The Union of Concerned Scientists, whose members included several Nobel Prize winners in the natural sciences, published a 1979 study describing in detail the possibility of a complete reorganization of US energy supplies towards renewable energy by the year 2050.[12]

Yet the energy business in the US was quick to counter the report, *A Time to Choose*, with its own report, *No Time to Confuse*, in which it attempted to turn fear of an actual energy crisis into fear of renewable energy.[13] In order to undermine renewable energy's development, the energy business pulled out all the stops, down to the systematic purchase of small solar companies that were eventually shut down. Apparently all that mattered was lowering costs and takeovers by professional big business. In his book *The Sun Betrayed*, a thriller about business crime, Ray Reece describes how this 'three billion dollar business' deliberately thwarts the solar breakthrough – with tactics that include the friendly embrace of solar actors in order to crush them.[14] Both President Carter and Congress got cold feet and flinched about carrying through with pro-solar decisions they had already initiated. This was a surrender that Barry Commoner, the pioneering thinker of the US solar movement, was already noting in his 1979 book *The Politics of Energy* when he remarked that there was apparently a political taboo about offending the interests of the private energy business.[15] Finally, there was a definitive backlash when Ronald Reagan became President in 1981. Programmes were radically cut, research institutes were collapsing along with businesses, and the solar movement petered out. 'Who owns the sun?'; this question, posed by Daniel M. Berman and John T. O'Connor, was given a clear-cut answer by the

conventional energy powers that be: since the sun cannot belong
to any individual – in other words, not even to the conventional
energy business itself – it should not belong to anyone.[16] This
is how the solar technology revolution in energy supply was
thwarted. A project in the making was rigorously demolished.
The US – and with it the world, which lost its solar model in
America – thereby squandered irretrievable time. Instead of
taking bigger steps towards a 'Solar America,' the US became
more of a 'Fossil America' than ever before, and today the risks
of traditional energy supply are incomparably greater than they
were in the 1970s

   Starting in the early 1990s, especially in Europe, a
movement arose like that earlier US one. Independent solar
organizations and local solar initiatives were shaking up the
public. Opinion surveys soon revealed that these enjoyed
enormous sympathy. In Germany this led to laws promoting
renewable energy that, for the first time, facilitated speedy initi-
ation into the market. In 2004, as a result, Germany alone had
35 per cent of the world's total installed wind capacity and
19,000 megawatts of newly installed electricity production
capacity using renewable energy, built on the basis of the EEG
law as well as a previous law (the 1991 Act on Feeding
Electricity from Renewable Energies into the Public Grid). Yet
the more this development makes visible headway, the greater
the vehemence with which established energy businesses attempt
to turn things back. Vastly exaggerated assertions about
purported increases in electricity costs are made public, with
shrill warnings that this would threaten the national economy's
competitiveness as well as isolate Germany internationally.
Influential media shaping public opinion, like the *Frankfurter
Allgemeine Zeitung* (Germany's newspaper 'of record') and *Der
Spiegel* (the weekly news magazine noted for its political coverage) loudly join in the chorus.

   The opponents of this law even start acting like fundamentalist conservationists over the ostensible issue of wind power
stations' destructive impact on the landscape; this, in spite of
the fact that these self-styled preservationists are otherwise
advocates of economic growth unfettered as much as possible
by environmental encumbrances. While they call loudly, out of

one side of their mouths, for technological innovations, they discredit the very innovations that are more vital and dynamic than all the others. They swear by new economic growth and admonish on behalf of creating new jobs. Yet although the growth rate for producing renewable energy facilities is 30 per cent annually, and even though more jobs are created there than in any other sector, this new branch is denounced as 'unfriendly to business'. The attempt is made to inflame public outrage about the additional costs for introducing renewable energy. This campaign is not only way out of proportion, it is also eerily irrational. It has all the features of the kind of 'political neurosis' that the writer Arthur Koestler detected in the 1960s among those who had come to terms with the real danger of an nuclear war 'with an empty grin on their faces and a totem in their hands'.[17]

Current efforts to roll back nuclear energy are strikingly similar to the situation in the US 25 years ago. Germany is experiencing a repeat performance of what happens to a country that has the greatest success mobilizing on behalf of renewable energy: that country also becomes the stage for the most vehement campaign reacting against the progress of renewable energy. This seems like a contradiction only to those who underestimate the dimension of conflict accompanying a shift in energy, and who are therefore incapable of fending off the counter-reformation. If a backlash were to succeed in Germany today, as it did in the US over two decades ago, this would again blunt the spearhead of the breakthrough to renewable energy not just in the pioneering country, but internationally as well.

As always, the dominance of the current energy system is so great, and its sphere of influence so far-reaching, that a fresh setback cannot be ruled out. To be sure, in the long run it will prove impossible to stop the changeover to renewable energy. The bottlenecks and limits of nuclear and fossil energy supplies are just too obvious for that. But every setback results not only in additional lost time; it also breeds social-psychological discouragement. It is difficult for people who have taken the initiative in a spirit of high hopes, only to suffer repeated setbacks and disappointment, to summon up the energy and take a second go at it. That lesson is also something demonstrated by the experience of the first backlash in the US. Only now, and only slowly, is the enthusiasm that once existed there during the 1970s being renewed by a new generation of activists.

Every social movement needs a productive mutual relationship among impulses, legislation that takes up these impulses, and entrepreneurial initiatives. This is confirmed by developments in Denmark, Austria and Switzerland, where a solar movement arose at the beginning of the 1990s (and in a manner analogous to developments in Germany). In Austria and Switzerland, however, the outcome was not a set of laws that might have given these impulses additional stimulus. In the absence of legislation, the movement's initial atmosphere of a new dawn gave way to overcast skies. Similarly, when the laws promoting solar energy in Denmark were allowed to lapse in 2000, many active groups immediately disappeared from the scene. A social movement needs visible successes to keep going. When there is a political setback, it succumbs to decline and stagnation before new forces begin to stir again after a lengthy interlude.

Mental hurdles

Given an attitude towards renewable energy that remains overwhelmingly hesitant, the world is living well under the threshold of urgent imperatives and given opportunities. By contrast, when it comes to nuclear and fossil fuel energy, the world continues to live well beyond its means. Nor is this contradiction something that can be explained solely by the power and influence of an energy system oriented around fossil and nuclear fuels, a system whose interest in self-maintenance and structure-conserving behaviour render it relatively calculable. The traditional energy economy is a prisoner of its own energy supply chain. The technological, economic, social and (not least of all) political entanglements of that energy supply chain were the subject of my book *The Solar Economy*.[18] But it is not an omnipotent system. It is not capable of intellectually guiding and corrupting the entire political and economic system, including science and the media.

So what is preventing those who are not directly or indirectly implicated in the traditional energy system from pressing ahead, resolutely and with the necessary willingness to engage in conflict, with the shift to renewable energy? Why, thus far, have there been no political initiatives promoting renewable energy as a future economic project with the same kind of clear-cut ambition that made it possible to build the modern railway, space travel, nuclear technology and (most recently of all) information technology? Why are there still no European institutions for renewable energy comparable to EURATOM or the European Space Agency (ESA) in their respective fields, or global institutions like the International Atomic Energy Agency (IAEA)? These questions about the actors and fields of action for and against renewable energy must be answered if we want to learn how the shift to these new forms of energy can be decisively accelerated.

These are questions about what proportion of responsibility should be given to political institutions or to 'business', to 'science' or 'the media', but also to the range of actors engaged in environmental protection. Questions, for example, about the lack of standards whereby, for reasons of local land conservation, approval for building wind and water power facilities is frequently and doggedly denied, in spite of the fact that nature overall has long been threatened much more seriously by the waste products that come from nuclear and fossil energy use. Or about the absurd standards whereby action programmes promoting renewable energy are made dependent on whether they match up with certain market dogmas. Or think about the massive funds, in flagrant contradiction to the meagre results they produce, expended on lavish international governmental conferences, with their caravan of environmental diplomats and non-governmental organization (NGO) representatives who make sure to weed out every standpoint that doesn't command a consensus. At these conferences the delegates seem to talk about just everything, though usually while talking *around* the most explosive issues.

A significant example of this was the climate conference that took place in July 2004 at San Rossore, a large estate near Pisa, organized by the regional government of Tuscany. At the beginning of the conference there was a talk by Al Gore, who in the 1990s had captured the world's attention with his book *Earth in the Balance*,[19] which elevated him into an international champion of global climate protection policy before he became US Vice President in 1993. Gore gave a brilliant lecture about threats to the climate and showed frightening charts about the catastrophes that had already set in or were about to happen. The speech made it vividly clear that comprehensive measures were long overdue. Yet as the cause of these catastrophic scenarios Gore named not fossil energy use, but rather the population explosion, scientific and technological developments, and the lifestyle of affluent countries – factors for which everyone, and therefore nobody, is accountable. He received enormous applause from his audience, mostly Italian environmental activists. Yet this way of describing the causes of environmental degradation can only lead to a sense of helplessness: nobody can demonstrate how, in the short or medium term, population growth can be contained, people's lifestyles changed, or how scientific and technological developments with their concomitant demand for more energy can be turned back. The conference participants skirted the subject of renewable energy as a real, tangible key to warding off all these dangers. In my talk at this conference, which came after Gore's, I did address this central issue. My remarks met with a divided response; for some of the conference participants, my statement was not 'fundamental' enough: it was considered too concrete and therefore too much of a direct challenge.

Of course, in order to bring about a shift in energy sources, numerous practical hurdles have to be overcome, impediments that exist alongside the familiar sources of resistance (administrative, technological and economic). But the greatest obstacles are mental, inside peoples' minds. These are the hurdles establishing the contradiction whereby the use of renewable energy has been progressing much too slowly (on the whole) even though everyone perceives the dangers of continuing to use nuclear and fossil energy. These mental hurdles, more than anything else, are what stand in the way of acknowledging and seizing upon the prospects for renewable energy. They are the source of insufficient planning and of evading the decisive question: who are the most suitable social groups – that is, the ones best motivated and most capable of acting competently and independently – to act as carriers of this energy transformation, who want to and are able to put this change into action? Both things – the plan and the carrier – are directly related to each other. No plan can have just any carrier, and not all the available carriers are suitable for every plan. And, depending on the plan and the carrier, the sources of resistance and the methods to be used may vary in each case. It is of the utmost importance that these questions be clarified in order to establish a strategic profile for renewable energy, which is the subject of this book.

These mental hurdles result from questionable premises that pervade the discussion on renewable energy and cannot withstand closer scrutiny. They have an axiomatic character; that is, they are based on fundamental assumptions that are regarded as established facts and are therefore held to require no additional justification. For better or worse, whoever does not contradict any one of these premises will have to submit to their (quite logically derived) consequences, even if these turn out to be highly unsatisfactory. When it comes to contentious issues with a broad impact, one generally confronts a number of such premises. The American sociologist Amitai Etzioni calls this the 'community of assumptions'. These assumptions are shared by society's functional elites, who practically close ranks around them; they represent their view of things and are 'usually held without awareness of their hypothetical nature'. It is assumed that 'the world really is the way the internalized and institutionalized images depict it', and the assumptions are granted 'absolute validity'. Differences of opinion are then 'tolerated only within the limits of fundamentally the same interpretation'.[20] Thus there arise 'prevailing opinions', carefully cultivated and even respected by those who know better.

Quite apart from all the notorious technical disinformation about renewable energy that has been spread around (though also refuted in numerous writings), there are essentially seven dubious technological or economic premises and six questionable premises of political action that get taken for granted as if they were predetermined, established, almost rock-solid facts. Whoever adopts these assumptions – or even just a few of them – ends up adopting perspectives and plans that recognize just part of renewable energy's potential, and which therefore leave this potential untapped.

The questionable technological and economic premises are:

- *Insufficient usable potential* – renewable energy's usable potential is not enough for us to afford the luxury of doing without nuclear and/or fossil energy. This premise makes conventional energy's long-term use appear as if it were an objective constraint, something to put up with in spite of all the obvious dangers.

- *The lengthy time requirement* – activating renewable energy on a large scale is only possible over the long run. And therefore, even in the long run, massive investment in conventional energy is indispensable in order to satisfy peoples' energy requirements. This premise, articulated under the guise of advocating renewable energy, is meant to suggest that we take our time about introducing renewable energy and that, in the meantime, we should tolerate continued use of traditional energy supplies.

- *The absolute necessity of large power plants* – the volume of energy demanded by a major industrial and urbanized mass society, this premise goes, could not be met without giant-sized technological facilities; renewable energy, which mainly uses facilities based on small-scale technology, is not suited to meet this volume of demand. This premise, too, serves to assure the acceptance of large energy plants. It is a seductive argument that directs renewable energy technology towards centralized facilities, to the neglect of decentralized applications, which are substantially more diverse and easier to introduce more rapidly.

- *Conventional energy's greater environmental benefits due to increased efficiency* – investing in the enhanced energy efficiency of conventional energy plants and of energy-consuming appliances would be much more cost-effective and contribute faster to solving the problem that renewable energy is supposed to address. This is a premise that exploits improvements in the energy efficiency of traditional technologies in order to play them off against initiatives for renewable energy, as if both are not simultaneously possible and necessary.

- *The functional priority placed on existing energy supply structures* – renewable energy needs to correspond to existing structures of energy provision, in other words, be compatible with these. The existing structure may be regarded – especially when it comes to power supply – as an objective technological requirement. This premise turns the status quo into the standard for determining how much renewable energy can be tolerated; and it asserts an innocent neutrality towards all energy sources even though this kind of neutrality has never existed and never can exist.

- *Protecting economic resources* – all energy policy decisions should be careful to avoid destroying capital in the energy business. In this way, the interests of the economy as a whole are identified with those of the energy business. Behind this premise there lurks the notion of a planned economy that is indelibly associated with the self-image of the traditional energy business and its energy policies. It is also a premise that assumes, almost self-evidently, that the energy business is the general carrier for every kind of energy supply – an assumption that is absolutely erroneous when it comes to renewable energy.

- *The economic burden of introducing renewable energy* – this premise systematically diverts attention from traditional energy's consequential damages in economic terms and from renewable energy's widespread economic and social usefulness. It attempts to play off current interests against future interests and encourage members of society to indulge in egoistic behaviour against the common good.

These fundamental technological and economic assumptions all create the impression of objective constraints that stand in the way of a full-scale reorientation towards renewable energy.

The six other premises relate to political fields of action and methods:

- *Renewable energy's dependence on subsidies* – this premise is not only used to divert attention from the fact that subsidies for nuclear and fossil energy have been (and still are) – as we shall see – many times higher than subsidies previously provided for all forms of renewable energy. It also diverts attention from the fact that there have long been opportunities for using renewable energy that have not depended on subsidies, but simply on ending the privileges accorded nuclear and fossil energy.

- *The need for consensus with the energy business* – the standing and (therefore) the influence of the established energy business are so great that it has made itself indispensable for any successful shift in energy use. In spite of major conflicts, therefore, one needs to arrive at a consensus with the energy business. This premise accepts the energy business's monopoly on action in every question of energy supply, as if the energy business alone were capable of providing people with energy. The status of the energy business thereby acquires an intellectual 'guarantee of eternity', as if we were dealing with a constitutional institution.

- *Fixation on competitiveness in energy markets* – since liberalization of energy markets is the general trend, even the programmes promoting renewable energy need to be arranged around a liberalized energy market. This premise gives 'the energy market' priority above all other decision-making criteria. It overlooks the fact that mobilizing for renewable energy primarily has to do with technological markets and only partly with the energy market.

- *The indispensability of global treaty commitments* – since energy problems arise globally, solutions to problems can only reside – for reasons having to do with economic cost distribution in international competition – in global community solutions that are negotiated as treaties and are binding for everyone, solutions whose inevitable compromises have to be accepted as a limit on action. This premise pushes the social utility advantages of renewable energy into the background. Furthermore, this premise overlooks the fact that no technological breakthrough has ever arisen from action coordinated by an international treaty, and all the evidence seems to indicate that no breakthrough is ever likely to emerge this way. This is a premise that focuses public attention and environmental actors' efforts on international treaty conferences, in spite of their highly unsatisfactory outcomes, to the neglect of other initiatives.

- *Environmental pollution caused by renewable energy* – since using renewable energy can also lead to environmental pollution, its introduction has to be scrutinized for environmental soundness in exactly the same way as nuclear and fossil energy. This premise blurs elementary distinctions between actual environmental damage and relatively marginal environmental disturbances, between irreversible and reversible environmental burdens, or between energy facilities that produce harmful substances and those that are pollutant-free but take up space.

- *The realism of taking small political steps* – since small steps elicit minimal resistance and are therefore easier to implement, it is a precept of realism not to scare off political institutions, business, and the general public with approaches that go too far. This premise is tantamount to capitulating in the face of real problems, since small political steps quite obviously do not suffice to solve the world-threatening problem of continuing to supply our economies with traditional fossil and nuclear energy.

All these one-sided premises obstruct our view of renewable energy's real potential and of promising approaches to solving our energy problems. They are prejudices that confound discussion and lead to reductionist strategies as well as to accepting energy conditions as they are. The muddle they coagulate in favour of the status quo creates a hidebound mind-set not only among actors in the energy business, but also in politics, economics, science, the general public, and even the strategic thinking of environmental groups and organizations advocating renewable energy. Prejudices are relatively easy to overcome for individuals, who benefit from information and leaps of recognition that fall like scales from their eyes. In society at large, however, overcoming bias is much more difficult to achieve, especially when prejudices keep getting cultivated and updated – cultivated above all by those who profit from their persistence and therefore loudly confirm these prejudices at every opportunity. Not coincidentally, these are the very energy specialists who find it especially difficult to overcome mental obstacles towards renewable energy. Pushing these hurdles aside, and thereby leading the entire energy discussion out of the intellectual confinement within these obstacles' perimeter, is the most important precondition for a shift in energy use.

One of the consequences of starting from false premises is that discussions end up referring only to a section of the total problem, that guidelines for action are developed relating only to that part of the overall picture, and that these guidelines are subordinated to all other problems – so that one loses sight of solutions to other problems. These patterns of reducing large problems to their smallest components pervade the energy debate. If this debate is mainly conducted from the viewpoint of climate threats caused by fossil energy emissions, the dangers of nuclear energy and questions about energy security are pushed into the background. If it is mainly conducted from the viewpoint of nuclear dangers, this then confines perceptions about the dangers of energy usage. If it is conducted solely from the viewpoint of depleting oil stocks, this will cloud awareness of potential dangers arising from other fossil energy sources and from nuclear energy.

These ways of reducing the overall problem to one of its components always lead to neglect of the diverse and grave reasons that speak on behalf of a general shift to renewable energy. The broad spectrum of reasons for a comprehensive strategy – the motifs of the renewable energy movement – emerge from four elementary differences between nuclear and fossil energy, on the one hand, and renewable energy, on the other:

- The use of nuclear and fossil energy entails massive environmental disturbances, with tectonic consequences across the board, starting immediately with these fuels' initial production and continuing until the by-products of their consumption are emitted into water, air and the Earth's atmosphere generally; by contrast, the use of renewable energy is, in principle, free of such consequences. From this contrast there emerges a general environmental motif for renewable energy that transcends the narrower climate protection motif. Even if the climate problem did not exist, there would still be a mass of ecological reasons speaking on behalf of an energy shift.

- Fossil energy can be depleted, which is why its continued use must inevitably lead to rising costs and supply bottle-necks and emergencies. Only inexhaustible renewable energy opens up the prospect of a permanent, secure energy supply for people everywhere. From this there emerges the motif of permanently secure energy availability, which speaks for renewable energy.

- Nuclear and fossil energy reserves lie in a relatively limited number of producing regions around the globe, so that their use requires lengthy supply chains. This inevitably entails major outlays in infrastructure, leads to growing dependence, and provokes economic, political and military conflicts. Every form of renewable energy, by contrast, is a type of energy that fits in with its natural surroundings and can be recovered directly with much smaller requirements in the way of infrastructure. From this there emerge such motifs of renewable energy as macroeconomic efficiency, political independence and peacekeeping.

- Fossil and atomic energy, as a result of the above-mentioned differences, are becoming increasingly expensive, both with respect to their direct and their indirect costs. Renewable energy, by contrast – if only because it accrues no fuel costs (with the exception of bio-energy) – becomes increasingly cheaper in the course of continuous technological improve-ment, industrial mass production, and intelligent new forms of application. From this there emerges the motif for renew-able energy having to do with social welfare and economic strategy.

All these motifs coalesce into a single grand motif – as compre-hensive as it is existential – of surmounting and avoiding crisis, a motif that (in light of the different worldwide crises discussed in Part II) is as explosive today as it ever was. The key to solving energy-determined crises is the shift to renewable energy. Focusing on this is not a 'one-issue' but rather a 'multi-issue' approach.

The unexhausted social potential

'The problems that exist in the world today cannot be solved by
the level of thinking that created them.' This statement by Albert
Einstein also means: they can hardly be solved by the same actors
who brought them about. Those who want to replace nuclear
and fossil with renewable energy, and who are actively pursuing
this goal, are – whether they want to or not – more than merely
economic competitors in the established energy business. They
are the established energy's structural opponents. There has
always been economic competition between energy suppliers,
always a struggle for market share: between electricity and fuel
suppliers in the heating market, among coal, petroleum and gas
suppliers, or between one energy corporation and another. Yet it
is striking how these competitors stick together when it comes
to opposing new forms of renewable energy; not letting renewable energy make it is their common cause. As far as the Lord
Privy Seal of the established energy business is concerned, the
stakes go beyond simply maintaining a supply monopoly and
keeping the infrastructure designed to corner that market
operating at capacity; also at issue is the conservation of established energy's social role, of its deep-rooted technological world
view.

The faster conventional energy is depleted, the more its
suppliers will rely on giving each other mutual support. For this
reason alone there has been an intensification of the trend for
former competitors in the supply of conventional energy to
merge into integrated energy companies. Although one may
discern thoroughly divergent attitudes towards renewable energy
crystallizing within the energy business, a hard common core is
unmistakable: the status and structures of conventional energy
dare not be shaken.

In his work *The Art of War*, written 2500 years ago and
regarded as a literary and philosophical masterpiece on methods
for settling conflicts, the Chinese general and philosopher Sun
Tzu wrote: 'If you know the enemy and know yourself, you need
not fear the result of a hundred battles. If you know yourself
but not the enemy, for every victory gained you will also suffer
a defeat. If you know neither the enemy nor yourself, you will

succumb in every battle...'[21] Decades ago, in officer training, I learned what is required for successfully settling a conflict: defining a goal. This means gaining a genuine picture of one's opponents, recognizing their strengths and weaknesses. It means analysing the field on which conflicts are settled and making an appropriate estimation of one's own forces; attacking where the opponent is weakest, using the instruments with which one is superior to him at this particular site; securing one's own surroundings in order to stand firm against counter-attacks. When, in the parallelogram of antagonistic positions, resistance against renewable energy proves too strong, its protagonists must attempt to change the field of forces in their favour. This requires making an effort at conceptualizing and communicating, and it means that coalitions have to be forged. Whoever accepts a disadvantageous constellation as inalterable fact is condemned to a Sisyphean labour, to surrender or being co opted.

In the energy debate, 'energy carrier' is a technological or economic concept. It refers to energy sources and technologies. With respect to renewable energy, distinctions are drawn here between 'natural potential', 'technological potential' and 'economically usable potential'. Yet the most decisive thing heading the list of what it will take for renewable energy to prevail is the *societal* potential: the people who can be won over to solar initiatives. Every proposal, no matter how appropriate, remains barren for as long as a 'carrier' cannot be found to sponsor it. In saying this, I do not by any means wish to diminish the value of analysing problems and finding creative solutions. But strategy is implementation, and there is no implementation without active carriers who have adopted prospects for action as their own because these correspond to their values and interests. Therefore the question of who will be the potential carriers of the shift to renewable energy must lie at the heart of any strategic discussion. This also sheds light on questions about, first, to whom proposals for action might be addressed, and second, if, and under what conditions, those carriers deemed indispensable for implementation are even movable. If the fundamental assumptions of a strategy are too one-sided at the very outset, it is also usually the case that the circle of actors derived from the strategy will prove to be ill-suited or too small. Paying attention to these connections is something that is lacking in many analyses and proposals from the debate on nuclear energy – and this includes some prominent writers on the subject.

Thus, in his book *Plan B*, Lester Brown from the Earth Policy Institute calls for efforts that are analogous to 'wartime mobilization' and 'greatness' in the book's political ambitions for an ecological economy, after the model of the Marshall Plan following the Second World War.[22] Yet he does not pursue the question as to why similar calls repeatedly run dry – including the plan presented by Al Gore in 1989 for a Strategic Environment Initiative (SEI), which was not even taken up by Gore himself after he assumed national office in 1993. The 'Global Marshall Plan' for a worldwide eco-social market economy – an elaborate plan promoted by (among others) futur-ologists Franz-Josef Radermacher and Ervin Laszlo as well by Mikhail Gorbachev, by the Club of Rome as well as by the Club of Budapest – is addressed generally to the governments of the major industrial states, as if the only thing they've lacked so far has been a plan.[23] But then why didn't these same governments ever get around to implementing a programme already elabo-rated by the task force on renewable energy appointed by the G8 Summit in 1999, which submitted an implementation plan for supplying energy to a billion people in the poorest develop-ing countries?[24] The ambitious recommendations of the EU Commission White Book on renewable energy from 1997 also remained on paper because the Commission has not assumed sponsorship for it.[25] And why, in spite of negotiations about global climate protection that went on for years, was the result such a meagre Kyoto Protocol? What has become of the celebrated, earth-shaking final declarations delivered by the UN World Summits at Rio and Johannesburg?

Mainstreaming Renewable Energy in the 21st Century, a publication by the Worldwatch Institute, describes the policies – few in number – that have proven successful.[26] But even this publica-tion does not mention which carriers it was who prevailed against the kind of resistance one finds everywhere, and how they managed to do so. The same goes for the book *Energy Revolution* by Howard Geller, in which the various policy approaches, along

with their respective successes or failures, are described, though
(again) without reference to the play of forces underlying each
case.[27] This lack of strategic assessment also applies to the
'Policy Recommendations for Renewable Energies' of the
Renewables 2004 conference.[28] These recommendations contain
an overview of numerous conceivable approaches to action, a
menu à la carte. But no distinction is made between hors d'oeu-
vres and main courses, nor even between their respective
nutritional values. Not everyone can digest everything, and to
some extent the entrées are not compatible with each other.
Some have stood the test, like the plan to introduce renewable
energy by legally guaranteed input rates. By contrast, trade in
certificates for renewable energy only brought about a few
ripples in the water, without making any major waves. Yet both
plans are discussed alongside each other. So what is the 'political recommendation'? Accentuating the plans and broadening
sponsorship for renewable energy are apparently necessary in
order to achieve a definitive breakthrough that is broad and
durable. To this end the character of the resistance and the intentions and methods should be acknowledged. Only then is it
possible to brace oneself adequately against these adversaries.

If an about-face to renewable energy cannot be pulled off
over the next two decades, the world can be expected, in the
foreseeable future, to slide into resource conflicts rife with
violence. An about-face means not only expanding renewable
energy, but also cutting back on the consumption of fossil and
nuclear energy. It means preventing additional trillions from
being devoured on the construction of new fossil and nuclear
power plants and thereby from cementing the conventional
structures of energy supply. It requires renewable energy to be
activated much more quickly and in a manner that is more forced
(both qualitatively and quantitatively) than is currently
envisioned by government action programmes – especially since
it can be foreseen that the goals most of these programmes
proclaim cannot possibly be achieved given the plans and carriers they envision.

This book is mainly addressed to the growing number of
renewable energy advocates, and to the even greater number of
those who are simply curious about it. It is meant to outline

approaches and mobilize forces that can make an unstoppable breakthrough succeed in the near future. According to the Swedish Nobel Prize winner for economics, the sociologist Gunnar Myrdal, it is possible for a social project to prevail if it is purposefully and tirelessly pursued by a impassioned following of just 5 per cent. These will then bring an additional 25 per cent of the society in tow. That is sufficient, because the majority of people is habitually indifferent – but, in principle, they are ready to go along with movements and the forces behind them if these can offer the general public a persuasive prospect.

'How long? Not long!'. During the 1960s this resounding reply to an equally brief question was hammered by Martin Luther King into the consciousness of the US civil rights movement, in order to persuade that movement that its chance to realize its goals was not far off. It is with this kind of determination and confidence that the imagination of many is stirred, the social atmosphere is revived and practical new ideas sprout up. Then, in no time at all, unanticipated leaps of development become possible. 'How long? Very long!'. This is the kind of thinking that, unfortunately, has been dominant in previous discussions about the time frame for a shift in energy. Even convinced ecologists behave this way to show that they are 'realistic'. But lengthy time horizons release people from direct responsibility and lead them to surrender matters to professional experts. Then the most important resource for renewable energy – the social resource – remains untapped. This is why my main interest is in discerning those approaches to renewable energy that permit the frequently posed question 'how long?' to be answered with 'not long!'.

The leitmotif for all of this is energy autonomy. It is a theme intended to be, in equal measure, political, economic and technological. It is, as a generalizable plan, only possible with renewable energy. But energy autonomy is not just the outcome of a shift to renewable energy; it is, at the same time, the hard core of a practical strategy: autonomous initiatives by individuals, organizations, businesses, cities and states are required in order to get everything moving. The new politics of renewable energy is about opening up spaces for these initiatives, spaces in which the initiatives can develop unhindered.

References

1   Friedrich Dürrenmatt, *The Physicists* (New York: Grove Weidenfeld, 1991)

2   International Energy Agency data are available from http://data.iea.org/ieastore/statslisting.asp

3   International Energy Agency, *World Energy Outlook 2004* (Geneva: OECD/IEA, 2004)

4   James Lovelock, 'Nuclear energy is the only green solution', *The Independent*, 24 May 2004

5   George W. Bush, Speech at the National Small Business Conference, 27 April 2005

6   David Freeman, *A Time to Choose, America's Energy Future* (Cambridge, MA: Energy Policy Project, Ford Foundation, 1974)

7   *New York Times*, 18 April 1977

8   David Morris, *Self Reliant Cities* (San Francisco, CA: Sierra Club Books 1982)

9   Rebecca Vories, *Reaching Up, Reaching Out: A Guide to Organizing Local Solar Events* (Golden, CO: The Branch, 1979)

10 Denis Hayes, *Rays of Hope: The Transition to a Post Petroleum World* (New York: W. W. Norton & Company, 1977)

11 Denis Hayes, *Blueprint for a Solar America* (Washington, DC: Solar Lobby, 1979)

12 Henry W. Kendall and Steven J. Nadis, *Energy Strategies: Toward a Solar Future. Report of the Union of Concerned Scientists* (Cambridge, MA: Ballinger, 1980)

13 Morris Albert Adelman, *No Time to Confuse* (San Francisco, CA: Institute for Contemporary Studies, 1975)

14 Ray Reece, *The Sun Betrayed* (Boston, MA: South End Press, 1979)

15 Barry Commoner, *The Politics of Energy* (New York: Random House, 1979)

16 Daniel M. Berman and John T. O'Connor, *Who Owns the Sun? People, Politics and the Struggle for a Solar Economy* (White River Junction, VT: Chelsea Green, 1996)

17   Arthur Koestler, *Die Armut der Psychologie* (Bern: Scherz Verlag, 1980), p317
18   Hermann Scheer, *The Solar Economy* (London: Earthscan, 2002)
19   Al Gore, *Earth in the Balance* (New York: Plume, 1993)
20   Amitai Etzioni, *The Active Society* (London/New York: Collier/Macmillan, 1968), p179
21   Sun Tzu, *The Art of War*, ed. by James Clavell (New York: Delacorte Press, 1983)
22   Lester Brown, *Plan B. Rescuing a Planet Under Stress and a Civilization in Trouble* (New York: W. W. Norton & Company, 2003), p203 et seq
23   Franz-Josef Radermacher, *Global Marshall Plan. A Planetary Contract for a Worldwide Eco-social Market Economy* (Hamburg: Global Marshall Plan Initiative, 2004)
24   *G8 Renewable Energy Task Force: Chairman's Report* (2001, available at www.g8italia.it/UserFiles/347.pdf)
25   EU Commission, *Energie für die Zukunft: Erneuerbare Energieträger* (Brussels: EU Commission, 1997)
26   Janet L. Sawin and Thomas Prugh, *Mainstreaming Renewable Energy in the 21st Century* (Washington, DC: Worldwatch Institute, Worldwatch Paper 169, May 2004)
27   Howard Geller, *Energy Revolution* (Washington, DC: Island Press, 2003)
28   International Conference for Renewable Energies, *Conference Report. Outcomes and Documentation* (August 2004, available at www.renewables2004.de/pdf/conference_report.pdf)

Part I

Sun or Atom: The Fundamental Conflict of the 21st Century

There is one forecast of which you can already be sure: someday renewable energy will be the only way for people to satisfy their energy needs. Because of the physical, ecological and (therefore) social limits to nuclear and fossil energy use, ultimately nobody will be able to circumvent renewable energy as the solution, even if it turns out to be everybody's last remaining choice. The question keeping everyone in suspense, however, is whether we shall succeed in making this radical change of energy platforms happen early enough to spare the world irreversible ecological mutilation and political and economic catastrophe.

How far we remain from recognizing the signs of the times is something that developments in the 1970s showed us. Before the outbreak of the global oil crisis in 1973, world energy consumption, according to statistics from the International Energy Agency, came to 6034 million metric toe. In 2002 the figure was 10,213 million metric tons – an increase of 69 per cent, more than two-thirds. Throughout this period renewable energy's share remained constant at barely 14 per cent. Actually its share is substantially smaller than that. The renewable share consisted of 85 per cent biomass in 1971 and then 80 per cent in 2002 – and in developing countries this was largely based on ruinous exploitation of local vegetation, without replanting, which is why the label 'renewable' is so misleading here. The share of nuclear energy during these three decades, by contrast, rose from 0.5 to 6.8 per cent of world energy consumption as captured by statistics. It would have been substantially higher had it not been for the setback brought about by public protest movements against nuclear energy, public referenda, the reactor catastrophe at Chernobyl, the collapse of the Communist bloc, and the (partial) liberalization of electricity supply in the interim.

The objection that technology was not advanced enough during these decades for renewable energy to be feasible is a flimsy excuse. This is even corroborated by the size of the Organisation for Economic Co-operation and Development (OECD) countries' research and development (R&D) expenditures for renewable energy research, which have stood at around 8 per cent of energy research funds for three decades. For nuclear research, by contrast, the OECD country average was 51 per cent. These proportions would turn out looking even more favourable to nuclear energy and slanted against renewable energy if the statistics compiled by the IEA had also included R&D spending by the EU Commission, especially the EURATOM (European Atomic Energy Community) agency's funds, as well as France's unpublished expenditures. There are only sporadic published figures about practical market-launching programmes going beyond R&D. At the end of the 1980s, Brazil started its bio-alcohol programme for fuels. Vehicles were introduced that could cover over 90 per cent of their petrol requirements using bio-alcohol. Between 1983 and 1987 alone, more bio-alcohol than petrol was used in Brazilian cars; bio-alcohol production rose from about 2 million (metric) tons in 1980 to 12 million (metric) tons in 1986. But then this trend stagnated for a long time because the worldwide drop in oil prices again dampened any motivation to save petrol, while there was simultaneously a sharp rise in the number of cars – so that, as early as the 1990s, gasoline consumption was again much higher than bio-alcohol consumption. The Brazilian programme was not even imitated by other countries that enjoyed similar opportunities for cultivating sugar cane.

Since the beginning of the 1990s, 350 megawatts of capacity have been available in California for solar-thermal power –

but then there was a worldwide stop to any new solar-thermal investment until 2004. Small hydroelectric power plants using running water have been around for over 100 years, yet there has hardly been an effort made to multiply their numbers. In Denmark, the share of wind-powered electricity in total electricity supply grew from 0.1 to 16.4 per cent between 1980 and 1999, all this without the cost of Danish electricity climbing disproportionately. Yet in spite of this practical demonstration that there is a different way of doing things, the share of renewable energy in overall demand among the other industrial countries' power supply sank noticeably during this time period: in Australia from 18.5 to 8.3 per cent, in Canada from 75.5 to 57.9 per cent, in Finland from 42.1 to 29.1 per cent, in France from 39.4 to 14.4 per cent, in Italy from 38.3 to 20.1 per cent, in Portugal from 80.5 to 34.6 per cent, in Spain from 49.4 to 21.9 per cent, in Switzerland from 88.9 to 59.8 per cent, in Turkey from 37.1 to 19.8 per cent, in the US from 15.5 to 7.4 per cent, in Ireland from 13.8 to 4.2 per cent and in Greece from 26.8 to 5.5 per cent. Apart from Denmark, Germany was the only country in which there was an increase in the share of renewable energy starting in the 1990s. All this goes to show that the growing demand for energy everywhere was met almost exclusively by fossil or nuclear energy, so that the share of renewable energy — most of which continues to be managed using old power stations at dams — kept getting smaller and smaller. Thus, Greece preferred routing electricity from coal-fired plants on the mainland to its wind-swept islands via underwater cables instead of erecting on-site wind power facilities.

Renewable energy — as Wolfgang Palz, long-time division chief for renewable energy at the EU Commission, had already explained in 1978 in a UNESCO publication *Solar Electricity* — was often better poised for introduction into the market than nuclear energy had been in its day.[1] But, even in the 1990s, every other conceivable measure seemed more important to political institutions than slowing down the trend of utilizing conventional energy sources: measures such as liberalizing electric power markets for the sake of lowering the price — and therefore increasing the consumption — of environmentally damaging energy sources. Or measures like easing international powers' access to fossil raw materials by making them duty-free. An additional factor has been the rapidly forced industrialization of Asia, with China and India in the lead, two countries that together make up more than a third of the world's population. Craving a share in the world economy's biggest potential growth market has shunted aside our understanding that this development is incompatible with sticking to traditional energy supplies. There are no tenable justifications for the various denials of renewable energy in mind and deed. All these excuses have one thing in common: they are untenable in view of all the crises brewing worldwide, crises whose origin lie partly or wholly in nuclear or fossil energy. This is especially true of the standard argument that renewable energy would not 'pay off' in the market-place — as if fossil and nuclear energy would have been able to prevail entirely and solely without political assistance in the past, and as if they would be capable of holding their own today without political support.

The long-ignored signals

The keynote of the signal to liberate us from our dependence on fossil energy was sounded by universal-minded scientists even before the Fossil Age had fully unfolded. At the dawn of the 20th century, Wilhelm Ostwald, who received the Nobel Prize for chemistry in 1909, spoke of the 'unexpected legacy of fossil fuels' that (mis)leads us into 'losing sight temporarily of the principles of a durable economy and into living from one day to the next'. His clear-sighted conclusion was that a 'durable economy' needed to be based 'exclusively on the regular influx of energy from the sun's radiation'.[2] In those days Ostwald was probably thinking in terms of a longer time period before this 'energy imperative' would have to be realized. Nobody in his day could have foreseen the growth in world population, which quadrupled over the last century. Nor was it possible to foresee the century's explosive economic growth, including the rise in consumption that (especially in the second half of the 20th century) triggered a worldwide orgy in fossil energy consumption. The industrialized world plunged into an energy delirium — a sustained state of intoxication that animated the rest of the world to imitate it and obscured everyone's senses in a kind of smokescreen. In the 20th century Ostwald's oracle was increasingly suppressed as more evidence piled up corroborating it. The Swedish scientist Svante Arrhenius, who won the Nobel Prize for chemistry in 1903 and later became director of the Nobel Institute, also wrote this in his 1922 book *Chemistry in Modern Life*:

> Concern about raw materials is already casting a dark shadow over mankind. Concerns likes those about petroleum are also warranted owing to the future of almost all raw materials. Every industrialist seeks to push his production as high as possible in order to achieve the largest conceivable profit, and he gives no thought whatsoever to how things will be after fifty years or half a century. The statesman, however, needs to apply a different standard.

Arrhenius was already warning about brutal international conflicts over energy:

> States lacking [in raw materials] cast covetous glances at their neighbours, of whom it is said that they have more than they need. And the result is that profit-seeking will be increasingly lured into those countries whose interests are not guarded by judicious men. Future historians will bring to light how much craving raw materials for the future is to blame for [our] great misfortune.

Fossil raw materials should therefore not be abandoned to 'national egoism' and 'industrial profit-seeking'. Mankind needs to arrive at the insight that it must 'replace [those raw materials] with the manpower that the sun pours out over us in inexhaustible amounts', whether directly or 'indirectly via the amounts of energy originating from the sun, amassed in streams of water and greening plant life'.[3]

Natural scientists — for whom it was more than self-evident at the beginning of the 19th century than it is today to think about the universal picture — were not the only ones who had an early awareness of these problems. In 1908 President

Theodore Roosevelt convened a governors' conference in order
to initiate compiling an inventory of raw materials not yet
exhausted and to catalogue the health defects and destruction
of natural resources caused by raw materials exploitation. In
1909 the National Conservation Commission he designated for
this purpose submitted its report, which called for resolute
measures to reduce emissions and save energy, to substitute
water power for coal, and to use solar heat, alcohol and other
organic fuels. Roosevelt called on 45 world governments to come
to an international conference in The Hague in order to discuss
the worldwide consequences of resource exploitation.[4] This
conference never came about, and even the National
Conservation Commission discontinued its work because
Congress refused to fund it any longer. Roosevelt was the same
man who had an early grasp of the danger to the US's democratic constitution emanating from the petroleum trust run by
Standard Oil boss John D. Rockefeller, and he started a
campaign against the Rockefeller monopoly. That campaign
ended in 1911 when the Supreme Court decided to enforce the
Sherman Act against Standard Oil and dissolve the conglomerate into several independent corporations (such as Esso, today's
Exxon).[5] This first large-scale political initiative against the
fossil industrial energy complex remained a mere episode,
however. There followed a century rife with environmental
destruction caused by the use of fossil energy and of an increasingly internationalized concentration of power in the energy
business. New discoveries and new drilling and mining
techniques repeatedly provided new excuses for brashly repress-
ing awareness of the mounting dangers.

Falling back on the sun was felt to be a relapse back to a
time before the Industrial Revolution and, by extension, to the
conditions of 10,000 years of civilized history in which human
beings satisfied their energy needs almost exclusively with renewable energy. The opportunity to use renewable energy optimally
by taking advantage of modern technology was not taken into
account — this in spite of technologies that had already been
developed for this purpose in the 19th century.[6] Yet the limitations of fossil energy were known to the world of the physicists.
Once atomic fission was discovered, the prevailing view was that

there was an historic path from using solar energy in pre-industrial times, to utilizing fossil energy created over millions of years inside the Earth, to nuclear energy. The possibility of acquiring colossal amounts of energy from nuclear fission or fusion fascinated scientists as much as it did governments and the public. It seduced them into a sense of omnipotence that regarded all risks as manageable — at least the risks associated with the 'peaceful use of nuclear energy' or even of nuclear weapons, which were assigned the role of deterring wars.

In this way the basic pattern was woven for worldwide energy conflict in the second half of the 20th century, the pattern that is also shaping the first half of the 21st century. Nuclear energy became the reinsurance policy needed to resume the world's intoxication with energy consumption even when claiming, all the while, that the environmental sins of fossil fuels could be ended some day. Atomic energy also rationalized ignoring renewable energy as something supposedly backward-looking. An arrogant fossil/nuclear world view emerged. Its sponsors could not concede that they had misjudged and were being haughty. They steadfastly invoked the indispensability of nuclear energy.[7] The cost for its expansion could go as high as one liked so long as its world view would never have to capitulate before renewable energy. The expense incurred for its introduction dare not have been in vain. The conflict between 'solar' and 'atom' — between embracing renewable energy or continuing down the path taken in the 1950s, initially by way of nuclear fission, later via nuclear fusion — is, above all else, a structural conflict linked to world views. It is played out using superficial technological and economic rationales that conceal the very things for which the advocates of renewable energy are reproached: ideological fixation and technological pipe dreams. This basic conflict was not apparent for some time, or to put it more precisely, it did not become visible until nuclear energy became discredited by the fateful warning of Chernobyl in 1986.

The smouldering fires of seven
energy-determined world crises

Yet the supporters of the fossil/nuclear world view have been making their calculations without taking into account the world-wide crises that, in spite of all the attempts at cover-up, keep getting generated (directly or indirectly) by nuclear and fossil energy. Seven grave crises may be discerned. Every one of these is well-known, yet each is usually only viewed in isolation rather than in the required synoptic perspective.

The global climate crisis

In 1988, the final declaration of the World Conference on the Changing Atmosphere (the upshot of an initiative of the Intergovernmental Panel on Climate Change established by the World Meteorological Association and the United Nations Environment Programme) stated that the world, because of its fossil energy consumption, was letting itself get involved in an experiment whose consequences would come to resemble those of a nuclear war. The number of individual catastrophes – storms, floods, droughts – is on the rise, and they are going to become more severe. They are even taking place earlier than most meteorologists have predicted. The major impending threats are probably those relating to the rise of the sea level, warming water, and changes in ocean currents. Attempts at placating concerns about these dangers by pointing to similar occurrences in the history of the Earth do nothing to remedy the climate crisis. These precedents took place in periods when only a few or no humans at all populated the Earth. What humans create today also needs to be avoided by doing everything humanly possible. We are threatened by the prospect both of major areas of settle-ment becoming uninhabitable and of gigantic expanses of land becoming degraded – and all this means mass movements of people in flight. These kinds of damages ensuing from today's climate catastrophes do not show up in any energy bill.

The exhaustion and dependence crisis

The most explosive problem about fossil energy supplies is the growing dependence of more and more countries on fewer and fewer production sources, especially for petroleum and natural gas.[8] Today the US is dependent on imports for up to 56 per cent of its energy requirements, Germany for 80 per cent and Japan for up to 95 per cent of their respective energy demand. The days of 'easy oil', of petroleum deposits that can be extracted relatively effortlessly and cost-effectively, will be coming to an end in just a few decades. The same goes for natural gas – although this is readily overlooked – which largely comes from the same oil-producing countries.[9] This means that about 60 per cent of today's global energy consumption will be up for grabs over the next several decades. Declining reserves on the one hand and growing demand on the other inevitably lead to rising energy costs, which harbour drastic dangers for the world economy and threaten to tear apart the social fabric. Increasing conflicts over these reserves' availability, including wars over 'cheap' residual resources, are pre-programmed into this development. The major portion of petroleum reserves still available resides in the arc of Islamic states that – not least of all owing to oil – has become an overheated crisis region, while another major portion of additional reserves may be found in the Islamic-Caucasian area, also a crisis region. This imparts an even greater explosiveness to the dependence crisis.

The poverty crisis in the developing countries

Developing countries without fossil resources of their own, and this is the world's majority, have to pay the same amount for energy imports on world markets as all the other countries, and each one has do this with a per capita gross national product (GNP) that is well under 10 per cent of the Western industrial countries' GNP. De facto, therefore, developing countries as measured by their economic efficiency face a burden that is greater by a factor of 10 or more because of their energy imports. At the same time, owing to a lack of networked infrastructure for energy supplies, these countries are economically even more dependent on non-pipeline-connected petroleum than the industrial countries. The consequences of energy poverty are ruinous exploitation of biomass, increasing steppe land, rural flight into the cities' overflowing slums, the destruction of social structures and the disintegration of states, and crises that spill over into international conflicts.[10] And yet, in a grotesque misjudgement of reality, using indigenous renewable energy to overcome this energy-determined poverty crisis is deemed economically unreasonable.

The nuclear crisis

Since the 1990s, more and more countries have wanted to equip themselves with nuclear weapons. The essential reason for this is that the nuclear powers (the 'haves') continued to insist on their own nuclear armament even after the Cold War was over. Above all, the US has insisted on this stance (and, as part of the US retinue, NATO strategy has also clung to this position), in spite of the overwhelming quantitative and qualitative superiority of its conventional weapons and troops. The result is that the international two-class system of 'haves' and 'have-nots' established in 1970 by the Non-Proliferation Treaty is less and less accepted by up-and-coming regional powers, and especially among the countries of the Islamic region. They see an additional legitimation in the belief that they would never be treated the way Iraq was if they had nuclear weapons. The US's gentle behaviour towards North Korea, which has a nuclear weapons potential, confirms this.

Access to a nuclear weapons potential and hiring experts to build one have become easier than ever: whether covertly, by finding scientists from the ruins of the former Soviet Union and hiring thousands of unemployed nuclear weapons specialists, or officially, by using the right inscribed in Article IV of the Non-Proliferation Treaty guaranteeing all (currently 138) signatory states technical assistance when it comes to 'applications of nuclear energy for peaceful purposes'. Whoever possesses the essential components of the nuclear fuel cycle, meaning reactors and the opportunity to enrich uranium and reprocess nuclear fuel (even if only on a small scale), is just a few quick steps away from possessing nuclear weapons. The deadline for giving notice on abrogating the Non-Proliferation Treaty is just three months. Not only can the technological boundary between civilian and military applications be quickly crossed, it is just as easy to transgress the political demarcation between 'peaceful' and military uses. There is also the growing danger posed by nuclear terrorism. On 11 September 2001, the world found out that fundamentalists do not shy away from mass murder at the cost of sacrificing their own lives. They could use nuclear terrorism to become a world power – not through the relatively complicated deployment of atomic weapons, but by means of less complicated kamikaze attacks on nuclear power plants or via acts of sabotage producing large-scale nuclear radiation.[11] The civilian use of nuclear power is a 'child' of its military application, and this is not a paternity easily shaken off.

The water crisis

The total amount of water on the planet has, to be sure, remained constant. Even evaporated water directed into the atmosphere returns to the Earth's surface – although not necessarily to where it is needed. Condensed fresh water that falls as rain into the oceans becomes salt water there. The freshwater crisis in many regions of the globe (increasingly a problem in the northern hemisphere as well) is attributable in large measure to nuclear and fossil energy. Three-quarters of Germany's water consumption as registered in statistics, and about 50 per cent in the US, originates from the demand of nuclear and fossil steam power stations![12] This water escapes into the atmosphere or is returned in heated form to rivers, which thereby impairs water ecology. The problem is even more serious in water-poor regions. The competition between people's immediate need for water and their indirect water needs because of agricultural production is a conflict that has frequently been described. By contrast, the competition that exists between these needs and the water requirements of the nuclear and fossil energy system has largely been overlooked thus far.[13]

In addition to what is required for steam power plants, there is a significant demand for water to wash coal that has been

mined or for oil production (in order to create the pressure
needed to extract petroleum). And then there are those serious
disturbances of ocean and water ecology with their negative
consequences for fish life and other habitats, or the damage
caused by tanker accidents and diesel leaks from motorized ships
and boats. One drop of fossil oil contaminates a cubic metre of
water. Nitrates from petroleum-based farm fertilizers also
damage the water table. The water crisis is to a large measure
the result of the nuclear and fossil energy system.

The farming crisis

The same goes for the crisis of modern farming. Because of
agriculture's shift away from using home-grown energy, including fertilizer, to chemicals, all the sectors bordering on
agricultural production have become steadily more dependent
on the energy business. The purchasing costs of fertilizer and
energy have grown enormously and diminished farmers' incomes.
The response to this cost-income squeeze has been heightened
production using more fossil-based energy and fertilizers – an
ecological and economic vicious cycle. In addition, the compulsion to increase production is a driving force behind the
transformation from a more peasant-rustic type of farming to
an industrial kind of agriculture – a development leading to the
destruction of rural livelihoods that increases the general level
of unemployment and destroys the culture of rural areas.
Moreover, soils become overtired – to the point of degradation.
Developing countries that are dependent on oil imports, furthermore, cannot keep up with this fossil-based increase in
agricultural production – and when they try to keep pace, they
can only do so at an economic cost that is disproportionately
high.

The health crisis

That health defects result from the normal operation of nuclear
power because of radioactive contamination is a fact that has
been repeatedly denied. But it is indisputable that this happens
in uranium mining. When it comes to health defects from fossil

energy, the results are even clearer, something that has been confirmed by the World Health Organization (WHO) and articles published in *Science*, one of the most reputable science magazines. Roughly one-quarter of humankind is therefore adversely affected by energy emissions. According to one study, which covered only Austria, France and Switzerland, these discharges lead annually to 800,000 cases of asthma and bronchitis and 40,000 premature deaths. And yet these countries have comparatively strict emission regulations. In China, premature deaths from 'outdoor emissions' are estimated at 290,000 annually, and in India at around 200,000. In China, according to World Bank research, fossil-based air pollution costs US$50 billion in health damage annually, which corresponds to 7 per cent of GNP. In the EU, these costs are estimated at US$70 billion.[14]

One WHO estimate puts the number of premature deaths at 1.8 million annually in Africa alone, where women and children are especially affected, in particular by 'indoor emissions', meaning traditional wood burning in houses and huts lacking technological opportunities for better energy use like energy-saving wood-burning stoves, solar collectors or solar electricity.

Reciprocal crisis infection

It is no accident that the crises sketched out here have shown up at the same time. The higher the level of energy consumption, the more this heats up all the accompanying problems (as in a system of interconnected pipes and ducts). A small harbinger of what can happen here was Italy's electricity supply crisis in the summer of 2003. A heatwave probably attributable to climate change had gripped half of Europe, especially Italy and France. Alpine reservoirs received less water, while rivers and streams dried out. The region's steeply rising power needs for electrical cooling systems collided with the hydroelectric power plants' sinking production. Even French nuclear reactors delivering electricity to Italy had to stop production for lack of cooling water from rivers. For weeks there were long stretches of time every day in which abrupt power failures were experienced. Industrial activity had to be stopped, computer systems crashed. Harvest failures, with their concomitant agricultural losses, reached all the way to northern Germany. The climate crisis had triggered a water crisis which, in turn, led to an acute power supply and agricultural production crisis.

This concatenation shows what awaits us over the next several decades if the world is unable to liberate itself post-haste from nuclear and fossil energy dependence. One need not even conjure up one of those oft-repeated horror scenarios about northern Europe losing its warming Gulf Stream and therefore entering an ice age, or about all the world's coastal regions becoming inundated and permanently uninhabitable, nor even about the dangers of a nuclear reactor meltdown. These dangers are more or less probable, but they are always assessed as hypothetical. No longer hypothetical is the kind of crisis escalation just depicted, a scenario quite likely to become more frequent.

Because of the climate crisis, the number of victims directly affected by catastrophes is bound to swell. The crisis will also increasingly impair both the ability of states to act and living conditions for the general public. Insurance companies will get into financial straits, from which they will be able to extricate themselves only by increasing premiums and removing climate risks from the protection their policies offer. Social compensation measures for people who have run into trouble, along with repair services for public infrastructure, are going to strain government budgets or compel higher tax burdens. The costs of compensating damages from environmental crises caused by outdated forms of energy reduce the financial leeway needed to provide for a future based on renewable energy. States that can summon up neither the financial nor the organizational energy to redress these catastrophic damages will be forced to abandon people to their fate. There will be more victims fleeing devastated regions for lands not yet endangered – and the number of uprooted and impoverished people will also be on the rise.

A political state of emergency is therefore pre-programmed into every oil and natural gas exhaustion crisis. There might also be surprises in store if a government were to be overthrown – for example, if Saudi Arabia's feudal regime with its hydra-headed monarchy were to be ended and replaced by a fundamentalist Islamic regime that might throttle and stretch out the timetable for oil production in its own long-term interest. Or there could be a political-military conflict encompassing the entire Persian Gulf region if the US should decide to use force to prevent Iran from acquiring nuclear weapons and thereby trigger a multi-country conflagration involving uncontrollable mass unrest. An additional scenario might be a rapid increase in relatively risk-free terrorist attacks on oil and gas pipelines, which run along stretches extending for tens of thousands of kilometres that are not reliably guarded. Attacks of these kinds could interrupt world oil supplies and plunge the global economy into a maelstrom. As early as 1980, one Pentagon study had already warned about this eventuality and therefore issued an urgent recommendation for conversion to renewable energy.[15] The political-military cost of securing oil supplies will rise in any case, as will political pressure from the US on other industrial countries to share in defraying this cost. It is no accident that China is rearming so that it can secure its international resource interests from a position of military strength.

But even if none of this happens (which we can only hope, though it is hardly a realistic expectation), the rise in the price of oil, because of its inevitable shortage, simply cannot be stopped by the evasive manoeuvre of falling back on non-conventional reserves. There will be increased domestic political pressure on governments to lower energy taxes so as to relieve citizens from the burden of drastically rising energy prices. A foretaste of this was supplied by the Europe-wide protest against fuel taxes in the autumn of 2000 after a rise in oil prices. A current event signalling the same problem is the legislation introduced by the Bush administration in April 2005, whose aim is to arrange tax breaks in the order of US$8 billion for companies producing coal, natural gas and petroleum as well as nuclear energy within the US.

If governments cave in to this pressure, they are endangering their public budgets. If they do not, economic and social distress will still be on the rise. 'Developing countries' will ultimately suffer economic collapse under the weight of price increases for oil imports, and this will accelerate their political institutions' decline to such an extent that industrial countries and international organizations will be hopelessly strained trying to provide assistance. Even those countries that have placed their bets on tourism as the sector carrying the burden of economic growth will suffer severe losses, since more expensive oil is going to stem the flow of international air traffic. The attempt made by the Gulf state Abu Dhabi to face up to the imminent drying out of its oil wells and adjust to the post-Oil Age ahead of time by building seven-star luxury hotels is probably condemned to failure if there are no longer enough tourists to sustain it.

And anyhow, what will happen with and inside the oil-producing states if their oil wells run dry quickly? Most of these countries have hardly taken precautions about the post-oil era, and they have carelessly neglected to promote small- and medium-sized industry as well as agriculture, as the political scientist Hartmut Elsenhans has noted.[16] And what are the prospects for Russia and the Central Asian oil- and gas-producing countries when their chief income source runs dry? Will they all follow the advice clamorously offered again to place all their bets on nuclear energy – and to do so in the midst of domestic turmoil, with fragile institutions lacking democratic foundations, and against the background of a newly rekindled Islamic–Western culture war? Will this not lead inevitably to the proliferation of nuclear powers? The world will be threatened by ruinous turbulence if, owing to unfounded fear of the shift to renewable energy, countries continue to play with nuclear and fossil fire. One is reminded of the pattern of behaviour in an ancient Greek tragedy, in which everything rushes towards a disastrous end. Everyone involved can see this coming, but nobody can release himself from his own behavioural compulsion contributing to the tragic denouement.

The many ingenious scenarios painted by conventional energy experts are built on an assumption that became unrealistic a long time ago – namely the possibility of somehow maintaining global stability in spite of energy crises flickering up all over the world and then shifting the costs for this onto the general public. Those who provide this kind of advice like to certify their own superior sense of 'realism', which they derive from the dominance of the traditional energy system and from the conventional prevailing wisdom (heavily influenced by that system) among political, economic and scientific 'elites'. Yet 'realism', above all else, is something that flows from a clear perspective on problems. Concepts and plans that do not provide any answer to these problems are not realistic; they are unreal. The basic requirement of realism is not being fooled by anything. The reality is that the world is now confronting the greatest challenge in the history of civilization and, in spite of this, has not faced up to this challenge in the appropriate manner. By consorting with fossil and nuclear energy, the world has got itself entangled in two 'Promethean' grand experiments from which it has no inclination to extricate itself of its own accord. Prometheus, of course, is that figure from Greek mythology who stole fire so he could take over the power of creation. For this he was terribly punished, and the fire was ripped from his hands by the gods. Since we do not live in a world of mythological sagas, we need to rely on social forces to put the nuclear and fossil fireplace on ice. An orientation towards renewable energy does not require some grand new technological Prometheus, like nuclear fusion, to whom the energy technicians of the industrial modern age keep calling out.

What society is going to be capable of taking decisive action in order to create a new, survival-guaranteeing energy foundation when the wildfire of energy crises has completely spread out all around us? How many people in this interconnected world will then be swept along into the abyss? Will it take a variety of catastrophes whose consequences are still containable before a definitive breakthrough towards the necessary shift in energy resources is triggered? Or will we succeed in forestalling such developments with rational action just in time? Both of these possibilities – a comprehensive shift to renewable energy *or* its 'long-term' postponement – have revolutionary consequences, albeit in extremely different ways. It is the difference between a positive and a negative vision – if the standard by which we measure policy and political action includes the human right of everyone to energy, climate and environmental protection, economic and social stability, and securing life and peace.

Enough energy for all: The sweeping potential of renewable energy

The fact that renewable energy can satisfy the world's entire energy needs has been explained repeatedly in detailed scientific scenarios since the 1970s: on a global scale, for the US, repeatedly for Europe, for Germany and Japan, for Sweden or Austria – and also for regions within individual countries.[17] What all these studies have in common is that they get systematically ignored in discussions about energy, even by relevant environmental institutes.

The different scenarios were drawn up using an 'inductive' method: they proceed from assumptions about current and expected supply and demand potentials for energy and then calculate in the possibilities for saving energy and increasing energy efficiency. At the same time, they shed light on the different forms of renewable energy according to their specific supply opportunities within the different sectors of energy consumption. Yet all energy scenarios, even those for renewable energy, are inevitably a glass bead game; no economist from the vantage point of today – even assuming that developments are relative – can estimate what the costs of traditional energy compared to those for renewable energy technologies will be in 2025 or 2040, and it is especially difficult to estimate expenses for technologies that are still young or have only recently been introduced. Yet even if no energy scenario can ever cover every facet of future developments, in principal it can at least sketch out what is possible and describe goals that are achievable so that appropriate action may be encouraged.

The opportunity for a complete shift in energy

In order to demonstrate the plausibility of energy supply based exclusively on renewable energy, therefore, it should suffice to employ a much simpler method. Based on a natural potential that vastly exceeds all traditional energy sources in quantitative terms, on technologies already available today (including opportunities for applying them), and with a little willingness to join in some creative practical thinking, one could plausibly make the case that it is possible to replace traditional energy with renewable energy.

Electricity as an example

In 2001 annual commercial electricity consumption worldwide came to 15.5 trillion kilowatt hours. In order to make this amount of electricity available exclusively through wind power, one would need to install – based on 2.5-megawatt facilities that produce 6 million kilowatt hours a year at medium-range wind speeds – 2.5 million wind power facilities around the globe. In order to create the same amount of electricity with photovoltaic facilities, one would need to install – assuming a production rate of 75 kilowatt hours of electricity per square metre of solar cell area and per year, which is a relatively small value under German insolation conditions – around 210,000 square kilometres of solar cells worldwide. That is much less than the built-over surface area of the EU alone, an expanse into which solar cells could be integrated in a variety of ways. When it comes to solar-thermal power plants, 155,000 square metres of collectors would have to be installed – based on a calculation that about 10 million kilowatt hours are produced per hectare of collector space – especially in desert regions or on areas otherwise not used.

Thermal heat as an example

In order to satisfy the world population's current need for heat using solar heat, it would suffice – as measured according to consumption from the year 2001 at 3.34 trillion kilowatt hours – to have 15,000 square metres of solar collectors, calculated on the basis of just 2.25 kilowatt hours of solar heat production per square metre of collector space.

Bio-fuel as an example

If today's 21 trillion kilowatt hour demand for fossil fuels were to be met by bio-fuels, the amount of forest or farmland acreage that would have to be made available for continuous energy harvests, calculated at an average energy yield of 50,000

kilowatts per hectare, would come to 4.19 million square kilometres. This corresponds to using about 8 per cent of the world's
forest, field and farmland acreage for this purpose – with
regrowth cultures for which annual harvests would have to correspond to the biomass potential that would be regrowing again
the following year. But in semi-arid regions there is an additional
cultivatable potential of well over 10 million square kilometres,
and above all there is the usually overlooked potential of water
plants in the form of algae cultures or water hyacinths.

These are projections of individual renewable energy options
for which (as adumbrated) there is no demand that they be
implemented – something that can be seen simply by looking at
the case of electricity, where the requirements for meeting world
demand are quantified with each one of the three options cited.
One therefore needs significantly less from each option than
indicated above. Additional options that supplement this picture
of a technological potential already within our reach are: 1)
water power (already long in use), which currently covers about
18 per cent of the world's electricity consumption and which,
in the form of small-scale water power – in other words, without
damming up flowing water – can frequently be developed; 2)
wave and tidal energy; and also 3) geothermal energy. That this
natural energy potential enables an even wider range of technologies to be activated is something that emerges from the basic
fact, described elsewhere, that the sun and its derivatives (wind,
waves, water and biomass) 'deliver' a daily dose of energy that
is 15,000 times greater than what we now consume in the form
of nuclear and fossil energy. To speak of insufficient energy
potential is therefore downright laughable. It is also nonsense
to speak of some limit set by technology, for the issue at hand
(given the required volume of production for energy facilities)
is the kind of production capacity that has been customary in
other industrial sectors for a long time – and in the future even
the energy required for these facilities' production can and will
be renewable.

What, therefore, is the principal obstacle supposed to be?
The projections introduced above serve only to open up our
thinking on the subject. The practical attractiveness of renewable energy becomes greater with each step taken towards a closer

and more differentiated consideration of its potential for natural and technological application. This attractiveness includes: technological and structural enhancements of efficiency through the avoidance of transmission and transportation costs; the opportunity renewable energy provides for regional and local energy provision; new building forms that drastically lower active heating costs in houses; and major opportunities for mining bio-fuels from the biological waste products of the agricultural and timber industries and from foodstuff production or leftover wood from forestry, expanded by way of new biomass cultivation plans using crop rotation, annual multiple harvests, new gasification and fermentation techniques. The magnitude of all these opportunities expands in regions with above-average insolation, natural water reserves, especially good wind conditions, soil conditions and forest yields. The scale of opportunities also grows with continuous optimizing of application techniques already tested and the development of new ones, and it increases with improvements in techniques for energy facilities' production, for increasing their efficiency, and employing new materials.

Just this spectrum of current opportunities illuminates how supplying the world with renewable energy, even taking into account developing countries' growing energy needs, is something we can already describe. The proportions in which the individual options are mixed will be different from country to country, region to region, from one local community to another, and from house to house. Which mixture is realized in each case cannot be predicted and will depend on many factors: on the effects of energy savings that are achieved, which will lower energy demand parallel to the expansion of renewable energy; on geographical conditions and natural supplies in each instance; on the developmental maturity of each technology, on each technique's degree of industrialization, and on its cost trajectory; on the open-mindedness of economic enterprises and, not least of all, on the state of public consciousness – in other words, on social factors. The only sure thing is that today's widespread uniformity in energy supply structures and energy consumption, which developed on the basis of fossil energy, will become a thing of the past. Every country, indeed every region

Table I *'100 per cent scenarios' for energy supply with renewable energy*

Title	Year of publication	Organization	Target country/region
Solar Sweden: An Outline to a Renewable Energy System	1977	Secretariat for Future Studies (Director: Professor Thomas Johansson)	Sweden
ALTER: A Study of a Long-Term Energy Future for France Based on 100% Renewable Energies	1978	'Le Groupe de Bellevue' Scientific group of leading research institutes	France
Energy Strategies: Towards a Solar Future	1980	Union of Concerned Scientists	US
Solar Energy Futures in a Western European Context	1982	International Institute for Applied Systems (IIASA)	Western Europe
Renewable Energy Supply under Conditions of Globalization and Liberalization	2002	Survey Commission of the German Bundestag	Germany
Energy Rich Japan (ERJ)	2003	Institute for Sustainable Solutions and Innovations (ISUSI)	Japan

Target year	Energy carrier mix	Recommended instruments
2015	100% renewable energy: biomass 61.8%; active/passive solar heat 12.5%; water power 11.4%; PV (photovoltaic) 8.8%; wind power 5.3%; oceanic energy 0.2%	No data
2050	100% renewable energy: solar (photovoltaic, solar thermal, CSP (concentrating solar power), passive) 49.5%; biomass 27.2%; water power 13.7%; tide power 5.1%; wind power 4.6%	No data
2050	100% renewable energy; sectoral distribution: building sector 35% (active and passive solar use; short-distance heating, biomass); industry 30% (wind, PV, CHP (combined heat and power, or cogeneration)), CSP; transportation 25% (biomass, H_2, electricity); other 10%	Efficiency standards; tax policy; interest-free credits and subsidies; tax exemption or allowance; renewable energy usage obligation in the building sector; 'Solar Development Bank'; R&D; information policy
2100	100% renewable energy: wind power 33.9%; on-site 28.3%; biomass 15.1%; PV 9.4%; water power 8.5%; solar-H_2 3.4%; wave power 1.4%	No data
2050	94.6% renewable energy: import renewable energy 15.4%	Increase in efficiency: Renewable Energy Sources Act; Renewable Energy Heat Act; expansion of short-distance and long-distance district heating; import of renewable energy; R&D
No data (depends on politics / policy)	100% renewable energy: solar 35.1%; wind power 28.4%; CHP 17.7%; geothermal 13.5%; water power 5.2%	Efficiency standards and labelling; efficiency and renewable energy regulations for building sector; legally binding extension rules for renewable energy; input reimbursements; consumption reduction in transportation

will be getting a specific, and also diverse, energy foundation. Supplying the world with renewable energy will be 'multicultural' (see Table 1).

Of course, all sorts of individual efforts will be necessary in order to realize this vision. But what is required is no more complex or more expensive than the development and production of satellite, aerospace, communications, medicine or weapons technology – and it is less complex by far than nuclear technology. The assertion that it is not possible to arrive at a comprehensive energy supply using renewable energy is an insult to the creativity of physicists, chemists and engineers. And if there are any scientists who assert this, they are only discrediting themselves.

Countless practical examples show that this can work. Since 1994 the most illustrative and outstanding projects have been honoured with the European Solar Prize awarded annually by EUROSOLAR.[18] These include residential homes, for example, but also old buildings, prefabricated houses, school and local government buildings, office buildings, and production sites that meet their entire energy needs – electricity and heat – autonomously using renewable energy. A few of these (like the 'plus energy house') even produce surpluses. The vast majority of these buildings' owners are people earning average incomes. Imagine what can happen if more and more homeowners rethink their energy use along these lines – and, ultimately, if everyone does so because it becomes the social norm. People would be rid of their worries about rising energy prices, city air would be cleaner, the number of the infirm would sink. The city landscape would be changed, especially rooftops, since there would be lots of crystal blue and multicoloured solar panels instead of the kind of red roof tile dominant in German cities. After all, what we are dealing with here – if we add up home demand for electricity, heating and cooling – is nothing less than half of the solution to the problem.

The prizewinners have also included farmers and vintners, who not only meet their energy needs with renewable energy they produce on their own but have also become energy suppliers themselves, as well as firms who tank up their entire fleets of vehicles with vegetable oil; producers of synthetic bio-fuels like 'sunfuel' or bio-ethanol and of the drive assembly technologies related to these fuels; cities and municipal works who supply their residents with electricity and heat from biomass power plants and can completely heat housing developments using solar heat that they store in the ground for the winter. The list includes businesses that have developed passenger boats driven exclusively by electricity from solar cells installed on each boat, entirely noise- and emissions-free, and which transport up to 100 people along the Neckar river in Heidelberg, on Lake Constance, or around the Alster river in downtown Hamburg. Other winners are cities that have bought back their electricity grid and are operating it either themselves or with a municipal civic cooperative. EUROSOLAR also issued awards to islands and small local communities who made themselves energy-autonomous for all their electricity and heating needs. All these award winners instigate others to follow suit.

With a little bit of 'sociological imagination' (to borrow a term from the late C. Wright Mills and the German scholar-activist Oskar Negt), we can appreciate how countless small achievements can be bundled together into a whole new and larger entity. All these examples show that the hurdles are not, at core, technical and economic barriers. What matters are ideas and attitudes that can unleash initiatives. In any event, the basic assumption of an insufficient technological potential is untenable.

The opportunity for rapid implementation

Take Germany's Renewable Energy Sources Act: about 10 per cent of Germany's entire electricity supply was achieved using renewable energy, of which about 7 per cent came from 'new' forms of renewable energy, meaning without water power from dams. This 7 per cent represents about 19,000 megawatts of power plant capacity initiated because of the Renewable Energy Sources Act. The annual growth in capacity promoted by the Renewable Energy Sources Act and its forerunners comes to about 3000 megawatts, of which wind power has the largest share. Assuming that Germany experiences the same annual growth over the next few decades, capacity would increase to 48,000 megawatts in 2015, 78,000 in 2025, 108,000 in 2035, 148,000 in 2045 and 178,000 in 2054 (note, what we are describing here is an introductory tempo for which there already exists practical proof). At 16,000 megawatts, wind power currently already has the greatest overall potential for renewable energy in Germany. Further developments will make the renewable energy spectrum more pluralistic. The tempo of change that has already been reached does not even have to be sustained for decades on end in order for us to arrive at a situation, 40 to 50 years from now, in which nuclear and fossil energy will have been completely replaced by renewable energy. Renewable energy's still youthful technologies will continuously increase their level of efficiency, and new storage technologies will follow. What matters, by the way, is not so much installed output as the amount of electricity actually produced. Whereas traditional energy technologies tend to be nearing the end of their potential for technological development, so that we can only expect diminishing returns from their optimization, renewable energy technology is at the start of its development, so that each of its varieties harbours a huge potential for optimization.

The speed of introduction for renewable energy also depends, of course, on the cost situation. In every cost comparison between renewable and conventional energy, the basic question has to be whether we are dealing with an isolated microeconomic or with a macroeconomic type of cost accounting (including ecological follow-up costs), and whether this is a short- or long-term calculation. Yet even individual facilities will find that the comparative cost situation is continuously improving in favour of renewable energy when they take a look at its greater potential for innovation. Fixed costs for fuels from traditional power plants, by contrast, can only be expected to rise.

Whoever asks about the amount of time needed to introduce renewable energy will have to compare this time requirement with the time spent on new conventional energy facilities. By way of illustration, between 2000 and 2004, in just five years, Germany experienced the creation of about 14,000 megawatts total capacity for electricity production from renewable energy. Investors had as yet little practice in this new technology, and the power plant industry was not even equipped to handle this kind of growth. Let us imagine, by contrast, that the electricity conglomerates had decided in 2000 to build new large power plants and commenced with the initial preparations. Not a single power plant would have come on line by the year 2004. By contrast, installing solar and wind power facilities took place in a matter of days, and for small water power plants it was only a matter of weeks. In every situation where providing new capacity is the issue, decentralized energy has a clear time advantage. This is especially true for developing countries, because by using the appropriate technologies they can avoid what is not only a costly but also a time-consuming construction of infrastructure (such as for electricity grids) and thereby considerably shorten their pathway to a reliable energy supply.

The thesis that there is an enormously long time requirement for introducing new kinds of energy is a misapprehension that energy experts derived from the history of conventional energy systems. This experience is based not so much on the long construction times required for large power plants as it is on the even more time-consuming process of completing the wide-ranging transportation and distribution structure needed to supply conventional energy. This experience, however, would be applicable to renewable energy only if the choices about its expansion were to be oriented around the traditional model and its trajectory of large-scale technology. Yet, with a few exceptions, this is precisely what renewable energy renders technologically unnecessary and economically meaningless. The fundamental technological-economic assumption behind the excessive time requirement, therefore, is also untenable.

The real time problem for renewable energy is truly neither technological nor economic, but rather political and mental: the political problem takes the form of countless arbitrary administrative hurdles, and the mental problem lies in the need for a change of attitude.

The dispensability of large power plants

The assertion that a secure electricity supply depends in some compelling way on large power plants cannot be maintained if only for the simple reason that there is only one really decisive fact: one can only feed as much electricity into a grid as is taken out of the network. Once electricity is fed into the grid, its origin is no longer physically observable. When grid-based electricity production is decentralized, its geographic dispersion must be broad enough to guarantee a proper voltage balance. But above all, a large power plant is by no means the best guarantee of a more secure and more efficient energy supply. If it breaks down, at one fell swoop there is a danger of large-scale supply interruptions, which can only be avoided by maintaining an extensive reserve capacity. That is the reason why, in Germany for example, only about 60,000 megawatts out of 100,000 megawatts of conventional power plant capacity is used. By contrast, one of the advantages (completely underestimated) of a decentralized application of renewable energy relates precisely to its use of numerous individual modules that operate independently of one another, so that the loss of a few units counts for less. It is therefore possible to do without the extensive reserve capacity needed for a large power plant. Bad planning can also be avoided this way; only when the need for electricity grows are additional modules installed.

The prerequisite for this, however, is achieving a relatively even expansion of electricity production using different forms of renewable energy, so that these can supplement each other reciprocally. Even in order to provide large industrial consumers with power consumption of around a few hundred megawatts, one need not hold on to large power plants if – as emphasized earlier – enough power is fed into the grid from decentralized production. Even a finely meshed supra-regional integrated network is not absolutely required, since each large consumer has the opportunity, should the occasion arise, to switch over to producing its own energy – especially if it has a chance to use combined heat and power cost-effectively or can avail itself in the future of its own storage battery capacity.

In a study for EUROSOLAR, *The German Expansion Potential*

for Renewable Energy in the Electricity Sector, written by Harry Lehmann and Stefan Peter, the authors refute the electricity conglomerates' assertion that there is an indispensable need, between now and 2020, for conventional large power plants with a total capacity of 40,000 megawatts as a replacement for other large power plants that will have been shut down by then.[19] The study calculates not only how much expansion of capacity will be required for renewable energy, but also the actual compensatory output associated therewith for each power plant. When it comes to wind energy, the study estimates a somewhat reduced additional annual expansion until 2010, which was pegged at around 2500 megawatts in 2003 and will level off between 2010 and 2020 by increments of 2000 megawatts annually. With respect to photovoltaic energy, the study calculates a steep increase until 2010, and after that annual new installations of 1000 megawatts. The same is assumed for biomass, in association with the expansion of CHP facilities, which will increasingly be operating with biomass. When it comes to geothermal electricity production, owing to the time required to set it up using test drills, the assumption is that there will only be a very small expansion up to the year 2010, after which there will be a steep rise (see Table 2).

Table 2 *Capacity expansion for renewable energy in Germany (megawatts)*

Energy source	Year	Capacity expansion	Power plant compensatory output
Wind energy	2010	28,600	4000
	2020	48,600	12,000
PV	2010	10,000	1000
	2020	20,000	3000
Biomass	2010	10,000	18,000
	2020	20,000	
CHP	2010	19,000	
	2020	32,000	32,000
Geothermal	2010	100	
	2020	16,000	16,000
Total in 2020			
Without geothermal			47,000
With geothermal			63,000

Table 3 *Compensatory output from renewable energy (megawatts)*

	Compensatory output via renewable energy	Compensatory output without renewable energy	Compensatory output with 1% gain in efficiency
2010	23,000	30,000–35,000	23,500–28,500
2020	46,000	40,000–65,000	43,000–48,000

Based on this, power plant output is determined using two variations: one, without any additional gains in efficiency from electricity-consuming appliances, and two, assuming a gain in efficiency of I per cent annually (see Table 3).

From this it follows that there is no need to build new conventional large power plants and also no need to extend the lifetime for operating nuclear power plants. Nobody can claim that this possibility is unrealistic from the standpoint of the potential inherent in nature or technology – especially since expanding the use of small water power plants, an equally plausible option, was not even taken into account by this study because it is an option currently crippled by absurd administrative barriers (of which we will have more to say later). Adding this potential, one could paint a picture of renewable energy's prospects that is even more favourable. It also cannot be imputed that this kind of switch to renewable energy would be economically 'unreasonable'. The cost to the electricity consumer would certainly rise, but this will also be the case with new construction for large power plants and as a result of their rising fuel costs.

Let us peer further into the developments the future has in store. The segments of electricity demand as we previously knew them are shifting. On the one hand, the demand for electricity keeps sinking the more that electricity for cooling, heating and warm water in buildings is replaced by solar-thermal energy and CHP, the more energy-efficient electrical appliances become, and the more these devices draw their electricity from integrated PV modules, so that they almost turn into appliances not dependent on electric current. These positive developments in energy efficiency are matched on the other hand, however, by additional demand for electricity in the area of heating and fuel needs, namely via growth in electricity-driven heat pumps. The overall demand for electricity is also going up because of the growing use of information and communication technologies. Electricity is the energy form that has the greatest variety of possible uses; it is, as the Swiss economist and member of parliament Rudolf Rechsteiner says, the 'reference energy' for any consideration of energy systems.[20]

The efficiency advantage of renewable energy

The thesis is that gains in efficiency and savings while continuing to use conventional energy are the most cost-effective and quickest path to lowering energy emissions and should therefore be given priority over mobilizing for renewable energy; however, this is a thesis conceived in isolation, and it construes a contradiction that does not even exist. Greater energy efficiency from motors, electronic devices or houses will function independently of whether one uses fossil/nuclear or renewable energy. The lower the actual demand, the easier it is to substitute renewable for conventional energy because the amount of energy that needs to be replaced in each case is smaller. Any such 'efficiency-based approach' may therefore accelerate the shift in energy from fossil/nuclear to renewable. If the thesis favouring priority for efficiency-oriented strategies refers only to the techniques for energy conversion, it is being imagined in much too simple a fashion. The only thing then being compared is the relationship between the financial input for technically optimizing a conversion facility and the output of energy and emissions. This simple approach neglects everything that happens within an energy flow, from the appropriation of energy to the expenditure of human labour and technologies. One needs to compare supply systems with reference to the entire energy flow and not just its individual elements.

In my book *The Solar Economy* I described in extensive detail the inevitably long supply chains of fossil and nuclear energy use starting with the production of coal, petroleum, natural gas and uranium all the way through to their final use in motors and appliances, and I compared these with the supply chains for renewable energy.[21] The latter are fundamentally shorter simply because –

aside from the use of energy crops – any expenditure to make primary energy available drops out of the picture. Such expenditure can, moreover, be shortened even further (extremely so) if the renewable energy converted in decentralized facilities is also used at the same site or in the same region. Therein lies the systematic advantage of renewable energy, which has not been noticed nearly enough. It has, not least of all, a decisive advantage when it comes to efficiency, and one that has only been exploited in a preliminary way. The advantage is at its greatest whenever a new energy supply system emerges, as in the rural areas of the South, where 2 billion people live without any hook-up to an electricity grid. In this case, one can immediately skip the development that led industrial societies on the path towards ever more centralized energy conversion using large power plants and refineries (and with the sprawling energy supply structure this required).

The kind of autonomous energy that can only be made available to everyone using renewable energy is no makeshift solution; it represents, instead, the general prospect for the future. It gives developing countries an opportunity to get ahead of the game instead of having to undertake a protracted, costly and inefficient effort at copying the energy supply structures handed down from the industrial societies. In industrial societies, the systemic advantage renewable energy has in efficiency terms will only be fully revealed over the medium or long term. This is because the infrastructure expense that was indispensable to produce and supply traditional energy emerged slowly over several decades, has largely been paid off, and only needs partial supplementation, renewal and maintenance. For this reason it is possible to have strategies using this infrastructure – which does not mean this needs to be the standard for every other new approach. All strategic designs for renewable energy need to keep an eye on what constitutes the greatest potential for increasing renewable energy's productivity, which is the opportunity to avoid, whenever possible, the inevitable and wasteful expense associated with making fossil and nuclear energy available. An energy supply system based on renewable energy has efficiency opportunities that are definitely closed off to a system working with nuclear and fossil energy. These opportunities ensue from the following reasons, briefly outlined here:

- Since each instance of 'final energy' use always happens at that decentralized site where people work and live, every decentralized way of providing energy, as a rule, has an efficiency advantage over any centralized solution.
- Efficiency is greater the less technical refurbishing or conversion is required. When fossil energy is used as fuel or heating energy, fewer conversions are required than is the case when fossil energy is turned into electricity, which then has to be distributed. Therefore, proceeding from an input of primary energy, electricity supplied from fossil and nuclear energy in large power plants turns out to be the most inefficient way of making energy available. But since electricity, as emphasized earlier, is the most important 'reference energy', clinging to traditional forms of energy is the greatest obstacle to efficiency in the future of any society or economy. By contrast, the opportunity to turn solar radiation and wind or flowing water and waves into electricity in a single conversion step is tantamount to the greatest revolution in energy efficiency imaginable. The fact that this requires a separate electricity storage expenditure is neither an insurmountable impediment, nor does it reduce renewable energy's systemic advantage.
- If the issue is not the demand for electricity but rather for heating or cooling energy, the direct use of solar heat is the most efficient option imaginable. If the issue is fuel for mobile transportation systems, bio-fuels produced and marketed on a decentralized basis have a clear systemic advantage over hydrogen whenever it requires more technical conversion steps to be made available.
- If, in addition, the direct economic 'secondary effects' are taken into account, the efficiency advantage of a whole range of renewable energy applications becomes even more striking. For example, via the dual function of solar cells and solar collectors as a roof or facade, and the secondary or tertiary utilization of biomass (wood refuse, food leftovers, agricultural waste products) already used for energy elsewhere or of waste products from bio-fuel production (oil cakes for fodder, ashes from biomass gasification as fertilizer, the use of residues from bio-ethanol production for electricity production, and much more).

- By avoiding climate, environmental and health damage and by saving foreign currency when domestic energy is substituted for energy imports, as well as by virtue of the permanent new jobs secured as a result, renewable energy has a higher macroeconomic efficiency that no one can seriously dispute.

Heightening efficiency is both a precondition and a consequence of all rational economic management. Efficiency criteria have to be guaranteed not only when comparing renewable with fossil and nuclear energy, but also when comparing fossil with nuclear energy or different types of fossil energy with each other – and, needless to say, also when comparing different possible uses of renewable energy. Hence, various plans that try to concentrate electricity production from renewable energy and bio-energy on specific regions – on regions where there is more sunshine (for Europe this means North Africa), where the wind gusts are stronger (for Europe this means the European or North African Atlantic coast or on the high seas), where the biomass harvest is larger (as in Brazil), or where more large dams might be built in order to transport energy from there, by way of lengthy transmission lines, to the sites of consumption where, if need be, they can be converted into other forms – such plans are certainly well-intentioned, but they have not been thought through to the end systematically enough. The economic factor of low production costs gets overvalued, and this leads all other factors to get neglected. These are unnecessary attempts at copying on the part of today's energy business. But, above all, it should not be forgotten that the urgent priority of countries that have a large natural potential for renewable energy lies in its use for domestic consumption. Thus, Morocco has one of the most favourable regions for wind in the world – but its energy dependence stands at 95 per cent. By exporting wind-based electricity it will not be able to earn as much as it can save in foreign currency (otherwise spent on imported oil) if it uses the electricity itself. The top priority for using large solar-thermal power plants in North Africa ought to be supplying this region's major cities with electricity – from Rabat, Casablanca, Algiers, Oman, and Tunis, through to Cairo or Alexandria. Only when this is achieved can they also get around to exporting should the occasion arise.

The independence of energy structures in teamwork

Centralized structures for supplying energy did not arise because they were more 'economical'. The real reason was that transporting electricity is something that can be done substantially faster and cleaner than moving fuel. This counts for a great deal, above all, when it comes to supplying cities with energy. In order to understand why, one needs to know the history of electricity supply.

At the beginning of electrification there were two different basic concepts represented by two pioneers that led to an entrepreneurial conflict that both sides fought with bare fists. It was the conflict between Edison and Westinghouse. Edison's vision was that of producing electricity on one's own – in other words, self-supply – in every house, while Westinghouse's idea was to provide electricity to houses via transmission lines. The latter had – under then-current conditions of electricity production using fossil fuels and water power – a better 'systemic' outlook. Electricity from water power cannot be produced in cities; it is only usable via electric transmission lines. These can supply electricity quickly and cleanly into the home. Edison's plan, by contrast, required delivering fossil fuels into every house, with the result that there would be numerous individual fireplaces in the city, which people were already fed up with because of their experience with heating from coal. His plan was, to be sure, more liberal, but for city dwellers it promised more immediate environmental damage and less comfort.

The conditions that led to the model of a uniformly networked energy supply using large power plants as production centres tend to become invalid, however, when renewable energy enters the picture: using solar energy for someone's own decentralized electricity production does not now require fuel transport. 'Delivering' sun rays happens all by itself and costs nothing. In addition, there are opportunities to make electricity from bio-gas and cities' own extensive food leftovers, as well as to produce electricity from wind power and biomass in urban environs and rural areas. Even if this takes place within an electricity cooperative network, no wide-ranging transmission networks will be needed. On the contrary, the more that decentralized electricity production and supply takes hold and spreads, the less need there will be to use existing networks to capacity. The costs for grid users will therefore rise when the network — within the framework of a liberalization that is fair to all market participants — is no longer co-financed by those who no longer use the grid (or who use it only part of the time). This will motivate many to switch over to decentralized production and marketing. The traditional system will lose its former economic edge. Electricity production will fragment. In addition to electricity that is supplied by a network, there will be decentralized production for the individual's own needs and for neighbourhood demand, area supplies for housing estates, insular supplies for smaller cities, either wholly autonomous or supplemented by spot transmissions. Supplying electricity will return — not fully and immediately, but increasingly — to the vision of its pioneer Edison, a vision that is only practicable on the basis of renewable energy.

How this process takes shape will depend on external factors (legislation), sociological factors (information, level of education, cultural and values consciousness), and technological factors. In order for the opportunities and limits of energy systems to be analysed and evaluated, however, one fundamental insight needs to be considered that is usually ignored: the most formative influence on an energy system is the energy source used. Whatever source is chosen first determines which techniques of energy production and conversion become indispensable, as well as, second, which infrastructure requirements actually exist, along with, third, the corresponding entrepreneurial forms that emerge. The widespread notion that the structure that arose for conventional energy is the standard for modern energy provision, and would therefore also be the best yardstick for renewable energy, is mistaken. This misconception sets in at the third stage in the development of an energy system — today's structures — in other words, after the first step — the choice of an energy source — and after the second, that of the technology that is necessary and possible for that source's productive utilization.

If this sequence is not recognized, today's structure will appear as if it is a sacrosanct and objective requirement setting narrow limits on the expansion of solar- and wind-based electricity. The central rationale behind this restrictive objection is the assertion that energy from solar radiation and wind cannot be stored. If no sun shines on the solar facilities and no wind blows on the rotors, fossil power plants would have to be on hand for constant reserve duty. That means they would literally have to be constantly 'under steam' so that they could jump in at a moment's notice. This would actually reduce the positive environmental impact of solar and wind power facilities, and it would cause pointless expense. These added costs (the argument runs) would become higher in proportion to how many more solar and wind power facilities would be attached to the network, especially if the electricity business were forced by arbitrary political decisions to store this current. This thesis is a key argument that many people found convincing during the campaign against Germany's Renewable Energy Sources Act.

Storing sun and wind power

Energy storage is always necessary when there is no simultaneity between the production and utilization of energy. In a strongly centralized and internationalized nuclear/fossil energy supply system, this simultaneity is, on principle, not possible. The storage warehouse for petroleum is the oil tanker, for coal it is the coal heap, for natural gas the major storage caverns and the gas tank, for nuclear energy the fuel rod store, and for water power (if necessary) the reservoir. Transport and distribution systems — pipelines, tanker ships and trucks — take on a supplementary storage function. Or else it is the power plants themselves that operate as steam power plants, that is, they produce steam, which they must then keep holding inside the power plants as a reserve in case there is a rapid increase in production. All nuclear power plants and all large fossil power plants are of this type.

In the current energy system, energy is stored prior to its conversion into electricity or heat. When it comes to renewable energy, this is also possible in the case of dammed-up water power and bio-energy. Geothermal energy even has the most perfect of all storage warehouses, namely the Earth itself, directly underneath the power plant. Otherwise this is possible only with natural gas, if the power plant has been installed directly above the production site. With energy from solar radiation and with power from wind, waves and un-dammed water, by contrast, it is not possible to store energy prior to its conversion into electricity or heat. These other forms of renewable energy need to be stored after conversion; that is the essential difference.

In any event, conventional power plants – independently of whether there is or is not any solar- or wind-based electricity in the network – need to be on constant standby to produce electricity so they can react to continuous fluctuations in electricity demand. This is the reason their energy consumption is inefficient. If feeding solar- and wind-based electricity into the grid does not achieve an order of magnitude conventional power plants must have simply in order to stand ready with a reserve that is uneconomical and unecological, this is no convincing reason to limit the expansion of renewable energy. The obvious step to be taken should be shutting down the entire operation of these conventional power plants and then organizing the reserve potential for solar- and wind-based electricity using other forms of renewable energy – such as biomass, water power and newly installed storage capacity. It is dissembling amateurishness for the electricity business to dispute these possibilities.

In its campaign against renewable energy, the energy business never mentions its own storage capacity, as if this were not just as easily usable as a reserve for solar- and wind-based electricity, for example, water power from dams, pump storage stations or frequencies available within the electricity grid. The possibility that the sun might not be shining or the wind might stop blowing just when these sources are most needed to produce electricity is presented as an insurmountable obstacle – as if, by way of contrast, extra coal or uranium could be hauled out of the mines at the very moment there is a spike in demand for coal- or nuclear-based electricity. Although the storage problem for solar- and wind-based electricity is exaggerated, it is necessary to devote more attention to it than has previously been done. Not every country can count on having laws that facilitate feeding this kind of electricity into the supply network without obstructions and in an economically attractive way, and one-third of the world's population lives without any hook-up to an electricity grid. In cases like these, both a general willingness to reorient electricity generally around the sun and wind as well as solar- and wind-based electricity's expansion depend on available services for reserves and storage.

An additional reason is that political setbacks are imaginable even in those countries where feeding the networks with electricity from renewable energy is currently guaranteed by law. Solar and wind power plants that have a plant-related reserve and storage capacity make it possible to overcome not only dependence on traditional structures but also widespread prejudices on this subject. The supply side-oriented approach to dispensing electricity from renewable energy can be supplemented by a demand side-oriented approach, which will substantially improve its profitability. The frailty of large power plants with their inefficient 'steam generators' will finally become apparent for all to see. From just a few supply structures exercising wide-ranging control over vast transregional and transnational grids there might emerge a great many small-scale supply structures. Opportunities for self-provision of electricity will multiply – extending all the way into private homes and even reaching as far as the countless electrical consumer appliances ('stand-by' or 'stand-alone' systems) that can produce their own electricity, either wholly or partially, using integrated PV modules. As it is, these devices already constitute 15 per cent of total electricity consumption – and this is a growing trend because of new information technologies, from mobile telephones to the notebook computer. Departing from the previous century's trajectory of supplying energy first in kilowatts and ultimately in gigawatts, a pathway that turned into a very broad one-way street, there will emerge a variety of pathways supplying energy first in gigawatts, then in megawatts, kilowatts and milliwatts.

It would go beyond the scope of this book to introduce the spectrum of storage variations and their respective fields of application. They range from new batteries – Toshiba has just introduced one that can be charged in three minutes – to flywheels, compressed air, hydrogen or thermo-chemical storage devices. They were introduced in the chapter 'Energy beyond the grid' from my book *The Solar Economy*.[22] Richard Baxter offers a comprehensive account of storage methods already in use in his book *Energy Storage: A Non-Technical Guide*.[23] In general, one can say that these become cost-efficient from the moment at which storage costs less than the energy delivered. Investments in storage capacity even begin to suggest themselves under conditions of conventional energy supply, so that it becomes possible to make substitutions for expensive deliveries of electricity at peak hours.

One practical way to have an independent 'island network system' has been demonstrated by the German wind power producer Enercon since 2004 on the Norwegian island of Utsira. Its point of departure was the local system of energy supply using diesel generators within the island's network cooperative. The alternative realized by Enercon is based on wind power plants, supplemented by a synchronous machine for regulating the line voltage and using a flywheel for short-term storage and batteries for long-range storage. The diesel generator now only needs to be used at just 10 per cent of its capacity – and its fuel needs for this lower usage can easily be met with biomass. At the same time there are tests going on – in case a substitute is needed – for a hydrogen generator in which the hydrogen is likewise produced from the wind power plant's electric current. The entire system guarantees a comprehensive, round-the-clock supply of electricity from renewable energy.

Increasingly, storage in the form of compressed air is gaining attention. Smaller amounts can be stored in compressed air containers. With compressed air receptacles – each about the size of a 10 cubic metre container – it is possible for homes to have their electricity supplied non-stop and autonomously on the basis of a PV system. A practical example of large compressed air storage is the Huntorf power plant in the German state of Lower Saxony, which has been in operation since 1978 with a capacity of 290 megawatts. Storage takes place in two ground caverns at a depth of 650 and 800 metres with a total volume of 300,000 cubic metres. At times when there is a surplus of electric current, air at a pressure of 50–70 bars is pumped into the caverns. These can be filled to the brim within eight hours. The compressed air power plant can be started quickly and reach

50 per cent of its maximum performance within three minutes. Another example is the 100-megawatt power plant in McIntosh, Alabama, which has been in operation since 1991. The compressed air is stored in several caverns with a total volume of 538,000 cubic metres. It operates at full performance for 26 hours. In both instances, it is fossil- or nuclear-based electricity that is stored, but their storage potential could just as easily be used for wind-based electricity. Some new compressed air storage facilities have made wind-based power their point of reference from the outset. The Iowa Stored Energy Project, which is allocating 84 megawatts of wind power for a 200-megawatt compressed air power plant, and using an aquifer 400 metres underground that previously served to store gas. In McCamey, Texas, there is a 400-megawatt compressed air power plant, which is fed by 270 megawatts of wind power capacity and can produce 10,0000 megawatts hours of electricity with a storage filling. It can furnish 37 hours of maximum performance. The number of caverns and aquifers that can be opened up is considerable and developing them would require a one-time investment. They fulfil the same function as pump storage works in which water gets pumped into artificial or higher-filled natural basins in order to produce electricity again.

Think about the many mountainous Greek islands that could organize their entire energy and water supply solely from wind energy. Wind power plants produce electricity for the inhabitants' direct consumption, for the operation of a seawater desalination plant, and for pumping this water into a storage basin. The latter, in turn, fulfils three functions: providing fresh water to the island's inhabitants, agricultural irrigation, and producing electricity to complement the wind power plant. Together with solar collectors and bio-fuels – produced from the leftovers of agricultural production that has been revitalized by freshwater irrigation and from food – this island would become energy-autarchic. Once the island was set up with this kind of installation, no energy bill will ever have to paid again to anyone outside the island.

What is possible on natural islands is, however, also possible in 'insular structures' – and this is even the case on a larger, indeed a very large, scale. Norway has so much water power from dams that its electricity needs are completely covered this way. This electric current is exportable via transnational transmission cables; the resulting shortage for purposes of domestic consumption is meant to be covered by gas power plants. But why not, as an alternative, use wind power plants along Norway's wind-rich fjords? Combining wind and water power alone should be enough to facilitate a functioning electricity supply system, one in which sufficient water power and an extensive electricity grid would be available. This is an opportunity that is available in numerous large regions inside Europe – in the Alpine countries or the Balkans, in addition to Scandinavia. The opportunity exists in Brazil, China, Canada, Ukraine, Japan, Central Asia, in large sections of Russia, India and the US – even if no additional renewable energy options were to be brought into play. China, for example, has 200,000 megawatts from coal-fired power plants and 100,000 megawatts from hydroelectric power plants on dams and, according to current plans, it intends to rush ahead with the additional construction of 70,000 megawatts for water power, 150,000 megawatts for coal-based power, and 30,000 megawatts for nuclear power. But it has a water problem in the big cities of the interior that is getting worse, a problem that is attributable not least of all to the enormous water consumption demanded by coal mining and power plants, and which is going to get even worse with more nuclear power plants. By replacing coal power plants with wind power, for which water power plants would provide compensatory storage, it might be possible within a short period of time to arrive at an emissions-free electricity supply. This immediate opportunity exists in countries with large water power plants that have already been installed and with extensive electricity grids. Just the combination of wind and water power from dams alone, in any event, makes it possible to have an energy supply available around the clock.

Bio-fuels and new drive-assembly technologies

Petrol, diesel and kerosene (for jet planes) represent 95 per cent of all the transportation fuels used worldwide today. For nearly a century, motor technology – whether for vehicles moving on

land, air or water, or for stationery use – came to be increasingly
oriented around combustion engines using petroleum derivatives. This did not happen for lack of other drive technologies;
at the beginning of the 20th century there were electric motors
with the same efficiency as combustion engines, and these were
also used for decades – like the delivery vehicle Opel Blitz or
the city bus systems hooked up to electric power lines (overhead
cable or trolley buses). Even Henry Ford's original idea about
the 'automobile for everyone' involved powering the vehicle with
bio-ethanol. That there can be alternatives to petroleum is
proven by the vehicles operated in Germany during the Second
World War using wood gasification motors, and by the Red
Army's off-road vehicles in the former Soviet Union, which were
able to work using pure vegetable oil. A diesel motor developed
by the German car engineer Ludwig Elsbett that runs on pure
vegetable oil has existed for decades, yet not one of the major
car manufacturers has tried to put it on the market.

What emerged over the course of the last century was a total
fixation on petroleum fuels in a period of cheap oil without
competition, the era of unrivalled petroleum that edged out all
other fuel options during the first few decades of the 20th
century. The petroleum business programmed the development
of drive technologies accordingly. It was a business that
expanded into the world's last isolated hamlet and acquired a
unique global monopoly. This also made it even easier for oil to
conquer the market for heating fuel. The car industry – which
cannot sell even a single car without there being fuel for purchase
– had to adjust the development of its motors to petroleum
fuels. Even environmental policy had to do this later on, when
it came to setting standards for improving fuel quality and
reducing pollutants. The result of all this was a monolithic
structure fixated on fossil fuels.

The problem with bio-fuels is not only that – apart from
Brazil and with the partial exception of the US – there is still
insufficient bulk production to entice the car industry into
offering suitable motors for them everywhere. In addition, so
long as specific drive technologies are required for each one of
the different bio-fuel options – vegetable oil, bio-ethanol or
sunfuel – this problem of a low level of interest on the part of

car manufacturers will remain. The car industry thinks in terms of producing large series — that is, apart from the prestige cars each manufacturer uses to cultivate its brand name. It was only when some diesel vehicles were first cleared for esterified vegetable oil use in Germany that there was finally a bit of market development. An additional obstacle is the petroleum industry, which sees its supply monopoly endangered by bio-fuels and wants to keep them at arm's length for as long as possible. Yet another obstacle has more of a social character, and this impediment is one that reaches all the way into the environmental movement: it is the notion that expanding the use of biomass will entail extensive competition with food production and nature reserves, and that this might intensify the trend to monocultures in agriculture. These misgivings are seized on by the petroleum industry — though the same apprehensions have hardly inhibited the oil business from swamping farms worldwide with petrochemical fertilizers and pesticides and from increasingly burdening the ecosphere with a growing supply of fossil fuels.

It is price that is regarded as the biggest obstacle. Yet the price barrier is the easiest hurdle to clear through a tax exemption for all bio-fuels, which has recently become the rule in Germany, Sweden, Spain and Switzerland. As a result, bio-fuels have already become cheaper than fossil fuels in those countries. Governments, of course, lose tax revenue this way. But in return they take in other taxes, because the production of bio-fuels leads to the creation of new jobs — and that means saving money on welfare transfers for people who had been unemployed — while simultaneously stabilizing the social consensus between business and labour owing to the additional employment effect. The way to dispel ecological misgivings about bio-fuels is to use production and marketing plans that, instead of mindlessly increasing bulk production in giant plantations, rely on multi-cultivation and multiple reuse of raw and residual materials. It is obvious, moreover, that there is an urgent need for a discourse about arranging ecological dangers in some kind of hierarchal order, a subject we shall deal with in Part II. The technological dynamic whereby the obstacles mentioned can be overcome in the vehicle and fuels markets, however, requires a reversal of the previous paradigm for motor manufacture. Instead of adjusting motors to fit one particular fuel, they should be geared to work with several different fuels and the possibility of a flexible mix. The 'flexible fuel' car that has been put on the market at no extra charge by all the major car producers in Brazil since 2004 fits into the category of essential new drive technologies. The catchword is the multi-fuel engine. Bio-ethanol can be added to become up to 85 per cent of the fuel mix, and 100 per cent is a technological option within reach. The proportions of the mixture can be determined by the driver anew every day; a meter displays the proportion in the mixture at any given time. If bio-ethanol is not offered at the filling station, it can be fetched from a special supplier. The petroleum business loses its monopoly. In order not to keep losing market share, it will begin to offer these fuels itself. A flexible variant of this kind is the Elsbett motor, which takes pure vegetable oil in addition to diesel fuel. The 'sunfuel' developed by the German chemical engineer Bodo Wolf and his firm CHOREN – which can be produced from solid biomass using high temperature gasification, so that a fuel with a diesel-like quality is produced – accommodates the car manufacturers' previous paradigm. Yet it would be a mistake for the car industry to insist on a single fuel – even if it is made out of biomass. The future lies in a mixture of bio-fuels, so as not to dictate one single route for using bio-fuels to every region in the world. Only if this route is not pre-ordained one-sidedly by this or that motor technology can the whole potential of bio-fuels be fully developed, based on a variety of ecologically compatible cultivation plans, and only then can the car industry keep producing cars in large series. This process will also be accelerated by hybrid drive technologies that reduce actual fuel needs through electricity produced in the vehicle itself.

The macroeconomic advantages

Its purported indispensability is what obtains a special political, economic and social position for the established energy business. This is how it validates its monopoly not only on competence but on action as well. Yet the energy business is hardly the only business capable of making the investments needed to supply energy. It is indeed barely conceivable that financing a comprehensive and effective mobilization of renewable energy would take place within the confines of the traditional energy business with its highly concentrated and interlocking structures. No company pursues its own loss of sales and therewith its own decapitalization. But in this case, one has to hazard the consequences. Taking this risk is the price of any wide-scale structural change. The world of renewable energy, with its decentralized usage, is no place for a monopoly of investment and operations. There are plenty of potential investors, and consequently there are also no limits on the financial resources that can be mobilized on behalf of renewable energy.

Even the counter-argument that introducing renewable energy entails a major economic burden is only correct if microeconomic burdens are equated with macroeconomic ones and if nobody distinguishes between short- and long-term burdens. Undoubtedly, the shift to renewable energy is a burden on the energy business, a burden that is greater the quicker and the more broadly the transformation takes place. For many actors, especially in the primary energy sector, this prospect poses an existential threat. Even energy consumers might be in for some temporary burdens. But to avoid them means to hazard even greater burdens in the future, because ultimately no one is spared the wildfires of the global crises caused by energy. Seen from a macroeconomic perspective, by contrast, the shift to renewable energy presents an enormous opportunity. Taking advantage of this opportunity, however, means recognizing new ways to proceed. Instead of simply extrapolating from the large-scale to the small-scale, one needs to see how the small-scale points to the big picture.

The macroeconomic advantages of renewable energy reside:

- in its indigenous availability and thereby in the currency savings it affords along with the improvement in the balance of payments from cutting back on energy imports;
- in the replacement of commercial fuels by free primary energy, that is, in the substitution of technology for fuel

costs – and thereby in the creation of new jobs for installing power facilities. Unlike large power plant construction, which cannot be distributed broadly enough, production of decentralized power facilities is possible in almost every country;

- in the avoidance of infrastructure costs through regional-ized energy production that is then used in the same region;
- in the promotion of crafts and agriculture that comes from solar construction and biomass utilization, which means permanent stabilization of small- and medium-sized businesses and thereby of regional economic structures;
- in the broad distribution of income because of the emergence of decentralized entrepreneurial forms;
- in the avoidance of ecological follow-up costs, inter alia by reducing health costs and costs for catastrophe prevention and compensation;
- in the avoidance of international security costs (see Table 4).

Waiting for Godot: Fossil and nuclear autism

The sponsors of the traditional energy system would prefer to carry on the same old way. They are in a unique position. They are pulling all the strings. Without the fossil energy business (as the people running this sector see things, based on their inveterate self-image), industrial society as it developed over the last 200 years would never even have existed, and our modern economy and society would simply have collapsed. For the economist Elmar Altvater, the industrial era is more accurately described as 'fossilist' than, say, 'Taylorist' or 'Fordist'.[24] Even more tellingly, the fossil era held its ground and emerged even stronger over the last 30 years, a time when sociologists had proclaimed the 'post-industrial era'. And the energy system's spokesmen now herald even more growth in fossil energy consumption, although others are already talking about the 'de-materialization of the economy' and the 'information' or 'digital age'.

But how would the history of the last two centuries have turned out if James Watt had not invented a steam engine for

Table 4 *The macroeconomic advantages of renewable energy compared to fossil and nuclear energy supply*

	Fossil	Nuclear	Solar electricity	Wind electricity	Small-scale hydraulic power
Domestic availability, currency savings and improvement of balance of payments because of energy imports avoided	No or limited	No or limited	Yes	Yes	Yes, with appropriate topology
Creating new jobs by producing own plants	No or limited	No or limited	Yes	Yes	Yes
Increasing productivity by avoiding commercial fuel costs	No	No	Yes	Yes	Yes
Increasing productivity by having fewer conversion steps	No	No	Yes	Yes	Yes
Avoiding infrastructure costs (transmission, transport, distribution)	No	No	Yes	Yes, except with offshore	Yes
Promoting decentralized economic forms (agriculture, skilled crafts)	No	No	Yes	Yes	Yes
Promoting growth through private investment, spreading ownership	No	No	Yes	Yes	Yes
Reducing climate damage	No	Minor	Yes	Yes	Yes
Reducing health damage	No	No	Yes	Yes	Yes
Safeguarding water	No	No	Yes	Yes	Yes
Avoiding security costs	No	No	Yes	Yes	Yes

Large hydraulic power	Waves	Solar-thermal electricity	Solar heating and cooling	Geothermal	Energy plants	Residual biological materials
Yes	Yes	Yes	Yes	Yes	Yes	Yes
No	Yes	Yes	Yes	Yes	Yes	Yes
Yes	Yes	Yes	Yes	Yes	No	Yes
Yes	Yes	Yes	Yes	Yes	Yes	Yes
No	No	No	Yes	Dependent on plant size	Yes	Yes
No	Yes	No	Yes	Dependent on plant size	Yes	Yes
No	Dependent on plant size	Dependent on plant size	Yes	Dependent on plant size	Yes	Yes
Yes	Yes	Yes	Yes	Yes	Yes	Yes
Yes	Yes	Yes	Yes	Yes	Dependent on use of modern technology	Yes
Possibly	Yes	Yes	Yes	Yes	Dependent on cultivation plan	Yes
Possibly	Yes	Yes	Yes	Yes	Yes	Yes

which coal was the most suitable energy supplier? What if, instead, he had come up with a solar-powered steam engine driven by a parabolic mirror (the forerunner of the modern parabolic dish collector), like the one presented at the Paris World Exhibition in 1878 – about 100 years later – by the Frenchman Augustin Mouchot? This machine was the sensation of the fair and aroused enormous interest, especially since France had just experienced supply shortfalls in coal. But new coal-mining technologies became available immediately after the exhibition, and the bottleneck became a thing of the past. Mouchot was forgotten, along with his 1869 book *Solar Heat and its Industrial Applications*; his solar steam machine can be seen today at a technology museum in Paris.[25] The machine did not stand a chance of being introduced into the market even though at that time people were not so small-minded and condescending as they are today, always checking to see if a new technology will 'pay off' from the start. Yet the coal-driven steam machine, the energy transformer of the 19th century – deployed in factories, steam power plants, in ships and locomotives – had already made itself so indispensable that a power structure quickly emerged from the coal economy and from the producers and users of the corresponding technology. A power structure like this does not give up the ghost simply because a better technology might fulfil the same goal in a different way. Rather, such a power structure is more likely to play off its lead, the advantage in technical maturity it acquired over several decades, and its influential political networking against anything new and different that it cannot control.

Like any other system, the energy system also strives for self-preservation. The more self-confident and powerful it is, the more effectively it acts. And what could convey greater self-confidence than identifying with the great success story of the Industrial Age (whose tale of woe, of suffering and misery, is hardly ever related in the same breath as the triumphalist narrative)? Electrical workers were regarded fairly early in the industrial era as the 'new masters of the world' – thus the title of a publication by the physicist Felix Auerbach from 1901.[26] And Lenin's famous sentence, 'Communism is Soviet power plus the electrification of the whole country', was matched in the

West by the writer Victor Hugo's statement that democracy equalled the general franchise plus electricity. The all-embracing role of the steam engine was ultimately focused on producing electricity. Down to this very day, steam engines drive the turbines of large nuclear and fossil power plants. The second key energy transformer was the combustion engine, which gave the petroleum industry of the 20th century its major impetus and turned oil into the vital elixir of the world economy.

Thus (and especially since the world's energy needs keep growing), it is outside the realm of the imaginable for the current system's sponsors to grasp that the energy they are supplying does more bad than good – and that renewable energy might take the place of fossil and nuclear energy. Society, too, can no longer just mentally dismiss today's energy business. At best the role of renewable energy is seen as one of satisfying the extra demand that cannot any longer be covered by nuclear and fossil energy. Finding a substitute for the latter, by contrast, is subject to a taboo. That is why even those 'scenarios' put out by the world's energy conglomerates and regarded as especially far-reaching stop short of envisioning this substitution. These are the ones put out by BP and Shell, scenarios that garnered enormous applause from the environmental scene over the last few years and were also frequently cited at renewable energy conferences: renewable energy can – according to what these studies say – meet half the world's energy needs by 2050. The assumption underlying this prognosis, however, is that world energy demand will have doubled by then. In plain language this also means that the core of conventional energy supply will not be shaken up in any way. For internal consumption within the company, the anonymous author of the Shell study had calculated a 100 per cent scenario, but he was given to understand by the corporation that it could not accept such a statement.

The economic pacemakers for renewable energy – leaving aside, as always, the big hydraulic power plants – are not the conglomerates that support the conventional energy system, but rather local and municipal energy companies that have stepped out of line, small technology companies and investor groups. One might object that this is typical for the pioneering phase of any industry, before the sturdy and experienced workhorses inevitably arrive on the scene. This is how the 'roll-back' in the US that was discussed in the Introduction got started. Has everything become different all of a sudden because energy-based crises are on everyone's mind and renewable energy is now within reach? In spite of all the forces of resistance just mentioned, can we now really expect to see more and more of the concrete walls blocking renewable energy start to crumble? There is much more evidence speaking against than for the possibility of the big energy conglomerates now becoming the driving force behind renewable energy. More and more oil drills and production licences need to be amortized. Pipelines, large power plants, refineries and grids need to be used to capacity. Investments in large power plants and infrastructure have amortization periods lasting two to three decades. The different individual invest-ments for each never occur at the same time. The number of major investments that are prefinanced is always roughly as high as the number of those that are depreciated. There is, accord-ingly, never a good time to flag down a travelling train and transfer to another one. At best it should suffice occasionally to uncouple one wagon and attach a new one.

The real calculation the energy conglomerates are making is different from the one they are presenting to the public. They simply do not want to admit this, which is what makes the energy debate so dishonest. To be sure, the system will continue to crumble because of ongoing energy-based crises. There will continue to be occasional openings towards renewable energy the more it is recognized that there is no stopping this new train. If one goes along for the ride, one can always, if need be, put the brakes on, turn around or travel on two different tracks. Some people will cooperate for reasons of public legitimacy, since totally abstaining from renewable energy can no longer be publicly justified. Be that as it may, this is no way for renewable energy to achieve a timely breakthrough. In the future, too, no one can expect a move to put renewable energy in the conductor's seat to come from the conventional energy system. Renewable energy will not be handed that locomotive role, that is, unless we lower our expectations and are satisfied taking a slow train.

And, in any event, there is a hard core that keeps pursuing the ongoing triumphal march of the nuclear and fossil energy system. This has been articulated, crystal clear, in the national energy report of the US from 2001, under the aegis of Vice-President Cheney. They are planning oil drills on nature preserves, large-scale dredging of oil sands, methane hydrate from the ocean as a successor to natural gas, new coal and oil production techniques in order to do a better job exploiting available reserves, new nuclear power plants, promotion of nuclear hydrogen, new transmission lines in the tens of thousands, and military protection for international energy resources.[27] Internationally the Bush administration is actually less isolated than it appears as a result of its refusal to ratify the Kyoto Protocol. What was discussed in 2004 at the nuclear conferences in Moscow broadly corresponds to the nuclear portion of the Bush-Cheney programme, and to the view held by Russia, Japan, China, India, EURATOM and sections of the EU Commission. The 'fossil' portion of the Bush-Cheney programme is broadly coterminous with the World Energy Outlook of the IEA and the statements of the 2004 World Energy Conference in Sydney. And as far as the military safeguarding of energy resources is concerned, UK as well as US practice is in line with the Bush-Cheney report, and the EU's security policy in its most recent formulation comes even closer to this line of thinking.

This autistic attempt at self-preservation, however, needs to be legitimized against a background of very public climate dangers. The catchword abused for this purpose is 'sustainability'. In the 42-sentence final declaration of the Sydney World Energy Conference, which declares that growth in fossil energy consumption through 2050 is unavoidable, the concept crops up ten times. It is apparent that the established energy system has regrouped. The plans they are following are formulated in such a way that they promise a way out of the world's climate traps without shifting to renewable energy. An attempt is being made to acquire conceptual sovereignty in responding to the world's climate dangers. The effort includes an official avowal of faith in the Kyoto Protocol. The thing that everyone finds disturbing about the attitude of the US government is its official rejection of this treaty. The plans and concepts brought into play against forcing the issue of renewable energy are an intensified argument in favour of natural gas, 'clean cool' power plants, large-scale plans for hydrogen, and – in a close though often only cautiously articulated association therewith – a renaissance of nuclear energy. In no way can a single one of these plans stand comparison with the opportunities renewable energy offers. The advocates of these last-ditch survival strategies for fossil and nuclear energy resemble the characters Vladimir and Estragon from Samuel Beckett's *Waiting for Godot* – two vaudeville figures lost in time and waiting in vain for someone they do not know and who possibly does not even exist.

Natural gas – a bridge to renewable energy?

Word has got around that petroleum reserves are expected to run out within the first half of this century. Denials of this realization keep getting toned down. Yet with new drilling and production techniques available, an unflagging attempt is being made to eke out from the ground even more of whatever promises to become economically attractive as soon as easily extracted petroleum deposits get scarcer and thereby more expensive. These, then, are the 'non-conventional' reserves: Arctic oil, deep sea oil, or simply what can be found in oil sands and slate. Fifty years ago even North Sea oil still had a reputation as 'non-conventional'. But since nobody could claim that these reserves might be portrayed as climate-friendly, there is now more talk about natural gas, as if this could be treated as a form of renewable energy. Because burning natural gas creates significantly less in the way of direct environmental pollution, it is also on the list of priorities drawn up by many environmental policy makers and scientists. Natural gas is even praised as a 'bridge' to the era of solar hydrogen, as renewable energy's natural partner. The natural gas networks of today as the hydrogen networks of tomorrow! As if it were now already self-evident that hydrogen is going to be the next step. And (furthermore) as if future production facilities for hydrogen could be installed exactly at those sites where gas is fed into the network today. This is how one kind of future for renewable energy is being solidly (mis)planned – a future that, in all probability, will have to look quite different.

It is certainly understandable that natural gas should be preferred to any of the other fossil fuels, especially in cities. Natural gas does significantly reduce current air pollution. In New Delhi this became immediately tangible as a matter of sight, sense and smell ever since the public bus system there converted to natural gas. Natural gas, moreover, is well-suited for combined heat and power cogeneration, and the efficiency of large power plants using natural gas is greater than when they use coal or oil. Building costs are lower and construction times shorter. But all these facts do not justify dismissing the grave problems that either relativize the advantages, both ecological and economic, of natural gas or negate these benefits entirely. Above all, in almost every discussion about natural gas the climate dangers are hushed up even though it is indisputable that a natural gas molecule has a climate-changing impact 20 to 30 times greater than a carbon dioxide molecule. A byproduct of extracting and transporting natural gas is a higher level of methane emissions. The precise order of magnitude is not known and probably also not registered. Some say that the Russian gas network, from which more than a third of Europe's gas supply comes, emits massive amounts of methane owing to leaks. This was denied in a study conducted by the Wuppertal Institute for Germany's largest natural gas supplier, Ruhrgas.[28] But the Institute certainly did not have its analysts pace off the many thousands of kilometres that make up that gas network. It can be neither confirmed nor denied that methane's contribution to rapid climate change over the last several years might be greater than previously assumed.

When people talk about the efficiency of natural gas, they should also look at the energy losses that go along with transporting it, for example, at all the pumping stations. Even greater are the losses that take place when natural gas has to be transported not across pipelines but in fluid form (liquid natural gas or LNG) on ships. These losses happen because the technology for LNG requires cooling temperatures as low as −160°C. The trend, however, is increasingly running in the direction of LNG because the expense of using pipelines over long distances only pays off after natural gas has been extracted from a 'giant field'. Transport opportunities for LNG are considerably more flexible than they are for pipelines, and this factor becomes more important the more that production and consumption expand. Natural gas is also running out, along a time line roughly parallel to petroleum, as Julian Darley has calculated in his book *High Noon for Natural Gas*.[29] How quickly it can run out (and how expensive it is to hire experts who assert the opposite) can be shown in the US, which since the 1990s has achieved a massive expansion of gas power plants with a total of 220,000 megawatts and now faces the problem that there is not enough natural gas available to have these new plants working at capacity.

Those countries and regions that have significant natural gas deposits are just as limited as those having petroleum deposits, and the two areas are largely coterminous. Essentially, these are the North African countries of Egypt, Algeria and Libya, plus Nigeria, Russia, the countries of the Caucasus or Central Asia, Iran and the Gulf state Qatar. Among two-thirds of gas producers, rates of production have already started to slow down. For this reason more and more countries are becoming interested in the increasingly scarce potential of Russia and the Central Asian countries. In addition to the EU, the countries lining up to exploit this shrinking supply include the US, Japan, China, Korea and India. The increasing bias of energy investments towards natural gas, investments that constitute a disproportionate share of the US$16 trillion the IEA regards as indispensable through to 2030, is therefore an orientation that clearly clashes with anticipated supplies. It is hard to see how the projected increase in worldwide demand, from about 200 billion cubic metres per annum currently to around 300 billion cubic metres by 2025, can still be satisfied.

The upshot could be that people will lose their inhibitions and become more inclined to fall for what might prove to be the world's most dangerous environmental adventure: exploiting gas hydrates above the sea floor – the 'fire from the ice', as Hans Schuh titled an article in the German weekly *Die Zeit*.[30] This oceanic hydrate developed from the putrefaction of algae and plankton. Under high water pressure and ice-cold temperatures, most of this potent mix was transformed over long stretches of time into gas hydrates that got deposited on the ocean floor instead of ascending into the atmosphere above the water surface. One litre of this hydrate contains 164 litres of methane gas. There are estimates promising volumes of gas from the ocean depths and permafrost regions of Alaska, Canada or Siberia that amount to double the entire reserves of petroleum, natural gas or coal, 12 trillion tons of carbon. That is mind-boggling. More cautious estimates – like those of geophysicist Alexei Milkov in *Earth-Science Reviews* – mention 'only' 500 to 2500 billion metric tons.[31] Perhaps this more sober figure will put a brake on the gas hydrate intoxication. For the dangers inherent in drilling are incalculable.

The gas hydrates, whose deposits are supposed to have an elevation of 1000 metres on some ocean floors, contribute to stabilizing the continental slopes. If they are broken down, there is a danger that oceanic mountains in the deep sea will collapse, on a scale as incredible as a tsunami. Geophysicists suspect that about 8000 years ago methane hydrate was released between Iceland and Greenland because of ocean water warming up, resulting in more than 5600 cubic metres of the continental shelf collapsing into the Atlantic (the 'Storrega slide'). This was how the Norwegian fjords arose, which gives one an idea of the kind of power this flood released. Gas hydrates could, at a minimum, raise the dangers confronting the globe's climate to a much higher degree:

- extracting gas hydrates, whether in the ocean or in permafrost regions, is hardly controllable overall and can lead to massive increases of methane escaping into the atmosphere;
- ocean warming resulting from carbon dioxide emissions could lead to a change of direction in the Gulf Stream's flow (an event long dreaded anyway) so virulent that this potential becomes like a tsunami – wherever that might be.

Nevertheless, work on extraction techniques for gas hydrates is taking place at a feverish pace, financed by oil conglomerates and public funds. In the Gulf of Mexico the Hydrate Energy International company is already active. And what will Russia, which today gets 20 per cent of its state revenues from gas sales, do when it can no longer satisfy international demand for gas with its conventional gas deposits? Can if afford to deny itself a hold on the Siberian frost regions or on the gas hydrates along its Pacific coast?

Emissions-free coal power plants?

Measured by the standard of 'statistical availability', meaning the proportion of estimated reserves to actual annual consumption, there is more certainty about how long coal will continue to be available than there is for other types of fossil energy: about 170 years. But since burning coal produces the highest level of emissions and is under enormous pressure from climate policy, 'clean coal' has become the motto for survival in that business, alongside attempts at increasing the efficiency of power plants, though this is only possible to a limited extent.

As a way of making coal 'clean', one fallback measure is CO_2 separation, already practised with natural gas extraction. How this functions in gas production may be shown by the example of the Norwegian firm Statoil: its natural gas, extracted from the North Sea, has a carbon dioxide content of 9 per cent, which needs to be reduced to 2.5 per cent before it can be sold. The surplus is separated and pumped into a layer of salt 800 metres under the seabed. The cost of the facility was 350 million euros. In this way Statoil has been able to save on CO_2 taxes levied by the Norwegian state. So long as gas production continues to exist, the separation procedure makes complete sense and is relatively easy to operate. If carbon dioxide has already been separated, it is better to store it than to pass it on into the atmosphere, still a widespread practice. In the case just depicted, surplus CO_2 is also transmitted on the spot into a depot near the source.

Things get substantially more complicated when the power plant is meant to be carbon dioxide-free. In this case the CO_2 that was separated and cleaned has to be brought via pipelines to a storage site, such as a salt cavern. There must be guarantees that the carbon dioxide can be stored here for thousands of years without leakage. Above all, what needs to be avoided is the possibility that large amounts of CO_2 might escape abruptly.

Other conceivable methods might be to liquefy the CO_2, at first using a large dose of cooling energy and then using tankers on the open sea to pump it into the ocean depths where it can dissolve. This, however, entails the danger of incalculable disturbances to the oceanic ecosystem, which Brad Seibel and Patrick Walsh have warned against in the journal *Science*. The carbon dioxide, they argue, would alter the acid content of the deep sea water, which is bound to have consequences for the organisms living there.[32]

The CO_2-less power plant, in any event, means extending the energy chain of coal utilization by several additional links. The costs are higher by a wide margin than in the aforementioned case of natural gas. In 2003 the German federal government's Council on Sustainability submitted guidelines for a 'modern coal policy' along with recommendations for a R&D effort. According to the Council's estimate, the costs for CO_2 separation and 'sequestering' are '20 to over 60 euros per [metric] ton of CO_2 higher than what it costs for efficiency measures, certification prices, and renewable energy', However, since the technology for CO_2-less power plants will not be available before 2020, the efficiency potentials for carbon dioxide reduction would largely be exhausted by that time, and the certification price for emissions trading would rise correspondingly. At that point, then, sequestering carbon dioxide could work 'economically' and motivate countries to adopt climate protection measures they would not otherwise be prepared to undertake.[33]

At the convention organized by the Council on Sustainability ('Innovative Technologies for Electricity Production – On the Way to CO_2-less Coal and Gas Power Plants'), the Council's chair Volker Hauff explained: 'The world's hunger for energy keeps growing – especially in developing and newly industrializing countries, which frequently have large stocks of the CO_2-intensive energy carrier coal. They are not about to renounce falling back on this resource. And who could blame them?'[34] The proper question, however, is this: why shouldn't we actually dispense with them – since, after all, we are talking about a power plant that might be CO_2-less only after 2020? Should one regard new coal-fired power plants as legitimate simply because a country still has large stocks of coal? Must every resource be exhausted down to the bitter end simply because that was the resource used at first? If there were still some 'economic reason' for this, like lower costs compared to renewable energy, it might make some sense. But even the report issued by the Sustainability Council admitted (indirectly, though clearly enough) that this rationale has disappeared. The point was conceded in the sentence cited above, stating that running a CO_2-less power plant today is more expensive than the cost of renewable energy. If renewable energy, however, is already more cost-effective than a hypothetical CO_2-less power plant, the cost comparison will turn out to be even more favourable in the year 2020. Should one, nevertheless, 'not blame anybody' for picking coal-fired power plants over renewable energy today? Especially since the latter brings with it even more ecological and economic advantages – such as saving enormous amounts of water and restabilizing the water cycle.

The only practical opportunity to avoid CO_2 would come from producing hydrogen from coal, an option pointed out by Amory Lovins.[35] This would be done by taking the hydrogen content of the coal instead of burning the latter; the 'hydro-' would then be separated from the carbon at the mining site and the carbon would either be deposited or used as a solid industrial raw material. Such an approach, however, needs to be measured (see my earlier remarks on hydrogen) against the opportunities presented here that derive from the spectrum of renewable energy fuels. But this approach would at least be more practical than the Sustainability Council's recommendation, which is fixated on coal-fired power plants.

That very Sustainability Council has, in spite of all its other recommendations and professions of loyalty to renewable energy, lent a good word to one of the current energy system's attempts at self-preservation, a survival effort for which there is no longer any plausible justification. It has shirked from the logical implications of its own declarations. A consistent conclusion would have to sound like this: even when the CO_2-less power plant becomes an available option, renewable energy will still be more economical; renewable energy, because it brings along additional ecological benefits, should be recommended as the highest-level priority that is in every country's interest.

Hydrogen economy?

Lately, numerous 'experts' have been raving about using hydrogen as the solution to every energy problem. Most people automatically associate hydrogen with renewable energy because they are thinking about 'solar hydrogen'. Just recently the hydrogen discussion experienced a major boost. Jeremy Rifkin published his book *The Hydrogen Economy* (in German it had the more dramatic title *Die H2-Revolution*).[36] Romano Prodi, President of the EU Commission between 1999 and 2004, told the Conference on the Hydrogen Economy held in Brussels in June 2003: 'Hydrogen is ... the focal point in an energy revolution.' And he added, somewhat less bombastically: 'The rational solution would be to turn resolutely towards renewable energies – provided we can find a way of storing them.' For this, he indicated, hydrogen would be the best candidate.[37] Hydrogen is not a primary energy. It is contained in water, fossil energy and plants. It can be recovered by electrolysis that splits water into its components, hydrogen and oxygen, or by detaching hydrogen from fossil energy forms or from plants. This always requires an expenditure of energy. Whenever renewable energy is involved, the procedure is emissions-free. If nuclear or fossil energy is used, this merely leads to a spatial shift in emissions.

There is, however, no valid reason to name an era after a secondary energy – and one, to boot, that cannot and will not be playing the main role in the foreseeable future. If hydrogen is going to be mined using renewable energy, then (intrinsically) it is the latter that is playing the lead role. Every kind of renewable energy that can be employed (whether as useful heat, as electricity or as fuel) without taking a circuitous and costly detour via hydrogen can also be used directly. There is really no need to store more than a share of all the renewable energy forms activated. Hydrogen is, as we have seen, by no means the only storage possibility; rather, it is one among many, and it is not in every case the economically most attractive or most efficient choice. For this reason alone there can be no justification for

the high-sounding concept of 'the Hydrogen Age', since hydrogen can hardly ever amount to much more than a side track on
the renewable energy path. The era in which hydrogen bred by
renewable energy will be able to play a more or less major role
should be named after the energy foundation actually sustain-
ing it; it will be a Solar Age, for the remainder of civilized
history.

When a concept becomes a fashion, it is inevitable that those
who discovered the topic will reveal their amateurishness. This
dilettantism includes proposals that plead for hydrogen made
from natural gas or bio-gas, or for using electricity to mine
hydrogen from power plants using biomass or located at dams.
But it is simply systematic nonsense to take energy that is already
(and therefore continuously) available in stored form and transform it again into another form of energy. Storage is not an end
in itself. These proposals demonstrate even more clearly how
reckless it is when actual problems of supplying hydrogen go
unnoticed. Perhaps this happens because it gives people a way
to philosophize, in a manner as unencumbered as possible by
facts, about grand perspectives, and to avoid taking any real live
initiative that might transform the way society uses energy.

In order for hydrogen to be produced from renewable energy
(the only process that is not tantamount to ecological self-
deception), the first thing needed is electricity. If this has to be
transported across great distances – say, from the Sahara or offshore wind farms – to a hydrogen production site, the energy
loss can be calculated as 10 per cent at the least. Once it has
arrived at the point of electrolytic hydrogen production, the
electric current separates water into hydrogen and oxygen. At
this stage of the transformation, by today's standards, energy
losses of 35 per cent can be expected. Should hydrogen in pure
form then be prepared for general energy supply, it would have
to be liquefied or compressed in special pressurized containers.
Liquefaction, for which temperatures of $-253°C$ are required,
leads to additional energy losses of about 50 per cent of the
hydrogen already produced in small facilities, and to 30 per cent
when it had been produced in large facilities. Compression, by
contrast, means energy losses of only 8 per cent at 200 bars of
pressure and 13 per cent at 800 bars. To transport hydrogen to

the consumption sites themselves, not only would a separate infrastructure be required, but there are bound to be additional energy losses, either via the energy that is consumed by the transport vehicles or because fluid hydrogen has evaporated in the pipelines or on transport ships, where long distances can result in losses between 20 and 30 per cent. If, after the hydrogen has been shipped, it is poured into filling stations, the result will be additional losses, and then there are even more losses when the hydrogen is turned into electricity in a fuel cell. In the optimal case, about 20–25 per cent of the electricity employed at the outset emerges as electricity again on the other side, and rather less in the case of liquid hydrogen. It is for reasons like these that Ulf Bossel, the organizer of the European Fuel Cell Forum, speaks of a 'hydrogen illusion'. This is also why Dirk Asendorpf, writing in the German weekly *Die Zeit*, concluded that, although 'heads of state and eco-visionaries' might be raving about hydrogen, this approach was tantamount to 'pure energy waste' from the perspective of physics.[38] And Robert Service has written in *Science* that this approach has been blown out of proportion and not been thought through – and he has criticized the US and Japanese governments, along with the EU Commission, for sinking billions of dollars into this endeavour.[39]

One field where applications for hydrogen are possible, therefore, has to do with storing those kinds of renewable energy that are not available in a stored form anyway or that cannot be conveniently stored. Hydrogen presents a special storage opportunity when, if possible, just one conversion step and no new infrastructure are required. In other words, it should be made available using the most direct links possible, both technical and spatial, to renewable energy facilities, that is, hydrogen that is produced within this framework – from surplus solar- or wind-based electricity – and then transformed back again into electric current. There is also an interesting opportunity for extracting it from biomass, by detaching hydrogen from vegetable hydrocarbons; that would be the bio-hydrogen variant.[40]

The other field of application playing a major role in this discussion is fuels. Fuels are only suitable for hydrogen, however, under narrowly defined preconditions. One application would be to synthesize the hydrogen directly at the site of its produc-

tion into the aforementioned 'sunfuel'. After electrolysis, there
would no longer be additional losses and also no additional need
for infrastructure. The supply of bio-fuels is expanded that way.
Uses in the form of 'pure fuel' also need to be oriented around
the guideline of avoiding additional conversion and transport
steps, something that is conceivable only for fleets or for a few
very specific fields of application. Hydrogen as an aircraft fuel,
for example, could be produced from nearby solar or wind power
facilities at an airport, then filled into the airfield's tank depots,
and finally taken from there and pumped directly into the planes.

Whoever understands hydrogen properly, viewing it in terms
of system analysis, can only conclude that plans for hydrogen
conceived in super-centralized and sprawling terms are mere pipe
dreams. Hydrogen will either be produced and also reused in a
decentralized way, something Amory Lovins also recommends[41]
– or it will turn into the next super-flop promoted by energy
business lobbies who recognize an opportunity for avoiding
structural change in energy supply: hydrogen as a way of saving
the conventional energy economy with its big business structure. Whoever talks grandiloquently about hydrogen's prospects
today without, in the same breath, advocating an immediate
expansion of electricity production from solar radiation and
wind power can only have one of three motives. The person:

- means well but is either uninformed or thinking with a one-
  track mind;
- wants to put off changes in the conventional energy system,
  and to reassure society, feeding it with false hopes for several
  decades to come; or
- has producing hydrogen with nuclear electricity in mind,
  though without wanting to admit this openly.

Most of the many conferences recently convened to discuss
hydrogen and fuel cells have that last-mentioned motive; they
serve, above all, to exploit the public's fascination with (and
fundamental sympathy for) hydrogen as a way of bringing
nuclear energy back into play. The greater the enthusiasm with
which hydrogen can be presented as an option for the future,
the longer the delay in expanding solar- and wind-based electri-

city, and the faster the realization on the part of a very environment-conscious and thoughtful public (or at least this is what the advocates of nuclear energy hope) that there is no way to bypass nuclear hydrogen. This is why many of those currently voting for hydrogen are actually functioning as part of a pro-nuclear campaign. The only government leader from among the industrial countries who openly and unmistakably acts this way is that 'honest soul' (at least in this respect) George W. Bush. His US$1.7 billion hydrogen programme is explicitly in the service of nuclear hydrogen; to produce nuclear hydrogen, funds are supposed to be diverted from the research budget for renewable energy. The hydrogen campaign is managed by the classic nuclear and petroleum lobby, which – as Rudolf Rechsteiner so aptly puts it – 'has kidnaped hydrogen in order to pursue its own goals'.[42]

This applies not only to the US, but also to the EU. The raucous tones with which Romano Prodi advocated renewable energy at the EU conference on the 'hydrogen economy' are just a superficial cover-up for Europe's complicity in the nuclear kidnapping of hydrogen. The conference was presented a paper from the 'High Level Group for Hydrogen and Fuel Cell' appointed by the EU Commission with the highly promising title *A Vision for the Future*. The paper does contain a statement to the effect that renewable energy is the most important source for hydrogen production. Whenever the documents gets more specific, however, it talks about 'zero carbon hydrogen', which includes nuclear hydrogen. By 2020, the prognosis runs, 5 per cent of all new vehicles would be running on hydrogen, in 2020 it would be 25 per cent, and 35 per cent by 2040. The report recommends employing 'advanced nuclear' fuel for hydrogen production at the outset, to be followed by 'new nuclear' after 2040. Between 2020 and 2030 an extensive pipeline infrastructure for hydrogen is supposed to be created. The EU Commission has already provided US$1.2 billion to this end.

How closely the EU concept resembles the Bush administration's plan is also demonstrated by the agreement reached in Washington during June of 2003 within the framework of the International Partnership for the Hydrogen Economy (IPHE), with the participation of the US, UK, German, French and Italian governments as well as of those of Brazil, China, India, Japan and Russia. Nuclear hydrogen is fully integrated into the IPHE's action list; only in Europe they talk somewhat more quietly about this than they do in the US or Japan. If we take a look at the composition of the 'High Level Group' from the EU, we find among the 19 members 14 companies represented, including car and petroleum concerns, technology conglomerates with a positive attitude towards nuclear energy, and one nuclear physicist in the person of Italian Nobel laureate Carlo Rubbia, as well as the French nuclear research centre CEA – but not a single scientist, institute or business from the field of renewable energy. Philippe Busquin, at the time the EU Commissioner for Research and Development, declared in an interview with the nuclear industry journal, *Atomwirtschaft*, that it was time to proceed with the production of hydrogen 'on a longer term' by using high temperature reactors (HTRs), meaning proceeding along a thermo-chemical path instead of by way of electrolysis.[43] The IAEA is participating in this project.

To be sure, not all of those in the 'hydrogen community' that is taking shape in this manner have the intention of achieving a nuclear energy revival through the back door. The High Level Group is clearly demonstrating, however, that this EU organization plans to pursue the production of hydrogen in a centralized way. To achieve this goal the nuclear energy community has offered its services, and it has done so by invoking the familiar, never-changing argument that not enough electricity could be supplied using renewable energy. The nuclear energy community is extremely well versed in directing billions of public funds onto its grist mill and then squandering them. By getting into the game as a potential hydrogen producer, the nuclear industry is hoping to weaken resistance against nuclear energy among an environmentally conscious public. Therefore the industry has become, though this is still unnoticed by many, the driving – and, from the standpoint of any constructive future prospects for hydrogen, counter-productive – force behind numerous hydrogen conferences.

Renaissance of nuclear energy?

'Solar or nuclear' was the title of a debate on Austrian television I conducted several years ago with a well-known professor of atomic physics. The professor was not one of those members of his guild who likes to whitewash the risks of nuclear energy. But he was convinced about its future prospects, and especially about the indispensability of nuclear energy. Fossil energy, he understood, carried risks that made its use prohibitive, and he regarded renewable energy as something that (unfortunately) did not have enough usable potential to satisfy people's energy needs. His remarks on the subject amounted to a lucky bag of grotesque prejudices, all of which were easy to refute with a few empirical facts – like his assertion that the energy expended on producing a solar facility would be higher than its energy output. The professor was highly irritated about his 'scientific' material, which he had evidently trusted. After the broadcast he told me in a voice that was both moved and moving, 'Measured by what you have said, my professional life was misguided.'

During the 1950s, virtually an entire young generation of scientists came to believe in a future that would be permanently freed of all material afflictions if only we succeeded in banishing the threat of the atom bomb and securing instead a role for the 'peaceful use of nuclear energy'. On the heels of the first nuclear reactors, the fast breeder reactor was due to come on line, a reactor producing its own fuel. And this would soon be followed by nuclear fusion and as much electricity as anybody would ever want, almost gratis and virtually residue-free, for people everywhere and for all time – a veritable vision of the sun on Earth. The philosopher Ernst Bloch wrote in his book *The Principle of Hope*: 'A few hundred pounds of uranium and thorium are enough to make the Sahara and the Gobi desert disappear, to transform Siberia and northern Canada, Greenland and the Antarctic into the Riviera.'[44] Bloch gave no thought as to which direction the water might be heading as it melted and left the polar regions. And in 1958 another philosopher, Karl Jaspers, wrote in his book *The Atom Bomb and the Future of Man*: 'If the atom does not bring us annihilation, it will place all of existence on new ground.'[45]

Nuclear energy seduced people into entertaining hyper-trophic notions about how all the limitations and troubles afflicting humankind in the eternal struggle for existence could be surmounted for good. In the 'Russell-Einstein Manifesto' issued in 1954, a statement signed by numerous famous schol-ars and scientists issuing an urgent call for the abolition of nuclear weapons, it said: 'Remember your humanity and forget everything else. If you can do this, then the way is open to a new paradise; if not, it will mean the end of life altogether.'[46] There was now only a choice between nuclear hell or nuclear paradise – perhaps as a way of restoring some mental balance for themselves in light of what nuclear physics had conjured up in 1945 at Hiroshima and Nagasaki. The promise of nuclear energy was regarded as an immense unfolding of productive forces that would bring adequate prosperity to people everywhere and radically shorten the pathway from the realm of necessity into the realm of freedom. It was envisioned as the place in which natural science might fulfil the ethical mission it had assumed ever since science – in the intellectual tradition of Francis Bacon's utopian novel *Nova Atlantis* – made mastery of nature in service to humanity its task.

Living with nuclear power?

Not much is left of those promises, which were as dreamy as they were presumptuous. Because of what actually happened at Chernobyl, the promises turned into nightmares. But what has remained are the national and international structures of the nuclear industry, which are struggling to survive and will not settle for the residual chores of managing atomic energy's phase-out. On the world stage the relevant structure is the International Atomic Energy Agency (founded in 1957), and in the European arena it is the European Atomic Energy Community (EURATOM). Also left over are several large nuclear research institutes, not just in Russia, Japan, France, China, India or the US, but also in Germany (though now under a different name); another residual structure is the budgetary priority accorded nuclear energy in the field of energy research;

and then there is the privilege, unprecedented in world history, that lets major nuclear accidents be insured by the states where they happen because the risks are too high for any private insurance company. Another leftover is the mental habit that makes a future bereft of nuclear power plants strike so many people, especially scientists and technicians, as unreal. Because nobody can turn the clock back on knowledge that is already out there, nuclear energy is a fact that cannot be thought away, so it is said. The world, according to this view, must therefore learn to live with nuclear power plants over the long run.

This is exactly how people have talked, and continue to talk, about nuclear weapons. These too, according to their advocates, are a reality that can no longer be eliminated, which is why we must learn to 'live with the bomb'. This attitude has even been the source of an attempt to consecrate the atom bomb with a higher purpose, as an instrument of permanent peacemaking. Nuclear deterrence was declared a unique means for preventing war, which in the future would deter anyone from ever starting a war again. The central piece of evidence adduced for this thesis is the fact that a cold war conducted for decades between two ideologically contrary world powers never led to a 'hot war' and then ended with the bloodless collapse of the Soviet superpower. Nobody will ever be able to furnish proof to the contrary, that a Third World War might not have broken out even without the nuclear deterrent of mutually assured destruction. No logical conclusions can be drawn from a non-event, in this case that of nuclear non-disarmament. Yet by way of this argument the attempt is made to de-legitimize appeals and initiatives for a worldwide supervised nuclear disarmament. What can be demonstrated (and not just as a counter-factual proposition) is that nuclear deterrence was unable to prevent the outbreak of numerous proxy wars throughout the second half of the 20th century. And what deterrence did give rise to was a historically unprecedented arms race accompanied by a misallocation of resources on a global scale — and to an intense ideological cultivation of enemy images on both sides of the cold war: better dead than red, or better dead than capitalist. And, coming soon to a political theatre in your neighbourhood: better Western than Islamic, or vice versa?

In spite of all the emphasis on how nuclear arms have a peacekeeping effect, an attempt was undertaken to prevent additional countries from acquiring the bomb. The political instrument used to this end was the Nuclear Non-Proliferation Treaty (NPT), which went into effect on 1 July 1970. It was meant to prevent, as permanently as possible, the emergence of additional nuclear countries, in return for which it would pave the way for the 'peaceful use of nuclear energy' worldwide. States with nuclear weapons committed themselves in this treaty to nuclear disarmament — an obligation that has never been concretized since the document was signed. States without nuclear weapons have committed themselves to renouncing nuclear armament, but they simultaneously obtain the right to assistance with civilian uses of nuclear energy. In Article IV of the NPT it says:

> All the Parties to the Treaty undertake to facilitate, and have the right to participate in, the fullest possible exchange of equipment, materials and scientific and technological information for the peaceful uses of nuclear energy. Parties to the Treaty in a position to do so shall also cooperate in contributing alone or together with other States or international organizations to the further development of the applications of nuclear energy for peaceful purposes, especially in the territories of non-nuclear-weapon States Party to the Treaty, with due consideration for the needs of the developing areas of the world.

This was meant to draw a clear line of demarcation between military and civilian uses; fencing in of one kind of use, expansion of another. The treaty became the working foundation of the IAEA. This organization was meant to be the worldwide monitor seeing to it that no nuclear material gets diverted to building an atom bomb while also providing governments with unlimited assistance in developing their nuclear power plant programmes.

The permeable line separating peaceful and military uses of nuclear power

The history of the IAEA demonstrates that it is not possible to talk about nuclear energy and remain silent about nuclear weapons. For a clean division between military and civilian use has become, as already mentioned, more difficult than ever. Nobody even tried to seize the chance of a lifetime that the epochal shift of 1990/91 provided for an initiative leading to supervised nuclear disarmament worldwide; at least there was no such initiative emanating from the cold war's victorious side. The argument that complete disarmament was rendered impossible owing to the worldwide dissemination of knowledge about how to build atomic weapons is just an excuse. After all, there is also a treaty ostracizing chemical weapons worldwide, a treaty whose observance is substantially harder to supervise because there are many more possibilities for manufacturing chemical than atomic weapons. As late as 2000, to be sure, at the conference held in New York to revise the NPT, the treaty had its previous time limit extended indefinitely – but only because the Clinton administration agreed to end all nuclear weapons tests. Clinton's willingness to end testing has since been rescinded by his successor Bush Jr, who has even taken official steps to develop new atomic weapons ('mini-nukes'). Because a new ideological world conflict is now brewing in the form of an Islamic–Western *Kulturkampf*, there is simultaneously a growing motivation for Muslim states to acquire nuclear arms.

Today the path to nuclear armament always goes by way of civilian use: with the backing of the NPT, it is possible to camouflage preparations for nuclear armament while getting some assistance acquiring these weapons. In the international arms control debate it used to be said, and quite rightly, that what matters more than anything else is the potential – and not just an assessment of whatever intentions the current government may harbour. That government may be entirely credible and not have the slightest intention of converting its civilian nuclear programme into a military one. But what will be done by the next government if it already has a technological potential for nuclear weapons ready to hand? At that point future atomic powers (in addition to the five permanent members of the UN Security Council, Israel is unofficially in the nuclear club, India, Pakistan and North Korea have joined, Brazil and Iraq nearly made it, and Iran might possibly belong in the foreseeable future) would only need to imitate the fine example others have set for them. In his book *Die Politik der latenten Proliferation* (*The Politics of Latent Proliferation*), Roland Kollert describes how the programme, 'Atoms for Peace', was rather more like a case of deception – or perhaps self-deception. Apart from the US and the Soviet Union, all of today's nuclear powers – including France and the UK – started out on the 'peaceful use' track and only acknowledged their military intentions at the 'last minute' of their transition to full-fledged nuclear armament.[47]

If for no other reason than this, propagandizing a renaissance for nuclear energy is hair-raisingly irresponsible. At a minimum, the prerequisite for a country to use nuclear energy is stability in that state's domestic politics and international relations. In how many of the world's countries can these be guaranteed and permanently maintained? The world situation is anything but stable. The bitter irony of nuclear history might some day turn out to be the story of how the wishful thinking of the 1950s – 'no' to nuclear weapons, but 'yes' to so-called peaceful use of atomic energy – turned into its exact opposite: ever fewer nuclear power plants, and ultimately no longer any at all, but in exchange for this more nuclear-armed countries than there are today.

There can be no doubt that nuclear physics is one of the most demanding scientific disciplines. The further along one is on the nuclear pathway, up to and including nuclear fusion, the greater the general respect accorded the outstanding scientific and technical achievement this requires – especially respect for the attempt to analyse the kind of nuclear fusion that takes place in the sun and then actually try copying it on Earth. It would seem inconceivable for this technological marvel not to have some social utility. This may be the reason why, to this day, nuclear fusion has been sheltered from the withering critique directed against nuclear energy, as if the one has nothing to do with the other. But it most certainly is the reason why, to this day, nuclear physicists and their institutions can afford to keep proclaiming one novel achievement after another in nuclear technology – promises that, only a little later, turn out to be completely irredeemable. These broken promises are, nevertheless, usually attested to have greater realism about the future than is the case with ambitious future-oriented projects using renewable energy that have already proven they can work.

In 1993 the University of Munich sociologist Ulrich Beck described the kind of psychologism whereby the attempt is made, at regular intervals, to launch a renaissance in nuclear energy. This is done, according to Beck, using a 'dramaturgy of risk' in the form of a 'competition to repress thoughts about major risks'. One need 'no longer deny' the nuclear danger – but 'only proclaim that other dangers are even greater'.[48] This is a way to enhance the opportunities for nuclear energy all over again, 'and it might even turn out that the environmental movement, yesterday's opposition, will become tomorrow's involuntary ally'. It is against this psychological background that the campaign for a 'renaissance' of nuclear energy is taking place, in a manner that is starting to impress political institutions and the media once more. The three elements of this campaign are the promise of new reactors with lower accident risks, the global climate catastrophe and the assertion that there is no opportunity for replacing fossil energy unless it involves nuclear energy.

The new pro-nuclear campaign demonstrates how fatal the impact can be on public awareness, as well as on the consciousness of political and economic decision makers, when the aims and opportunities of switching to renewable energy are not articulated aggressively enough. This lack of opposition clears the way for assertions like those made by the authors of a June 2004 article ('Back to nuclear power') that appeared in the German magazine *Stern*:[49]

> *A quick salvation is not going to come from nuclear energy. Its problems from the past will not be solved, nor will its plans for the future be available right away – should they even work as promised. To dispense with nuclear power altogether and for all time, however, also seems presumptuous. What we are left with, then, are plague and cholera: atmospheric warming*

*and the risks of nuclear technology. What we are looking for is
medication against plague and cholera.*

This splashy article from the magazine with Germany's second
largest circulation – which had been a platform for the
movement against nuclear power plants in the 1970s and 1980s
– appeared two weeks after the Renewables 2004 conference.
And yet this journal is now 'looking for' a medication against
plague and cholera. Apparently this conference did not convince
the magazine that renewable energy is the very medication its
editors are seeking. At that conference, too, only a half-hearted
effort was made to persuade anyone about the renewable cure.

Increasing instead of reducing risks

In the 1950s atomic energy garnered broad support because it
was portrayed in glowing colours as a great historical prospect,
as a project for all humankind. As late as 1974, the IAEA was
promising that 4.45 million megawatts of nuclear power capacity would be installed by the year 2000. That is almost double
the total capacity installed for electricity production worldwide
today. The 'nuclear community' applied no self-restraint of any
kind, neither with respect to the numbers it was forecasting nor
with reference to the speed at which it expected nuclear power
plants to be introduced. They have constantly had to scale back
their prognoses ever since. In 1976 the capacity forecast went
down to just 2.3 million megawatts, and by 1978 it had declined
to a mere 800,000 megawatts. And then came 26 April 1986,
the date of the Chernobyl accident. Today there are actually 439
nuclear power facilities worldwide, operating at a total capacity
of around 300,000 megawatts and distributed across 32
countries. For the 'higher class' of atomic reactors (the fast
breeders), the Karlsruhe Nuclear Research Center predicted in
1965 that installed capacity would come to 80,000 megawatts
in the Federal Republic alone, and 450,000 megawatts were
projected for the US in 1974 by the Atomic Energy Commission
(renamed as the Nuclear Regulatory Commission that year) –
both projections for the year 2000. And all those unfulfilled
predictions about the nuclear fusion reactor are also lined up

along an endless chain. When the UN sponsored a nuclear conference at Geneva in 1955, the first fusion reactor was announced for 1975. Today, 50 years later, the fusion reactor is heralded for 2060. Although the date for delivering on this promise keeps getting further and further away, the funds keep flowing copiously.[50]

The latest projection from the IAEA, which is the basis for the proclamations of a renaissance in nuclear energy mentioned in the Introduction, is even cautious compared to earlier projections. Specific decisions about individual projects are invoked as evidence, like the decision that a new reactor is going to be built in Finland; that France has announced new plant construction for 2007, with facilities that will run for 60 years and replace all of today's atomic reactors; that there are current plans to built 27 new plants worldwide, 18 of them in Asia; and that the US is extending the officially approved life span for 56 of its 102 reactors from 40 to 60 years.

In a parallel development, the consequences of the Chernobyl catastrophe are being downplayed. In the respected German weekly *Die Zeit*, that paper's science correspondent Gero von Randow wrote that there were only 45 deaths there and 'merely' 2000 registered cases of thyroid cancer.[51] Yet the figures came from interested parties. Independent investigations like those of the Radiation Institute in Munich established that there were 70,000 death victims, including suicides out of desperation, and these studies anticipate additional victims from delayed reporting numbering in the tens of thousands. The strategy of soft-pedalling Chernobyl's damage includes miscalculating the number of victims by setting them against those who have suffered from fossil energy emissions and coal mining.[52]

In order to put the alleged economic advantages of nuclear power in a more favourable light, not a word is said about how its economic foundation was and remains a machinery of political subsidies and privileges of the first order. In addition to tax-exemption for nuclear fuels and release from liability obligations, the companies building nuclear power plants have received preferential credit and, in many cases, investment grants of unknown magnitude. Most of the reasons why Electrité de France, which receives 85 per cent of its electricity production from nuclear power plants, is among the most debt-ridden companies in the world are 'atomic' in nature. From the 1950s to 1973, the OECD countries spent over US$150 billion (in current prices) on R&D in nuclear energy – but practically nothing, by contrast, on renewable energy. Between 1974 (when the International Energy Agency started collecting data) and 1992, it was again US$168 billion – for renewable energy, by contrast, the figure came to just US$22 billion. The EU's opulent promotion of nuclear energy is not even included in this count, and the French figures remain secret to this day. Together with the grants provided by non-OECD countries, especially from the former Eastern bloc, total subsidization worldwide comes to at least US$1 trillion; for renewable energy, by contrast, subsidies amount to US$40 billion at most over the last 30 years, including market introduction programmes. In Germany alone since the 1950s, atomic energy was subsidized with the following amounts: about 20 billion euros for building research reactors; 9 billion euros for failed projects like the fast breeder, the high temperature reactor and a reprocessing facility; 14.5 billion euros for plant closings, restorations, rehabilitating deposit sites and final disposal for materials; and about 20 billion euros in lost tax revenues because of tax exemption anticipated for final nuclear waste disposal. The calculation does not include police security measures and expenditures for university institutes or for basic financing of research centres.

By the mid-1970s nuclear energy had largely been thwarted, more as a result of massive cost over-runs than because of growing resistance. Since then, the boundary lines limiting its expansion have been drawn ever more tightly. Estimates that uranium deposits will only last a maximum of just 60 years are based on consumption from facilities currently running; that is, even if the number of facilities were to be doubled, the time available would inevitably be cut in half. Without an immediate transition to fast breeder reactors, which could stretch the fissionable material by a factor of 60, it stands to reason that not even the growth rate calculated by the IAEA could be achieved. Without switching immediately to breeder reactors, it would be impossible to have any kind of comprehensive expansion in nuclear energy, something already pointed out in 1980

by the Bundestag Survey Commission chaired by SPD parlia-
mentarian Reinhard Ueberhorst. Yet the history of the breeder
reactor is a fiasco. Thus far, these reactors' high costs and vulnerability to breakdown have made them unsuitable for commercial
operation. Klaus Traube — the manager of the German fast
breeder reactor project in the 1970s and, for a quarter of a
century, Germany's most prominent nuclear energy critic — has
documented the failure of the grand ambitions associated with
the fast breeder reactor:[53]

> *Germany's 300-megawatt breeder at Kalkar was started in
> 1972 and then abandoned in 1991 — after 19 years of
> construction that devoured seven billion marks (25 times the
> original estimate). An analogous project planned for the US
> was never implemented. It is true that some demonstration
> breeders designed for mid-range performance were put into
> operation in the mid-1970s in France, the UK and the Soviet
> Union, but they were shut down in the 1990s. During the
> start of a parallel Japanese project in 1995 a major accident
> occurred. That particular breeder plant has been out of commis-
> sion ever since; it is unclear if it will ever be put to work. The
> world's only large-sized breeder power plant ever put into
> operation, the 1200-megawatt Superphénix that France started
> in 1986, was shut down in 1997; in ten years of operation
> it produced a volume of electricity that corresponded to 7 per
> cent of its capacity utilization. All that remains is a 600-
> megawatt Russian breeder plant. In the mid-1980s
> construction also commenced in the Urals on two commercial
> 800-megawatt breeders, which were supposed to go into opera-
> tion in 2000 but were also actually abandoned. This pitiful
> end to the race for breeders, a competition staged with such
> lavish funding, is ultimately attributable to the enormous
> technical complexity and shortcomings in security technology
> associated with the breeder concept. These characteristics led
> both to enormous costs and catastrophic outcomes as a result
> of persistent breakdowns in the plants. Four decades of devel-
> opment in all the major industrial countries have reduced the
> breeder concept to absurdity.*

There are six additional reasons arguing against any kind of future viability for nuclear power:

- The water problem – nuclear reactors' enormous water needs for steam and cooling compete with the demand for water from a growing world population.
- Minimal efficiency – the waste heat produced by nuclear power plants hardly lends itself to combined heat and power cogeneration. The reason is that long-distance heating transmission from centralized power plant blocks is very expensive. That is why nuclear energy is the energy form with the most meagre opportunities for increasing efficiency.
- Risk vulnerability – in tandem with the growing risk of 'new wars' (wars no longer carried out between states) there is a parallel rise in the worldwide danger of nuclear terrorism – and not just from aircraft attacks on reactors.
- The wrong energy business plan – since investment in nuclear power plants is especially capital-intensive, building these plants clashes with the liberalization of electricity markets and their short-term amortization periods.
- The time perspective for final disposal – nuclear waste needs 100,000 years to be securely stored. In light of growing risks of social instability, what political system can provide guarantees for such a lengthy term?
- Creeping radioactive contamination – nobody can estimate the long-term risks that releasing radioactivity harbours for nature and for human beings, even on a small scale. The more nuclear power plants there are in operation, the greater the danger.

Nuclear fusion as the last straw

Thus, the only prospect that remains is the nuclear fusion reactor, of which nobody today can say for sure if it will ever work. The operating principle of this reactor is that two hydrogen atoms (deuterium and tritium) are fused in a hot gas. The gas has to be heated for a few seconds to 100 millions degrees Celsius – 'hotter than the heat of the sun', as nuclear fusion researcher Eckhard Rebhan titled a book on the subject.[54] To achieve ignition, an even higher temperature of 400 million degrees Celsius is required. Even if there were no other environmental risks and we based everything just on the costs estimated by nuclear fusion researchers (and let it be recalled, all cost projections made by nuclear researchers have consistently proven to be vastly understated in practice), there is no rational economic reason to develop and introduce these kinds of reactors.

Japanese fusion research, for example, puts construction costs at US$2400–4800 per kilowatt, which comes out to a price of between 14 and 38 cents per kilowatt hour.[55] The lower figure is already higher than average costs for wind-based electricity in Germany today; the upper figure is higher than what it costs today for PV cells in southern Europe. Alexander Bradshaw, Director of the Max Planck Institute for Plasma Physics and scientific director of Germany's nuclear fusion research, put the cost at between 6 and 12 euro-cents when he testified at a hearing of the German Bundestag.[56] But he, like the aforementioned Japanese study, did not mention that the walls for the reactor have to be replaced every five to eight years, and that the replacement itself can take one to two years. These would be radiated components that would have to be stored as nuclear waste. Because of the lengthy periods when the reactor would be out of commission, there would have to be at least one substitute reactor as a standby for every two or three reactors actually running, which quickly pushes costs up even higher.

One study not conducted by a fusion researcher was drawn up by Emanuele Negro for the EU Commission. This study arrives at costs for producing electricity that are seven times higher than the expense of a nuclear fission reactor, calculated over a term of 30 years. Negro compares these costs with the degressive costs calculated for PV energy through the year 2050 – in other words, before nuclear fusion would even be available theoretically. He arrives at the conclusion that PV costs can draw even with those for producing fossil electricity today, while to 'the best of our knowledge' nuclear fusion costs would be five times higher.[57] This confirms what the former deputy director of the Plasma Fusion Center at the Massachusetts Institute of Technology, M. L. Lidsky, had already said more than two decades ago: nobody will want this reactor the way it is meant to be built.[58]

It is a myth, moreover, that nuclear fusion reactors pose no environmental risks. While they are operating, the material inside the core reactor becomes highly radioactive, which entails very costly waste disposal. Although this material, in contrast to the nuclear fuel rods used in atomic fission reactors, is only active for about 100 years, the amounts are considerably larger. The tritium required for fusion is capable of penetrating solid structures, and it turns into tritiated water after contact with air, which can cause the most serious kind of biological damage once it gets into the water cycle. Nuclear fusion reactors have an enormous thirst for cooling water. If for no other reason than its need for cooling water, this reactor technology has an inherent disposition towards being employed in highly concentrated production centres. There is talk of building reactors on a scale ranging from 5000 megawatts to as much as 200,000 megawatts.

Between 1974 and 1998, total costs for nuclear fusion among the OECD countries were already around US$28.3 billion. The test reactor called ITER, planned for use in an international cooperative effort and meant to be finished by the mid-2020s, is estimated to have construction costs of US$3.5 billion. A follow-up demonstration reactor is meant to be built for US$8 billion. No matter how highly skilled nuclear fusion researchers have to be in their training and work, the statements they make when asked about renewable energy are inept. Renewable energy's technological shortcomings are subjected to denunciation as permanently insurmountable drawbacks, even though renewable energy already has a proven track record of productive performance. The fusion experts seem to think it is more realistic to develop materials that can withstand temperatures of over 100 million degrees Celsius than to contribute towards introducing renewable energy on a broad scale.

For nuclear fusion researchers, the breathtaking technological performance they expect from a fusion reactor (should it ever succeed) is matched only by the downright subterranean level at which they rate renewable energy. In the Bundestag hearing mentioned earlier, the physical chemist Professor Alexander Bradshaw had this to say in response to the question of whether nuclear fusion was even necessary in light of the prospects for renewable energy: 'The sermons preached by the mendicant orders of the High Middle Ages, seeking happiness in a simple and impoverished life, were only followed by a few people even at that time.'[59] The protagonists pushing today's nuclear energy renaissance are certainly not at a loss for cognitive ability, but they do lack the will to acquire knowledge about renewable energy. If they were ready and willing to learn about what renewable energy has to offer, they would have to come out on behalf of stopping the nuclear fusion programme and in favour of concentrating on optimizing technologies for renewable energy. But since they are not about to head down this path on their own, the only remaining option is to stop fusion research by political means.

The last rearguard action of the established energy system?

Today the world confronts an existential decision about how energy will be supplied in the post-fossil era: it faces a choice between 'solar' and 'nuclear'. In reality, the future prospects for nuclear energy – which the writer Carl Amery has called the 'lazy magic of the Sorcerer's Apprentice' – are anything but positive, even if there were no resistance to the nuclear option. That is why the projections associated with nuclear energy play such a big role. Projections serve as a kind of bail bond for the traditional energy system, which is on trial in the court of a public opinion that recognizes the need to reorient society around renewable energy, especially against the background of the global climate problem. The preference of big business for atomic energy arises from its belief that teaming up with nuclear power facilitates its domination of the energy sector. If we lived in a looking glass world where nuclear energy could only be used in a decentralized form and renewable energy only by way of large power plants, it is a safe bet that the suppliers of fossil energy would have rejected the former and always opted for the latter.

The motive for the propagandists of nuclear energy's renaissance may be tactical or just pure presumption. It would be tactical if they were merely working towards maintaining the status quo at current levels, knowing all the while that the clock is ticking for nuclear energy. Just to succeed at this modest goal, the 'nuclear community' needs to exaggerate its own importance in a systematic way and denigrate every alternative. But maybe it is also presumptuous enough to hope that the fast breeder reactor might be made to work so that modern societies, using current nuclear technology and the last ton of uranium, can still reach the saving shore of nuclear fusion. In the meantime (according to this scenario), fossil energy will continue to be the primary way of bridging the era between fission and fusion. These kinds of hopes were described satirically by Carl Amery in a conversation he had with me and *Die Zeit* editor Christiane Grefe that was later published as a book under the title *Klimawechsel* (*Climate Change*): They resemble the hopes of a penniless man who orders one course of oysters after another in a restaurant so he might eventually find the pearl with which he can pay for his gluttony.[60] Money is no object so long as the systemic shift to renewable energy can be prevented. 'Anything but renewable energy' is the secret motto.

Yet the atomic and fossil energy system can no longer be expected to win the last battle in its war for self-preservation. The attempt to prevent a practical reorientation towards renewable energy by loading the dice on future options is bound to fail. There is no way that the technological opportunities for using renewable energy can be permanently silenced and undervalued. The most one can do is keep holding them back – in much the same way that has already been happening long enough. This thought is hardly reassuring, for the danger is too great that the established energy system's impending decline will drag society down into the abyss along with it.

The world view that rested on the hope that all of society's problems could be solved by science and technology led to a reification of the latter and to a discrepancy that the philosopher-writer Günther Anders had already described during the 1950s – before we had any real experience with nuclear technology – in his book about 'human antiquatedness'.[61] The discrepancy Anders described was one between technological perfectionism and the persistence of human fallibility. How lasting our infallibility has proven to be is something the ethnosociologist Hans Peter Duerr has forcefully shown in his five-volume work, *Der Mythos vom Zivilisationsprozess* (*Myth of the Civilization Process*).[62] There are no safeguards on any aspect of civilized progress, and the danger of reversion to anarchy is omnipresent. Nothing demonstrates this more clearly than what at first glance seems to be the paradoxical core contradiction of our time: the modern world's flood of scientific knowledge has not been able to prevent human-made natural destruction from becoming steadily greater on a global scale. Günther Anders speaks of a 'Promethean shame' that afflicts humans in the form of a growing sense of insufficiency vis-à-vis the fruits of technology. Humans trust technology more than themselves and have developed a limitless faith in technological feasibility. Man has 'deserted into the camp of his appliances' and subjugated himself to their power.[63] This is no longer a matter of consciously choosing the appropriate technology, which would include a conscious renunciation of outdated technologies; instead, this is all about simply perpetuating technologies by mindlessly continuing to develop them.

Every linear development eventually reaches a breaking point when the cycles of nature, society and economics start to stand in its way, when the development no longer has sufficient feedback and its own control variables stop changing in response. If a system is overpowering, it can extend its existence unduly for a while. Yet, as they grow larger, the corporations that supply energy also become more immobile – not in spite of their capital and organizational power, but because of them. At this point their attempt at self-preservation persists even against the better judgement of those who are in charge of the system, to whom all the possible breaking points cannot have remained a secret. Today's energy system is capable of ignoring the limits set by global climate change longer than anyone. The Kyoto Protocol, a subject we shall soon address, is not preventing the system from acting evasively. The consequences of climate change do not immediately affect its perpetrators. But there certainly is an impact from other energy-determined crises. That is why there is growing reluctance on the part of capital markets to provide billions in credits for large power plants and the extensive infrastructure they would require. This anxiety was also on the mind of those attending that family reunion of the global energy business, the World Energy Conference. It issued a call to improve public acceptance of the energy system – through public relations.

The first sentence of the final communique from the 2004 World Energy Conference reads: 'All energy options must be kept open and no technology should be idolised or demonised.' What this meant was that renewable energy should not be idolized and nuclear and fossil energy not demonized. In other words, nuclear and fossil energy should be presented to the public consciousness as equivalent to renewable energy. This 'equivalence' can only be contrived, however, by trivializing the problems and dangers of nuclear and fossil energy and by systematically playing down the technological and economic opportunities associated with renewable energy as well as its manifold social advantages. A broad-based campaign is meant to persuade people that the system of nuclear and fossil energy supply is innocent of any role in energy-related crises and to dissuade governments and societies from turning to renewable energy. On the basis of that assertion about equivalence with renewable energy, the only thing then meant to be decisive is the market price for energy. In order to facilitate formulating this price to the detriment of renewable energy, control over the structures of energy supplies needs to be secured. In order to prevent alternative ideas from even occurring to anyone, the supposed technological and economic advantages of traditional energy compared to those of renewable energy – in spite of the former's untenability and lack of technological imagination – are meant to be chiselled in stone. These are the exculpatory lies that serve to conserve the established energy system, lies the system uses in its attempt to justify its continued existence. All this is a bad omen for 'rationality' in dealing with renewable energy. Lately, strategies of sowing confusion are being used not only to dispute the potential of renewable energy for replacing nuclear and fossil energy, but also to contest renewable energy's environmental edge.

The question is not just how long capital markets and insurance companies will continue to fall for this strategy of confusion when they prepare their risk analyses. It is also a question of how many governments and parliaments will

continue to want to support the established energy system's self-
preservation strategy – and, if they do, whether they then have
the financial clout to raid the state's coffers again for the sake
of a nuclear energy renaissance. It is also questionable as to how
long the public will let itself be deceived – and as to how many
of the forces inside the energy system will hold out in maintaining this self-deception and submitting to the esprit de corps of
the energy fraternity's old boys network.

There is no other choice except to break the structural power
of the established energy system, to block the artery keeping
them on artificial life support, and (quite independently of that)
to mobilize the forces for renewable energy. Yet what methods
of political, economic and social action should be used, and who
should the players be in this endeavour? In Part II we shall show
that change will not be possible based on the fundamental
assumptions that shaped previous activism. These assumptions
tend to cripple the players who are available and hinder the
activation of many additional players who will be needed for the
shift to renewable energy.

References

1   Wolfgang Palz, *Solar Electricity: An Economic Approach to Solar Energy*
    (New York: UNIPUB, 1978)
2   Wilhelm Ostwald, *Der energetische Imperativ* (Leipzig: Akademische
    Verlagsgesellschaft, 1912), p81 et seq
3   Svante Arrhenius, *Die Chemie und das moderne Leben* (Leipzig:
    Akademische Verlagsgesellschaft, 1922), p112 et seq
4   National Conservation Commission, *Report of the National
    Conservation Commission* (Washington, DC: Government Printing
    Office, 1909)
5   Günter Barudio, *Tränen des Teufels. Eine Weltgeschichte des Erdöls*
    (Stuttgart: Klett-Cotta, 2001), p192
6   Julian Darley, *High Noon for Natural Gas* (White River Junction,
    VT: Chelsea Green, 2004)
7   Wolfgang Sachs, Tilman Santarius, Dirk Assmann and Cecil
    Arndt, *Fair Future – Begrenzte Ressourcen und Globale Gerechtigkeit. Report
    des Wuppertal-Instituts für Klima, Umwelt, Energie* (Munich: C. H.
    Beck, 2005), p56 et seq

8   Martin Schwarz and Heinz Erdmann, *Atomterror. Schurken, Staaten, Terroristen – die neue nukleare Bedrohung* (Munich: Knaur, 2004)
9   Hermann Scheer, *Sonnen-Strategie* (Munich: Piper, 1993), p52 et seq
10   Gerd Rosenkranz, Irene Meichsner and Manfred Kriener, *Die neue Offensive der Atomwirtschaft* (Munich: C. H. Beck, 1992)
11   Richard Heinberg, *The Party's Over* (Munich: Riemann Verlag, 2004); Paul Roberts, *The End of Oil* (Boston, MA: Houghton Mifflin, 2004); Colin J. Campbell, Frauke Liesenborghs and Jörg Schindler, *Ölwechsel* (Munich: DTV, 2002)
12   Ole von Uexkuell, 'Wasser und Energie. Das fossil-atomare Energiesystem verschärft die Wasserkrise', *Solarzeitalter* 3/2003, p14 et seq
13   Peter H. Gleick, *Water in Crisis* (New York: Oxford University Press, 1993), p67 et seq
14   Howard Geller, *Energy Revolution* (Washington, DC: Island Press, 2003), p6 et seq
15   Energy and Defense Project, *Dispersed, Decentralized and Renewable Energy Sources: Alternatives to National Vulnerability and War* (Washington, DC: The Agency, December 1980)
16   Hartmut Elsenhans, Elmar Kleiner and Reinhart Joachim Dreves, *Gleichheit, Markt, Profit, Wachstum. Kleinindustrie und Expansion des Massenmarkts mit einer Untersuchung aus Algerien* (Hamburg: Deutsches Übersee-Institut, 2001), p286
17   Le Groupe de Bellevue, *ALTER: A Study of a Long-Term Energy Future for France based on 100% Renewable Energies* (Paris, 1978), reprinted in *The Yearbook of Renewable Energies* 1995/96 (London: James & James, 1995), p104 et seq; Thomas B. Johannson and Peter Steen, *Solar Sweden. An Outline to a Renewable Energy System* (Stockholm: Secretariat for Future Studies, 1979); Henry W. Kendal and Steven J. Nadis (eds), *Energy Strategies: Toward a Solar Future* (Cambridge, MA: Ballinger, 1981); Wolf Häfele, Jeanne Anderer, A. McDonald and Nebojsa Nakiceňoviç, *Energy in a Finite World* (Cambridge, MA: Ballinger, 1981); Deutscher Bundestag, *Nachhaltige Energieversorgung unter den Bedingungen der Globalisierung und Liberalisierung. Bericht der Enquete-Kommission* (Berlin: Deutscher Bundestag, 2002); Harry Lehmann, *Energy Rich Japan* (Aachen: Institute for Sustainable Solutions and Innovations (ISUSI), 2003). These 100 per cent scenarios are reproduced in detail in a

series published by the journal *Solarzeitalter*. See 'Leitartikel für eine Vollversorgung mit Erneuerbaren Energien' at www.eurosolar.org/new/de/artikel2003.php. One example of a 100 per cent regional study is this profile of renewable energy in the southwestern German region Hegau/Western Lake Constance (1000 square km., 300,000 inhabitants): Solarcomplex, *Erneuerbare Energien in der Region Hegau/Bodensee: Übersicht der Technisch verfügbaren Potenziale* (Hilzingen: Kugler-Druck, 2002). On local governments who have converted 100 per cent to renewable energy, or who have made this their declared goal, see '100 Prozent erneuerbar – Ansätze aus der Praxis', *Photon* 3/2005, as well as the internet platform designed by the Rosenheimer Solarförderverein (Rosenheim Solar Promotion Association) entitled '100 Prozent RENET' (www.100re.net or www.rosolar.de).

18 EUROSOLAR, *10 Jahre Europäische Solarpreise 1994–2003* (Bonn, 2004) and *10 Jahre Deutscher Solarpreis 1994–2003* (Bonn: EUROSOLAR, 2004)

19 Harry Lehmann and Stefan Peter, *Das deutsche Ausbaupotential Erneuerbarer Energien im Stromsektor. Studie für EUROSOLAR* (Bonn: EUROSOLAR, 2004)

20 Rudolf Rechsteiner, 'Die Referenzenergie der Zukunft: Strom aus Erneuerbaren Energien', *Solarzeitalter* 4/2004, p7 et seq

21 Hermann Scheer, *The Solar Economy*, (London: Earthscan, 2002), p37 et seq

22 Hermann Scheer (see Ref. 21), p173 et seq

23 Richard Baxter, *Energy Storage: A Non-Technical Guide* (Tulsa, OK: PennWell, 2005)

24 Elmar Altvater, 'Aufstieg und Niedergang des fossilen Energie-Regimes', *Solarzeitalter* 3/2004, p14 et seq

25 Augustin Mouchot, *Die Sonnenwärme und ihre industriellen Anwendungen* (1879; reprint in German translation, Oberbözberg: Olynthus, 1987)

26 Felix Auerbach, *Die Weltherrin und ihr Schatten* (Jena: Fischer, 1913)

27 National Policy Development Group, *National Energy Policy. Report of the National Energy Policy Development Group* (Washington, DC: Government Printing Office, May 2001)

28 Wuppertal Institut für Klima, Umwelt, Energie, *Treibhausgasemissionen des russischen Erdgas-Exportpipeline-Systems. Ergebnisse und Hochrechnungen empirischer Untersuchungen in Russland*

(Wuppertal: Wuppertal Institut, December 2004)

29 Julian Darley (see Ref. 6)

30 Hans Schuh, 'Feuer aus dem Eis', *Die Zeit* 30/2001

31 Alexei Milkov, 'Global Estimates of hydrate-bound gas in marine sediments', *Earth-Science Reviews* 66/2004, p183 et seq; Sabina Griffith, 'Wenn Eis Feuer fängt', *Süddeutsche Zeitung*, 8 December 2004

32 Brad Seibel and Patrick Walsh, 'Enhanced Potential Impacts of CO_2-Injection on Deep-sea Biota', *Science* 294/2001, p319 et seq

33 Rat für Nachhaltige Entwicklung, *Perspektiven der Kohle in einer nachhaltigen Energiewirtschaft. Texte Nr. 4* (October 2003, available at www.nachhaltigkeitsrat.de/service/download/publikationen/brosch ueren/Broschuere_Kohleempfehlung.pdf)

34 Volker Hauff, 'Perspektive fossiler Energiequellen für eine nachhaltige Energieversorgung' – address to the convention 'Innovative Technologien zur Stromerzeugung – auf dem Weg zu CO_2-freien Kohleund Gaskraftwerken' (May 10, 2004, available at www.nachhaltigkeitsrat.de/service/download/pdf/Vortrag_ Hauff_Kraftwerkskongress_10-05-04.pdf)

35 Amory B. Lovins, *Twenty Hydrogen Myths* (Snowmass, CO: Rocky Mountain Institute, 2004), p9

36 Jeremy Rifkin, *Die H_2-Revolution* (Frankfurt: Campus Verlag, 2002)

37 Romano Prodi, 'The Energy Vector of the Future. Conference on the Hydrogen Economy' (Brussels, June 3, 2003)

38 Ulf Bossel, 'The hydrogen "illusion". Why electrons are a better energy carrier', *Cogeneration and On-Site Power Production*, March–April 2004, p55 et seq; Dirk Asendorpf, 'Die Mär vom Wasserstoff', *Die Zeit* 42/2004

39 Robert F. Service, 'The Hydrogen Backlash', *Science* 305/2004, p958 et seq

40 Karl-Heinz Tetzlaff, *Bio-Wasserstoff. Eine Strategie zur Befreiung von der selbstverschuldeten Abhängigkeit von Öl* (Norderstedt: Books on Demand, 2005)

41 Amory B. Lovins (see Ref. 35), p23

42 Rudolf Rechsteiner (see Ref. 20)

43 'EU-Commissioner Looks Ahead to a New Nuclear Generation', *Atomwirtschaft* 1/2003, pp14–16

SUN OR ATOM   117

44 Ernst Bloch, *Das Prinzip Hoffnung* (Berlin: Suhrkamp Verlag, 1959), p775
45 Karl Jaspers, *Die Atombombe und die Zukunft des Menschen* (Munich: Piper, 1958), p242
46 *The Russell-Einstein Manifesto*, signed by Max Born, Percy W. Bridgman, Albert Einstein, Leopold Infeld, Frederic Joliot-Curie, Herman J. Muller, Linus Pauling, Cecil F. Powell, Joseph Rotblat, Bertrand Russell and Hideki Yukawa; issued in London, 9 July 1955 (text available at www.pugwash.org/about/manifesto.htm)
47 Roland Kollert, *Die Politik der latenten Proliferation. Militärische Nutzung 'friedlicher' Kerntechnik in Westeuropa* (Wiesbaden: Deutscher Universitätsverlag, 1994)
48 Ulrich Beck, 'Die vertraute Katastrophe' in Wolfgang Liebert and Friedemannn Schmithals (eds), *Tschernobyl und kein Ende?* (Münster: Agenda Verlag, 1997), p55 et seq
49 'Zurück zur Atomkraft?', *Stern* 25/2004
50 Klaus Traube and Hermann Scheer, 'Kernspaltung, Kernfusion, Sonnenenergie – Stadien eines Lernprozesses', *Solarzeitalter* 2/1998, p22 et seq
51 Gero von Randow, 'Mit neuer Strahlkraft', *Die Zeit* 31/2004
52 Otto Hug Strahleninstitut (ed.), *15 Jahre nach Tschernobyl: Folgen und Lehren der Reaktorkatastrophe* (September 2001, available at www.tschernobylhilfe.ffb.org/ohsi0901.htm)
53 Klaus Traube, 'Renaissance der Atomenergie?', *Solarzeitalter* 4/2004, p5
54 Eckhard Rebhan, *Heißer als das Sonnenfeuer* (Munich: Piper, 1992)
55 Koji Tokimatsu, Jun'ichi Fujinob, Satoshi Konishic, Yuichi Ogawad and Kenji Yamaji, 'Role of nuclear fusion in future energy systems and the environment under future uncertainties', *Energy Policy* 31/2003, pp775 et seq
56 Alexander Bradshaw, *Antworten zur parlamentarischen Anhörung Kernfusion am 28.03.2001, mit Beiträgen von H.W. Bartels, H.-S. Bosch, H. Bolt, D. Campbell, W. Dyckhoff, T. Hamacher, M. Kaufmann, K. Lackner, D. Maisonnier, I. Milch, M. Pick, J. Raeder, R. Wilhelm* (Berlin: Deutscher Bundestag, Ausschuss für Bildung, Forschung und Technikfolgenabschätzung, A-Drs. 14-383d, 2001)
57 Emanuele Negro, *Photovoltaics and Controlled Thermonuclear Fusion: A Case Study in European Energy Research* (1995, available at http://perso.orange.fr/energyconsulting/negroP1Nice.doc)

58 As cited by Jochen Benecke, 'Kernfusion ist keine Alternative',
    Bild der Wissenschaft 2/1987, p128
59 Alexander Bradshaw (see Ref. 56), 'Protokoll der Anhörung'
    (hearing minutes)
60 Carl Amery, Hermann Scheer and Christiane Grefe, *Klimawechsel.
    Von der fossilen zur solaren Kultur* (Munich: Kunstmann, 2002), p93
    et seq
61 Günther Anders, *Die Antiquiertheit des Menschen* (Munich: C.H.
    Beck, 1958)
62 Hans-Peter Duerr, *Der Mythos vom Zivilisationsprozess, Band V [vol V]:
    Die Tatsachen des Lebens* (Frankfurt: Suhrkamp Verlag, 2002)
63 Günther Anders, *Die Antiquiertheit des Menschen* (Munich: C. H.
    Beck, 1958), p31

Part II

Blockades to Action: The Unbroken Power of One-Dimensional Thinking

Almost anyone today who thinks critically about energy supply and its consequences, and who knows something about renewable energy's opportunities, is bound to ask questions such as: what is the source of those blockades to action that one finds even among people who are not tied in to the established energy system? Why has it taken so long to break free of one-dimensional thinking and acting, especially since the one-dimensional approach is obviously not solving any problems? Where does this fear of the new come from? In his book *One-Dimensional Man*, the philosopher Herbert Marcuse analysed the 'radical acceptance of the empirical'. The only thing acknowledged in the one-dimensional world of Marcuse's critique is that 'which is *given*' to the individual who 'has only the facts and not the factors'. But this 'experienced world' is merely the 'result of a restricted experience, and the positivist cleaning of the mind brings the mind in line with the restricted experience'.[1]

In the energy system, too, thinking has been reduced to the facts set up by the system itself. But this restriction contradicts the central role that physical energy plays in every vital question. The fact that this contradiction does not get recognized is a consequence of viewing any given problem in isolation and disregarding that problem's contexts; this is a trend one may observe in every sector of society. It leads to fragmented perceptions and, accordingly, to perspectives that are more one-dimensional than those evoked by one-sided ideologies. The different areas of activity within society mutate into hermetically sealed subsystems that can barely get running feedback from constantly changing external factors. The energy system has a life of its own that is especially cut off from the outside, and its categories of action are especially autistic. But even other actors – including those championing a fundamental change in energy – are mostly integrated into their own subsystems where the approaches to thought and action are equally one-dimensional. They, too, are often standing in their own way.

The obstacles to taking action on renewable energy may therefore be explained not only by the one-dimensional perspective of the energy business, but also by one-dimensional thinking in the fields of politics, economics, and environmental protection. Mentally dissolving this reductionist optic is the precondition for overcoming it in practice. The best recipe for dissolving it is to illuminate the reasons behind its formation and their specific consequences.

The cultural hegemony of the traditional energy business

Whoever is dependent, or feels that way, becomes submissive. The more exclusively energy supply was organized by the energy business, the greater was the dependence. Yet people initially experienced this as something overwhelmingly positive, since it brought them unprecedented convenience, economic growth and higher incomes. Dependence did not have to be coerced. To get energy delivered free into your house instead of having to make the effort to procure it yourself, and to have this happen so easily in the form of electricity with diverse applications, this was a transformation society could only regard as liberating. That is why the energy supply system of the industrial countries is viewed to this day as the very model of economic advancement – even for developing countries, in which the majority of people are subjected to the daily tribulations of procuring fuel.

The 'home team advantage'

And so the energy business moved into the role of an acknowl-edged social authority, in spite of countless scandals about monopoly pricing, political bribes and environmental catastro-phes. Even serious blunders that led to bad investments totalling in the billions did little more than scratch its reputation for a while. The energy business has a home team advantage. In soccer, the host team can afford more fouls than the visiting team. Only when the home team plays poorly or acts unfairly in a crude way are there catcalls. The visiting team's players, by contrast, cannot afford as many infractions; aggressive performance is greeted with a veritable concert of Bronx cheers. So long as the energy business can guarantee energy supplies and promises to improve things, it is forgiven time and again. Even the concept 'energy supply' earns the business an advance payment in psychological trust. The energy business is counting on public understanding that nothing be allowed to happen that might weaken it, thereby (supposedly) endangering the general energy supply. The energy business may take it for granted that its own interest is deemed identical with that of society. Even when it is organized privately, the energy business plays the role of a quasi-governmental insti-tution.

Its role is underpinned by the advantage of habituation that all existing things enjoy vis-à-vis what is new and unknown. Advocates of the latter always have the burden of proof on their side, the onus of demonstrating that their project might actually improve the status quo. The political scientist Martin Greiffenhagen has described this as a psychological advantage for all conservatives and a handicap for all the forces of reform. Conservatives usually succeed in branding reformers' goals as dangerous so long as there is an overwhelming perception that the status quo is acceptable – and also because conservatives will occasionally introduce 'moderate' changes and then attempt to create the appearance that these improvements are only in good hands when *they* are in charge. The system of energy supply already in place is widely regarded as a success, and only routine repairs and occasional additions are deemed necessary. It appears inconceivable that it could become untenable. The fear that this might yet happen after all can be played off against any alternative.

The hegemonic position of the energy business has a suggestive power that even casts a spell over people who are aware that the conventional energy system has become prohibitive – a power that causes them to recoil from decisive change. Whenever the word 'energy' is uttered, it is always associated – like a Pavlovian reflex – with something that, on principle, is the 'responsibility' of the energy business. This association is equivalent to intellectually recognizing its exclusive mandate on all energy questions. When it comes to energy, the energy business – especially as represented on government commissions and in the business media – is also (as a rule) the first (and often the only) party whose opinion is sought and respected.

The mental routines of reiterated energy semantics

Concepts shape how we think and act. Once a concept has been occupied by a concrete activity, and that particular usage has become part of everyday speech, the inadvertent result is a mental hierarchy. How far this can go in the world of energy semantics is illustrated by the story of a builder who had an office building constructed so that it would be heated exclusively using solar heat and who then hyped this as a 'house without heating'. In effect, he was unconsciously ceding the concept of heating to fossil energy, and in so doing he was conceptually devaluing a completely workable solar heating system. This habitually indiscriminate use of a few well-rehearsed energy concepts contributes towards blocking our view of renewable energy and of what makes it unique.

This linguistic abuse begins as soon as these well-rehearsed energy terms are perfunctorily assigned to the blanket concept of the 'energy business'. Even among conventional energy suppliers, this concept is applied arbitrarily. It is assigned, for example, to companies that build power plants or operate energy facilities – but not to the car industry, even though this is also an industry that does nothing more than produce energy facilities of a certain kind, or to car drivers, who are independent operators implementing an energy output or service. Even the diverse opportunities for independent energy supply using small power facilities are usually disregarded in discussions of energy business options. There is even less reason to transfer the conceptual fixation on 'the energy business' to renewable energy, whose facilities are as decentralized as those of cars. Once renewable energy is mobilized in all its diversity, the well-rehearsed social division of labour between energy suppliers and energy users is dissolved. For this reason even the concept 'energy market' leads to a constricted outlook. It is a concept that disregards those renewable energy options having nothing to do with commercial energy use, but which instead involve, for example, locally acquired solar energy.

Even the concept 'energy consumption' is only suited to conventional energy. It means that energy – dissipated into greenhouse and other gases, into ash or nuclear waste – gets 'consumed'. But renewable energy, by definition, cannot be consumed; the expression 'energy consumption' therefore renders its chief advantage invisible. Only the concept of the energy user can be neutral vis-à-vis different energy forms. The terminology applied acts like a semantic smokescreen for renewable energy.

In addition, marginalizing descriptions are deployed in a calculated way to make renewable energy part of some new generic term, and therefore to relativize it; these include such terms as 'future energies', 'clean energies', or – the term used most often internationally – 'sustainable energies'. These kinds of generic terms are – as the linguist Uwe Pörksen says – 'plastic words': euphoniously bombastic, 'capable of arbitrary shading', and generating uniformity because of the way they evade any kind of concrete pre-definition.[2] Conventional energy is sometimes smuggled into concepts that arouse associations with renewable energy – so as to lend a conceptual status of ecological equivalence to conventional energy. But how can a non-renewable energy be called a 'future energy' if its future lies in its exhaustion? How can an energy be called 'clean' if the goal is merely to reduce emissions?

From the very beginning, even the concept 'sustainability' concealed an intention to create a smokescreen. It has been on everyone's lips since the 1992 global Conference on Environment and Development in Rio de Janeiro. Yet at that conference it was almost taboo to talk about renewable energy. In the meantime, it is not just renewable energy that is regarded as 'sustainable', but also every other form of energy so long as it fulfils conditions such as enhancing energy efficiency or lowering noxious emissions. In this way the concept 'sustainability' became a commonplace, even though it can be clearly defined: 'sustainable' means a durable balance with cycles of nature; when something is sustainable, it means that economic use may not lead to more being taken out than can be returned in an equivalent fashion. For this reason, only renewable energy can be called 'sustainable'. So why is it that many ecologists do not state this clearly? Why don't they come right out, avoiding any circumlocution, and talk in a direct way about renewable energy?

In an article for *Le Monde Diplomatique* on 'The talk about sustainable development',[3] the French economist Jean-Marie Harribey wrote that this concept:

> *serves as a saving argument for many: for governments, who are simultaneously doing their utmost to promote intensive agriculture; for the executives of multinational corporations, who have no reservations about using up natural resources and who encumber the environment with refuse; for non-governmental organizations, who really have no idea what they are supposed to do; and for the majority of economists, who feel that they are caught in the act when they place a strain on nature.*

Yet another example is those everyday advances in productivity that would be taking place anyway because of ongoing technological developments and competitive behaviour that get consecrated as 'eco-efficiency' — even when the reduced consumption of energy and material they bring is more than outweighed by productivity increases. With the assistance of professional ad agencies, the energy corporations are highly practised in strategically occupying the rhetorical high ground of ecological 'buzzwords'. In the US — in order to confuse and undermine the activist scene of climate protection initiatives aimed against fossil energy consumption – they have founded organizations whose names sound like pure ecology: 'Alliance for Environment and Resources', 'Citizens for Environment', 'Environmental Conservation Organization', 'Global Climate Coalition'. In the US 'fudge' is what they call these manoeuvres of conceptual diversion meant to drive ecological concepts from the field. This is done, not least of all, in order to placate the general public, which does not see through this camouflage. There are two formulas that can be used against these attempts to occupy ecological concepts so as to foist a different content on them or discredit them. First, exposure, although this presupposes a readiness to face conflict, and second, vigilance and precision about one's own way of talking, as well as the creativity to use clear programmatic concepts oneself, for the sake of substantive clarity and distinguishability.

Another problematic case in point is Germany's 'eco-tax'. This refers to the taxation of environmentally damaging products, especially fossil energy. But since every tax is experienced as a burden, this concept directs people's attention away from environmental burdens to tax burdens, and in this way it encodes a positive effect as something negative. It would therefore be more apt to speak of a 'pollution tax' instead of an 'eco-tax'. Campaigns are always being launched against the eco-tax in which the aim is to reduce the general tax burden. Campaigns against a 'pollution tax', by contrast, would be much harder to stage. Whoever attempted this would be revealing that burdening people with pollutants is an offence that leaves him indifferent.

Equally counter-productive is the concept of 'passive solar energy use' or of the 'passive house'. This refers to the direct use of solar heat in a building in lieu of indirect use by means of a conversion technology. Only – the concept 'passive' generally has a negative connotation. Every advertising psychologist uses the word 'active' as frequently as possible. Additional dubious concepts in current ecological language are 'emissions right' or 'pollution right' – words that form the basis for emissions trading. In these words, the positively connoted concept of 'right' in the sense of a legitimate individual claim is linked with the negative concept of 'pollution' – so that the latter is awarded a conceptual upgrade.

Inferiority complexes by way of 'energetical correctness'

'PC' as shorthand for 'political correctness' has become a fashionable term. It criticizes willing conformity to the dominant behavioural norms of the 'mainstream'. There is also something, by way of analogy, one might call 'energetical correctness'. Its norms are established by the 'community' of conventional energy experts active worldwide. This group decides which outlooks pointing beyond their own horizons may still be discussed. Whoever wants to be inside this group or to be recognized by it is well advised not to be too presumptuous about discussing renewable energy. Anybody who not only pleads on behalf of promoting renewable energy but also thinks it is possible to replace non-renewable energy completely is simply not taken seriously and branded as naive or ideological. The more limited the commitment, the more one is tolerated and regarded as 'reasonable'. In the milieu of the energy business it is expected that its members acknowledge the superiority of conventional energy supply even as a long-term prospect, so that renewable energy is merely conceded a subordinate role. Whoever sticks to this 'EC' code inevitably internalizes an inferiority complex about his commitment to renewable energy, can only act with great reserve, and soon finds it embarrassing to demand major, rapid steps towards replacing non-renewable energy.

It is hardly surprising that the sponsors of the established energy system's interests ignore (or disqualify as out of the question) every scenario that depicts an opportunity for supplying society completely with renewable energy. Were they to concede this possibility openly, they would no longer have adequate justification for perpetuating conventional energy supply at any price. When so-called independent energy scientists refuse to take these renewable scenarios into account, however, the motives are opportunistic. They are anxious, for example, that they might no longer be commissioned to prepare a study or a report, or they worry about no longer being cited by the 'scientific' energy community, which is tantamount to scholarly disbarment. That politicians and even environmental organizations should shy away from advocating the goal of completely supplying societies with renewable energy is something that can usually be explained by their lack of knowledge or their strong desire for recognition.

When the petroleum companies Shell and BP published their studies depicting a renewable energy contribution to world energy supply of 50 per cent by the year 2050 as plausible, this projection became, even among renewable energy's champions, the measure of all things. Psychologically this is understandable, because these studies go beyond all previous 'official' statements coming out of the energy scene and are therefore seen as an opportunity to make a better case against the general disdain for renewable energy. For the same reason it is easily overlooked that these studies forecast a doubling of world energy consumption, so that they were actually meant to justify continued consumption of conventional energy at high and unchanged rates! Along with all the jubilation about what seemed like 'finally' getting the energy corporations to take renewable energy seriously, there was a simultaneous acceptance of the studies' contention that coal, oil and nuclear energy would not only remain indispensable, but that they would even remain indispensable at the same level! But there was more than that, these corporate studies are much more often cited as points of reference for renewable energy than is another scenario, sketched out in Part I, for completely replacing conventional with renewable energy. But when the advocates of renewable energy make no effort to broaden the spectrum of perspectives regarded as worthy of discussion, they are bound to remain on the defensive. Having the power to be persuasive and effective on one's own presupposes taking a stand against this informal energetical correctness. This is of decisive importance psychologically. For it is the only way to pull the ground out from under those who seek to legitimize further expansion of fossil and atomic energy.

So long as the established energy system merely succeeds in covering the traditional paradigm with the cloak of sustainability and lending that paradigm an eco-efficient image, it retains sovereignty over the debate. It is a secondary matter whether this happens intentionally, through carelessness, because of cowardice, or from intellectual complacency. Renewable energy represents a new paradigm, which is to say a new, scientifically grounded view of how to supply energy. This can hardly be explained in the categories of the old paradigm. So long as that attempt to explain things the old way continues, we will be bogged trying to make the paradigm shift we require.

The lost identity of energy policy

Guaranteeing the availability of energy in society is a permanent, inalienable, basic political function. No political order can afford to neglect energy or to abandon it exclusively to so-called 'market forces' or transnational corporations not subject to political control. Yet increasingly this is exactly what is happening.

The history of energy policy in industrial societies began over 200 years ago with the opening up of coal deposits. This was the starting point for constantly expanding legislation. In 'mining law', landed property was restricted in favour of the producers of energy raw materials. Thus, for example, 1865 saw the enactment of the General Mining Act for the Prussian State, whose substance has hardly been changed to this day although its form is now the post-war Federal Mining Act. The law regulates prospecting rights for coal and ore, which every property owner is forced to tolerate even on occasions when there is no expropriation procedure. In almost all countries with similar mineral deposits, mineral production projects have been declared to be something in the public interest, and private property provisos have had to take a back seat. Normally, in line with generally understood legal norms, expropriating property is only possible when local and national governments declare that this is in the public interest. But when it came to energy supply – beginning as early as mining law – many countries introduced a special legal construction: the possibility of expropriating from private owners in favour of, and sometimes even done by, private firms themselves. This meant that the peculiar status of the energy business, including its private commercial component, was pre-programmed at an early stage.

As the system of energy supply was expanded and consolidated, rights of way for 'energy streets' were introduced, meaning routes for electricity, gas and heat transmission. The construction of energy plants and transmission lines was juridically privileged. In the course of electrification, electricity companies received regional monopoly rights – in exchange for a general obligation to supply society and public price controls. In some European countries the electricity sector was nationalized: this happened in France in 1946, when the Nationalization Act created Electricité de France (EdF), consisting of 1700 production and 17,000 local distribution companies. In Italy, the equivalent event came in 1962 with the formation of the state enterprise ENEL, into which all electricity-generating and network-operating electricity companies were incorporated, with the exception of large municipal works and small self-suppliers. These developments were based on social and economic policy considerations: promoting electrification, equal electricity prices for all, independent of place of residence, as well as a broad-based promotion of economic growth, independent of where mines or power plants were located. Energy supply, whether organized publicly or privately, became an integral component of the economic and social welfare infrastructure. Not coincidentally, it tended to be the more socially minded political currents that pushed this development. The formation of the government corporations EdF in France and ENEL in Italy was promoted above all by the leftist parties.

In Germany, admittedly, no energy companies were nationalized. But the Energy Management Act of 1935 granted the electricity supply companies the privileges that shape their behaviour to this day. They were allowed to refuse network access, along with supplementary and reserve current, to self-suppliers they found disagreeable, which facilitated the elimination of these self-sufficient producers.[4]

Recently this exceptional position in business life, expanded to include the provision of infrastructure installations, has even outlasted the kind of liberalization initiated in the energy supply sector almost everywhere. In spite of liberalization, private companies have retained privileged transmission construction rights for electricity and gas networks. Their ambivalent role as ordinary companies with governmental rights remained untouched. Moreover, even at an early stage energy became part of the industrial nations' imperialist foreign policies. The occupation of the Ruhr region in Germany by French troops after the First World War happened because of the coal deposits there and their role in heavy industry. Before that war, the joint German-Turkish construction of the railroad line from Berlin to Baghdad – the biggest infrastructure project of its time – served the purpose of gaining access to Mesopotamian (today Iraqi) oil deposits. The division of the defeated Ottoman empire after 1918, with the establishment of the states of Iraq and Kuwait, was based on UK and French petroleum interests. Even the establishment of the EU goes back to the Common Market for coal and steel at the beginning of the 1950s. In order to secure fossil energy supplies, the European Coal and Steel Community was formed, which was not discontinued until 2001. It had supra-national responsibilities, which ranged from investment breaks to research incentives, from the establishment of production quotas and prices to the approval of cartels.

Regardless of how one evaluates this development (which the above account has merely outlined according to its main points), it makes one thing clear: it shows that a broad, strategically conceived power of design was at work securing the long-term position of the energy business. By contrast, no comparable exertion of political force has taken place thus far on behalf of renewable energy. This can be seen most clearly by way of contrast with the single-mindedness of nuclear policy, both national and international, since the 1950s, the most ambitious technology programme of all time. As early as the 1950s, all the major industrial countries had laws about atomic energy. The founding of EURATOM served the 'speedy establishment and growth of nuclear industries' so as to 'contribute to the raising of the standard of living in the member states and to the development of relations with the other countries' (according to Article 1 of the Treaty). EURATOM's task was to include promoting and disseminating technical knowledge, facilitating investment and free movement of capital, creating a common market for nuclear fuels, and guaranteeing tax and customs privileges as well as special credit lines. Like EURATOM, the IAEA immediately received generous funding to support the expansion of nuclear power plants in member countries. Inside the East Bloc's Council for Mutual Economic

Assistance, which was founded in 1949 and dissolved in 1990, nuclear and fossil energy promotion was institutionalized in the form of 'permanent commissions' for nuclear energy, coal, petroleum, natural gas, as well as for energy plant construction and transport.

In 1973, after the first oil crisis, the OECD sponsored the foundation of the International Energy Agency in order to help organize joint policies on energy security. The same purpose was served by the 1991 European Energy Charter, from which the Energy Charter Treaty later emerged. Its members are the European countries, including the former Soviet Union, along with Japan and Australia. The main aims of the treaty are to secure open trade in energy and investment security for energy production and transport networks. For decades, the World Bank and continental development banks provided energy investment credits of up to well over 90 per cent for the fossil energy business, and to this day hardly anything has changed about this policy.

Nuclear and fossil energy subsidies as the greatest case of corporate welfare in world economic history

In addition, there were and are ample subsidies for nuclear and fossil energy. The total amount has never been fully recorded. In 2001 energy scholar André de Moor presented a calculation of annual subsidies in the amount of US$244 billion, of which US$53 billion were for coal, US$52 billion for petroleum, US$46 billion for natural gas, US$48 billion for electricity, US$16 billion for nuclear energy, and US$9 billion for using renewable energy. OECD countries raise 34 per cent of all these subsidies; other countries account for the remaining 66 per cent. According to de Moor's calculations, subsidies for renewable energy come to a mere 3.7 per cent of the total.[5] Needless to say, the subsidies are not evenly distributed across all countries. But apart from that, wherever they are given out, they promote the maintenance of the atomic and fossil energy system. They cause a cost degression with a worldwide impact; the amount of fossil fuels supplied is kept artificially high and the energy price

level artificially low, and capacity utilization for transport infrastructure is secured.

Not captured by these statistical calculations are the subsidies that take place in the form of tax exemptions worldwide for
aircraft and ship fuels; their volume would seem to be around
US$250 billion dollars. Also not captured – because it is almost
impossible to calculate – are the subsidies that flow into the
construction of electric and gas transmissions in many countries.
The total of all direct and indirect energy subsidies, in all probability, is somewhere near US$500 billion annually.

If one adds public research and development funds for
atomic energy, which in Part I were estimated at around US$1
trillion, the result is a breathtaking picture of an enormous political he-man act undertaken in order to make nuclear and fossil
energy available – and a pathetic picture of political powerlessness for renewable energy, which received a mere two per cent of
the subsidies that conventional energy got. It is a double
standard that is accepted as a matter of course in a way that is
almost spooky. Nuclear and fossil energy subsidies constitute
the greatest case of corporate welfare in world economic history.
How did it get this way?

Energy consensus out of habit and weakness

As the energy business sector grew, so did its influence on
politics and policy. When it came to energy questions, politics
(after what seemed like some settled groundwork) degenerated
into mere sectoral 'energy policy' of a kind that granted the
energy corporations high-priority authority to act on all practical questions of energy supply. The traditional energy business
thereby moved into the role of a quasi-governmental institution. Politics was reduced to the role of a moderator between
divergent interests within the energy business. This explains why
so many political attempts at mobilizing on behalf of renewable
energy over the last three decades either barely got off the starting line, stayed put, or fell by the wayside.

For decades, the division of labour between the energy
business and energy policy formed the basis for an undisturbed

energy consensus. The consensus was broken up by protest against nuclear energy that arose in the 1970s. All of a sudden, the uninvited were meddling in the energy debate. The energy business and energy policy makers usually reacted to criticism and attempts at meddling by closing ranks. Ever since, the forces of the conventional energy system, who are accustomed to well-rehearsed teamwork, have been cultivating a quiet, nostalgic hope: that the barking of the dogs will soon cease so that their fully loaded caravan can move on down the trail. The call for a 'return to the energy consensus' is basically a way of saying, 'Please be so kind as to leave the supply of energy to the ancestral powers, so that they can go about their business undisturbed.'

The catchword 'consensus' generally has a major psychological effect. Consensus corresponds with a desire for harmony and has the ring of reasonable compromise. Conflict, by contrast, is trying and unnerving; the outcome is uncertain; conflict generates opponents. Because of the accumulation of energy crises, the public articulation of their causes, the identification of their creators, and the emergence of clear counter-positions, however, it becomes harder and harder to maintain or restore the comfortable consensus within the closed circle of the political-economic energy system – especially when the counter-position has arrived in the political system: in public political debate, in parties, parliaments and governments.

To get beyond the framework in which the energy business operates, it takes political inventiveness that is fresh and energetic. This inevitably means breaking up the decades-long intensive relationship between energy policy and the energy business. Any encouragement of renewable energy as part of a consensus package with the energy business is condemned to failure – unless, that is, one is content with promoting renewable energy in small homeopathic doses, as a mere 'additive' to traditional energy supplies. It cannot be expected that the energy business will agree to a consensus on behalf of mobilizing renewable energy in an expansive way, if only because this mobilization's success would spell the downfall of the energy business itself.

The political decisions made in Germany that led to a breakthrough on behalf of renewable energy in recent years did not come about because of any consensus with the energy business, but rather as a result of intense and persistent conflict. It was no accident that this breakthrough was not initiated by the executive branch of government, but as a result of parliamentary initiatives. The picture is the same for European institutions: all initiatives for renewable energy that led somewhere at the EU level were demanded and carried out by the EU Parliament and forced on the Commission and the Council of Ministers. The primacy of politics was claimed on behalf of renewable energy and in opposition to the energy business. The latter's role as the fourth estate was no longer accepted. In Germany, the electricity business even felt that this was a constitutional violation and lodged a complaint – unsuccessfully – with the Federal Constitutional Court and the European Court of Justice.

The consensus orientation is always rationalized by saying that fundamental decisions can only be made under cover of a broad consensus, with the inclusion of all organized interests. But on many questions this is tantamount to conceding a veto right to these interests, as if democratic constitutions gave them a seat and a vote in legislative institutions. In reality this consensual attitude is just an excuse for lacking the will, or the courage, to act on one's own. There are many groundbreaking decisions that were carried out by governments in fiercely contested conflicts, based on slim parliamentary majorities, against a barrage of media attacks and even against majorities from opinion polls. But a strategic initiative on behalf of the breakthrough to renewable energy could even count on broad popular support – in contrast to numerous costly new weapons or technology projects that were seen through to the end in spite of broad public criticism, such as the global armament programme of the US, the UK's Trident nuclear submarine programme, or the Eurofighter plane supported by the UK, German and Italian governments. It would not be hard to generate greater enthusiasm for a breakthrough to the Solar Age than there was 50 years ago for entering into the hoped-for Atomic Age.

In light of the magnitude of the challenge, the small-minded behaviour of politicians in dealing with renewable energy is downright shocking. An additional reason for lethargy and passivity has to do with fatigue in the political systems of the industrial countries. A half century of successful development and steady economic growth lies in the past, 50 years in which the political system was consolidated and became more socially conscious – albeit hand in hand with growing differentiation and institutionalization of special interests. Appreciation of coherent policy designs and competence about implementing them have got lost in the process. Political institutions became more interwoven and more bureaucratic, procedures incomprehensible and undemocratic. The obvious decline in government's productivity – which can be seen in the way that society gets fewer public services from the revenues expended by the state – is the clearest indicator of the declining power of governmental institutions to act. As can be seen from what transpires in other areas, these institutions have a significantly diminished capacity to undertake reforms and less resistance to organized interests.

Nuclear research illustrates the kind of self-paralysing consequences that arise from decisions already made. No cabinet minister in the administration that governed Germany between 1998 and 2005, and no member of either one of the parliamentary delegations from the two parties (the SPD and the Greens) that formed a parliamentary majority in the Bundestag at that time, supported this project. And there are hardly even any senior civil servants in the ministries who might have been counted as advocates of nuclear research. Yet there were no cutbacks in research funds for the nuclear fusion project. The major research institutes, especially the Max Planck Societies, cling to this project and justify their institutional self-interest by intoning the familiar high-sounding chant of scientific-ethical responsibility and precaution about the future of society. Since this project also gets a big push from EURATOM, and because there is an international consortium contract to build an experimental and demonstration reactor, nobody retreated from this commitment – out of hesitance about clashing with established interests. It is the same mechanism that takes hold time and time again whenever there is an expensive big project or a new weapons technology. A military requirement is always simulated that cannot withstand critical scrutiny. In reality it is all about expensive state-funded survival premiums for technology companies and institutes, premiums that betray a pathetic lack of political imagination and courage about changing technological priorities.

Governments already have more work to do coping with the consequences of energy-determined crises – whether it is environmental impacts or economic and political 'collateral damage'. Just paying for the direct costs of energy crisis management eats up more funds than the effort to get at the roots of these crises. With each passing day, crisis management as a substitute for rooting out crises is getting more difficult and more expensive. In order to dodge all the conflicts and be spared the pains of a system change, political and economic actors let themselves in for intolerable risks and even greater pains.

The perversion of energy security by securing resources through military means

The most short-sighted and (in every respect) most costly type of crisis management is the effort to secure access to depleting petroleum resources by military means. This kind of political power play is a faster route into the very debacle it is intended to avoid. Since the beginning of the 1990s, all US governments have devoted the greatest practical attention to militarizing the way they secure energy, and they have attempted to draw others into this risky strategy. It is something that has been discussed since the outbreak of the global oil crisis in 1973, which (especially in the US) led to a veritable oil paranoia. But at that time the emphasis was still on mobilizing the US's own energy sources. In presenting his energy independence project in 1973, President Nixon invoked the spirit of the Manhattan Project and the space programme, an enterprise he wanted to revive. In 1979, in addition to his initiatives for an energy conservation and solar programme, President Carter presented a plan for mass production of synthetic fuels from gasified and liquefied coal, for which he sought US$88 billion from Congress. The plan was never implemented, rather like the ill-fated 'coal refining programme' of Germany's Chancellor Helmut Schmidt at the beginning of the 1980s, which pursued the same end.

The strategic shift towards securing energy by military means took place in 1981, when Carter was succeeded by Reagan. What was decisive was not only Reagan's credentials as an oil industry man, but also the fall of the Shah in Iran in 1979 and the shift to a fundamentalist Islamic regime under Ayatollah Khomeini. From now on the problem was not just distant oil sources, but (over and above this) 'enemy oil'. Initially, the new strategy was tried using the method of the proxy war. Iraqi dictator Saddam Hussein received massive support in his war against Iran. Everyone knew he was a 'rogue', but he was 'our rogue'. A million people fell victim to this first great oil war. Then it was discovered that Saddam Hussein was not only an anti-Iranian bulwark, but that his occupation of Kuwait also revealed him to be striving for the role of a global oil power. Now the US intervened militarily on its own (without proxy); the Gulf War of 1991 became the second great oil war.

According to calculations by Professor Donald Losman from the National Defense University in Washington, annual expenditures for the US armed forces on the Arabian peninsula since then have been US$60 billion, although the value of the oil exported from the Gulf region to the US between 1992 and 1998 was barely under US$10 billion.[6] At around the same time, after the USSR collapsed in 1991, there began the build-up of a US military presence in all the oil- and gas-producing countries of the former Soviet Union outside Russia. With the US in charge, the NATO summit conference at Rome in November 1991 decided that the 'Alliance's New Strategic Concept' needed to prevent the 'disruption of the flow of vital resources'. This was reiterated in NATO's declaration on its 50th anniversary early in 1999. But no effort was made in the 2003 Iraq War – the third great oil war – to include NATO, because no majority could be found for this. Mass protest in Europe showed that such a plan would have split NATO.

In June 2003 Javier Solana, the EU's High Representative for Common Foreign and Security Policy, presented the European Council with the document, *A Secure Europe in a Better World*.[7] In the section on 'new threats in a new security environment' it reads: 'Energy dependence is a special concern for Europe. Europe is the world's largest importer of oil and gas.' Military initiatives are not recommended. But there is no convincing EU plan to overcome this energy dependence in the next 20 years. All that is recommended is an increase in the share of bio-fuels to 5.75 per cent by 2010, supplemented by a few percentage points for hydrogen. Yet that hardly suffices to ward off an oil supply crisis triggered by political developments in the producing countries. If the supply of oil should be cut short as a result of political events in the oil-producing countries, would Europe – and not just a few EU members like the UK – also fall in with the 'American line' of crisis management and take part in the military occupation of a producing country? After all, in a speech in November 2004, Germany's defence minister at the time, Peter Struck, already stated that one of the armed forces' future missions would be to secure these resources.

If the shift to renewable energy keeps getting postponed, especially in the fuels sector, we might start witnessing developments that are currently regarded as unthinkable. Twenty years ago no one would have imagined an energy war conducted without proxy by a democratic state. And removing a brutal dictator from power will not always be available as a rationale. What would happen if a major oil-producing country were to curtail its production in order to stretch out its reserves over time for legitimate reasons of self-interest? Or what might transpire if, as a result of a general exhaustion of sources, not enough oil is available for everyone? Will countries then be occupied so that the occupiers can at least secure enough resources for their own needs, while others have to stare into empty pipelines? What international tensions will emerge when the US, China and the EU pursue ambitions like this separately and in competition with each other?

Military methods of securing resources only end up depleting traditional energy reserves even faster. Public funds get wasted. A worldwide rearmament of the leading colonial powers is provoked. The moral consequences are disastrous. The militarization of energy security is a perversion of energy strategy. The military force used in this endeavour only reduces the political force needed to secure society's energy supplies, something that ultimately should be rooted in the rational application of energy and in a shift to renewable energy.

Evasive manoeuvres to avoid political responsibility

This critique of energy policy's militarization also holds true for the three other energy strategy plans currently in favour internationally, concepts discussed in the next three sections:

- the worldwide liberalization of conventional energy supply, which means more privatization of political responsibility for society's existentially vital need to secure energy;
- the attempt to try solving the world's energy problem by way of consensus-oriented global negotiations, in other words, globalizing political responsibility – which means generalizing and diluting that responsibility;
- the use of economic incentives to reduce energy emissions, based on the Kyoto Protocol for environmental protection, an approach that turns a comprehensive social and political challenge into a single-factor problem calling for a single-factor plan.

All these concepts enable political institutions to shirk more far-reaching strategies and the conflicts for settling them. Plans should not be measured by the standard of wishful thinking that underlies them; rather, they need to be assessed by their empirical outcomes and foreseeable developments. A sober look at these three concepts shows that concentrating on them means to run panting after a train of escalating energy-induced crises and never arrive on time at the right destination, which is renewable energy.

The pseudo-liberalization of energy markets

Since the 1990s, 'liberalization of the energy markets' has become the standard for all energy business and energy policy decisions – and people act as if this were also the panacea for an ecologically oriented shift in energy use. Ever since, each political initiative to mobilize renewable energy has been forced to justify itself according to whether it meets this standard, no matter how unsatisfactory the results might be. The concept of liberalization used here refers above all to the electricity sector and to gas supplies linked to transmission lines, since other parts of the energy market are regarded as having already been liberalized.

The core idea sounds impressive: those companies that are owners of networks should no longer be allowed to abuse this 'natural monopoly' as a way of privileging an energy supplier or – whenever the electricity producer is simultaneously a network operator – privileging themselves. The production of electricity, its transmission and its distribution should be separated from each other entrepreneurially. This is a concept that has been evaluated as a 'shock to the system' – thus the title of a memorandum by the organization, Resources for the Future (RFF) in the US.[8] The public regulatory role should be restricted to questions of how efficient the transmission and distribution of electricity is, as well as to price controls and network utilization. The price for electricity should then be a result of free competition among suppliers. This is meant to establish a direct relationship between producer and supplier.

Every conceivable blessing was expected to come about as a result of liberalization. Thus, the following promises were made: declining energy prices would provide relief for electricity customers, promote economic growth and improve competitiveness; energy services would become more flexible; electricity customers would be able to choose freely among energy suppliers; and the electricity corporations would be deprived of power. Even in the environmental movement this step was mostly welcomed, against the background of unpleasant experiences with both private and public supply monopolies who were notorious for baulking at environmental-friendly energy supply. The prevailing impression was, it can't get much worse.

In her book *Power Play*, the Australian social scientist Sharon Beder analysed the practical consequences of liberalization in different countries.'[9] She comes to the conclusion that the brief history of liberalization is a story of broken promises. Prices for average households and small business have gone up almost everywhere. The reliability of service has suffered because investments in maintenance and training tasks have been neglected. Blackouts have increased. Environmental quality has, on the average, got worse; running times for old power plants with lower transformation efficiency have been artificially extended, investments in greater energy efficiency have mostly been cut – and each upshot of liberalization has contributed towards artificially propping up the price difference to electricity from combined heat and power facilities and renewable energy in favour of an environmentally harmful energy supply. In countries where there are no special laws to promote it, investments for renewable energy went down. At the same time, R&D efforts within corporations were reduced.

The victors of this development have been big industrial consumers who are able to negotiate lower electricity prices on the basis of their purchasing power – and especially the electricity corporations, who have been elevated into transnational enterprises. Liberalization facilitated an unprecedented process of concentration on their behalf. This was even something the EU Commission explicitly wished. It expressly wanted larger electricity corporations; in the common European electricity market that was envisioned, smaller suppliers were not regarded as sufficiently functional. It was a curious and highly contradictory concept: 'more market' through consolidation in the field of electricity companies, because large enterprises were seen as more 'marketable'.

What is happening, therefore, is pseudo-liberalization as a vehicle for self-interest. There are three reasons in particular why liberalization in the electricity sector has taken this turn:

- the dogmatic equation of the idea of liberalization with the privatization of supply networks;
- the incoherence of the approaches to liberalization, since fundamental aspects of integration in the energy business were not taken into consideration and have remained undiscussed to this day;
- turning the current market price for energy into an absolute, as if the idea of the market economy applies only to, and is exhausted by, low prices.

The dogmatic equation of liberalization with privatization

After the collapse of the Soviet bloc and its planned economy, there was a worldwide denunciation of all direct or indirect forms of public economic management as inefficient, inflexible and bureaucratic, as relics of an outdated politics. The state, the planned economy, monopoly, regulation, bureaucracy, inflexibility, inefficiency and spoon-feeding were regarded as negative synonyms – freedom of choice, the market, deregulation, liberalization and privatization, by contrast, as positive guiding concepts. With the Washington Consensus (formulated in 1990), this zeitgeist became the dominant economic doctrine. International financial institutions like the World Bank and the International Monetary Fund (IMF) made the uniform orientation of all national economies to the principles of state-free management into a global programme. The privatization of public service companies and the opening of these sectors to international investment capital became a condition for credit. The electricity sector was regarded as one of the choice pickings. That a planned economy can also emerge within a private economic system is a fact that lies outside the mental horizon of these apologists for a so-called neoliberalism, the doctrine that has emerged unchallenged in spite of all the criticism directed against it over the years. In reality it has led to a neo-feudalism run by large transnational corporations that interact with each other in limited oligopolistic competition and concede just one role to national institutions: opening markets for them. Thus, homage is rendered to a notion of the market economy that crassly contradicts the idea of the market economy as a framework for a social welfare-minded public order. Equating liberalization with privatization has contributed decisively to the rebirth of the conventional energy business, rising in tandem with liberalization like a phoenix out of the ashes. The most important levers of power these forces have wielded were unbridled internationalization and the privatization of networks undertaken in many countries.

Public ownership of a business enterprise can only be justified on the basis of an indispensable public interest that one ought not subject to the profit motive or expose to the risk of bankruptcy inherent in private enterprise. Whenever negative social effects result from the way a public corporation does business – for example, because of serious environmental contamination – that company's claim to further the public interest becomes dubious. Hence, privatizing publicly operated and environmentally damaging power plants can even help make governments more consistent about championing the kind of energy supply that is more environmentally appropriate, since governments will then no longer have a self-interested business interest preventing them from being more environmentally conscious. The function of power grids, however, needs to be evaluated in a completely different way. Their existence as a generally available infrastructure remains a permanent public interest. Everywhere electricity networks were privatized the role of electricity corporations has been strengthened, since (after all) they retained ongoing power to prevent any shift to renewable energy (in spite of losing their regional monopolies).

This is especially applicable to those countries in which the three functional areas of production, transportation and distribution of electricity were broken up ('unbundled') without simultaneously breaking up the integrated property structure of power plant and network operators. Inside the EU, after all, the latter was prescribed in a few countries – in the UK, Sweden, The Netherlands, Spain and Portugal. Where – as in Germany – this was not done, the electricity corporations have tried as much as possible to bring the natural monopoly of the networks under their control – in other words, to dominate precisely that part of electricity supply that fulfils a classic public purpose. With the coffers they filled during the era of regional monopolies, the electricity corporations went on a frenetic shopping spree, buying up regional and municipal networks. When state and local governments – either for ideological reasons or in order to improve their short-term financial situation – accommodate the energy companies, they open the way for liberalization to be undermined just as it is getting started.

To be sure, the liberalization laws require the electricity corporations to operate their networks by way of independent network companies. At first glance, therefore, it seems like a question of secondary importance as to who owns the networks so long as a public regulatory authority sees to it that network use is open to all market participants on equal terms. There are other reasons, nevertheless, why the electricity corporations want to bring the networks under their control. One reason is that network operation, even under conditions of publicly controlled remuneration for usage, remains the only secure source of income. If the companies – continuing the tradition of teaming up with governments – succeed in 'securing' lax public control, they can also continue raking in excessive profits effortlessly. This goal was most easily reached by Germany's electricity corporations. Through excessive usage payments at the trans-mission network level, they were able to rack up extra profits in the billions. In 2003 transmission network operators in Germany made sales of 19 billion euros. Of these, a mere 1.8 billion euros were used for investments in the networks; profits came to 6 billion euros.

But even if a public regulatory authority should succeed in preventing these kinds of excesses and in guaranteeing network operation that does not discriminate against any market partici-pant, the electricity corporation still gains from its ownership of networks a strategic advantage that is ultimately decisive for the company. Whoever has power over the networks also occupies a key position. The layout of the networks influences investment decisions for power plants. Investments by competi-tors can be prevented or delayed by failing to provide the necessary new network capacity. Where new production sites are required, as in the case of renewable energy, and where existing network capacity is insufficient, opportunities to obstruct emerge. Refusing to expand a network can be justified by claim-ing that this cannot be accomplished right now, or that it can only be realized later, or that, 'in the interest of all electricity customers', one cannot take responsibility for any increase in network operating costs. Additional network costs for renew-able energy are denounced as a macroeconomic burden. Conversely, the available network's workload, which is tailored to existing conventional large power plants, is regarded as an 'economic' reason for the 'need' to replace old large power plants with new ones. Never do the electricity corporations talk about how much network capacity might prove superfluous or might be saved by switching from conventional to renewable energy production.

Whoever has the network can assert that there is a need for large power plants in order to maintain line voltage and frequency. He can also induce artificial supply shortages in order to exact higher prices for reserve current. Arbitrary blackouts were induced in California between November 2000 and May 2001, the energy corporation ENRON took power plants out of the network on ostensibly technical grounds in order to derive a justification for its claim that it needed to draw substitute current from its own subsidiaries at drastically higher prices (higher, at times, by a factor of 10 to 50). In the *New York Times*, Princeton economist Paul Krugman talked about a 'US$30 billion robbery'. Energy scientists Woodrow W. Clarke and Ted Bradshaw suspect that this was a deliberate political manoeuvre in order to provoke a government crisis in California.[10] Conceivably, it is just a matter of time until one (or several) of the four electricity corporations in Germany who have the transmission lines under their control, and who simultaneously operate large power plants, might undertake a major campaign in which they strike a blow against the Renewable Energy Sources Act (EEG) by staging a blackout in one of Germany's major supply regions and then blaming it all on wind power plants. It is entirely conceivable, too, that a 'disciplinary shut-off' against wind energy or a 'blackmail shut-off' against the legislature might take place, with the goal of openly discrediting and overturning the EEG legislation. Another method for blockading renewable energy might be to refuse feeding electricity from renewable energy into the system, as required by law – only this time no longer in isolated incidents, as heretofore, but on a grand scale, all the while invoking the energy corporations' concern for their 'public responsibility'.

In this case the attempt is made to derive a rationale for perpetuating the old power plant structure by deriving it from the 'logic' of an electricity grid already built on conventional large power plants. In spite of the current annual growth rate of 3000 megawatts for renewable energy in Germany, the electricity corporations, most of the business press and the majority of 'economic policy' experts talk incessantly about the need to replace obsolete large power plants with entire new ones – as if renewable energy were not even an option. The electric companies are even demanding that the federal government give them 'investment security' – a completely anti-market demand. What they mean are plant utilization guarantees for these new power plants lasting several decades. This demand garners applause from the industrial lobbies, and most of the business commentators in the media are sympathetic. If the car industry were to issue a similar guarantee to the federal government about capacity utilization for new production facilities, they would be accused of wanting to replace the market with a planned economy. Guaranteed investment security for new large power plants would only be conceivable if regional monopolies were re-established – and the EEG were throttled. Apparently it is the latter that Germany's electricity corporations have in mind. It is no accident that, in the conferences they sponsor and the relevant media reporting on the electricity business, the EEG is constantly being discredited in a way that suggests a public campaign.

Economic planning wearing a market economy suit

Even this narrow-minded liberalization has already proven one thing, and a functioning market would confirm it: investments in large power plants are becoming an incalculable risk. Many investments have failed to materialize, something especially applicable to nuclear power plants with their high investment costs and correspondingly long amortization periods. And yet the energy corporations' resistance to renewable energy has hardly let up. In addition to the aforementioned reasons, this is attributable not least of all to an inconsistency in the liberalization laws that has hardly been a subject for discussion thus far. A consistently thought-out plan to break up the energy cartels would have to aim at an entrepreneurial separation of electricity production from fuel delivery. An electricity company that simultaneously maintains coal mines or delivers natural gas is not about to switch to wind power facilities and away from coal or gas power plants if it can produce electricity more cost-effectively with the latter.

In the integrated energy business, there is almost no such thing as an isolated transaction; instead, there are multiple transactions within a single enterprise – auto-erotic 'one-stop shopping transactions', so to speak. The duopoly of fuel delivery and power plant operation within a single corporation is the structurally conservative hard core of the energy business.

This is why it is also naive for some of renewable energy's advocates to entertain the wishful notion that the energy companies would, almost as a matter of course, switch over to producing electricity in giant offshore wind parks or in the Sahara from solar power plants installed there. If electricity can be produced more cost-effectively this way than in traditional power plants, it is assumed that corporations will voluntarily build thousands of kilometres of new transmission lines in order to support this prospect. In fact, the corporations are actually bristling at the mere suggestion that they might have to build just 10 kilometres for a wind park! It is illusory to expect that electricity producers would undertake multi-billion dollar investments that would cause them not only to shut down their own conventional large power plants, but also to end their coal, natural gas and nuclear fuel transactions – in other words, to undertake investments that would run counter to their own best interests.

The petroleum sector has been completely ignored by the apologists of liberalization, even though the oil business is the most monopolistic of any sector in the energy business. Its product dominance extends from production to the gas pump. The global corporations running this business produce large amounts of their petroleum themselves on the basis of production licences; they maintain the pipelines and refineries, organize distribution and monopolize gas stations. Transport by ship is the only thing they delegate, not infrequently to dubious shipping companies that travel under cheap flags in order to get around liability risks in the event of tanker accidents. The form of liberalization that the petroleum industry uses most of the time became prevalent a long time ago: duty-free status for energy raw materials. But there is something that has been

completely overlooked: in the petroleum sector, too, a break-up
should have been undertaken long ago separating raw oil suppliers, refinery operations and petrol stations from each other so
that, for example, every petrol station would be at liberty to
determine its suppliers on its own.

The fact that the petroleum sector has been left out of the
general trend towards liberalization demonstrates once more
that there has been a preference for implementing liberalization
in a way that does not stand in the way of established interests.
Liberalization is delivered on the backs of weakly organized
interests. The powerful business players clamour loudly for
liberalization whenever and wherever it suits their interests, and
they evade or undermine it when their interests are adversely
affected. That is why the liberalization of energy markets –
which sounds so convincing in every paper written on the subject
– is always subject to the danger of mutating into pseudo-
liberalization in practice; into a privatized, internationalized
planned economy wearing a market economy suit.

The mentality of the planned economy that underlies the
policy of a guaranteed energy supply is an ironclad and systemic
characteristic of the nuclear and fossil energy business. That
business is so dependent on far-flung international resource
streams, so integrated and large, that it is not capable of behaving any differently. It has at its disposal, furthermore, the
appropriate machinery for protecting its market segments. Even
if energy corporations are ready to adapt to renewable energy,
the time, place and mode of their adaptation are choices dictated
by overall corporate strategic interests. But these cannot be
identical with the political interest of countries and with
environmental interests worldwide, not to mention with the
interests of renewable energy providers operating on a decentralized basis. This is why the German electricity corporation
Eon may sell and distribute decentralized facilities for producing energy in the UK – outside its home market territory –
although in Germany the same corporation tries to torpedo this
kind of development. That is why the commitment of BP and
Shell to renewable energy is not primarily in their home-grown
field of fuel delivery, but in the area of solar electricity installations – in market territory outside their own. And that is why,

although they may be prepared to produce bio-fuels, for now these companies will only introduce bio-fuels into countries where the appropriate political parameters have been created – and, even then, only when new suppliers have emerged who might take away their market shares.

Starting as early as the 1980s, analogously, the car corporations that operate on a worldwide basis have been offering cars for sale in Brazil that can run on bio-alcohol – only not in Europe. The Bundestag, Germany's parliament, passed a law making all bio-fuels tax-free as of 1 January 2004; this makes it possible to offer bio-fuels for sale more cheaply than fossil fuels, so that the way has been cleared to introduce these new fuels quickly and on a broad basis. In direct opposition to this move, in the autumn of 2004 a working group set up by the federal government to craft a 'fuels strategy' – a group dominated by civil servants from the relevant ministries and representatives of the petroleum and car industries – articulated the view that introducing bio-fuels and vehicles to match was advisable only for certain regions in the world, such as Brazil, or for fleets of cars, but not for the market in general.

All these examples show that every effort at 'harmonizing' big corporate interests from the energy business with society's interests routinely ends up producing even more refined designs for a planned economy that, directly or indirectly, counteract the idea and practice of a liberalized energy market – even if these are constantly being invoked rhetorically. The guardians of the old time-sanctioned energy structures are aided here by a simplified, mutilated notion of what the market economy is, a notion that turns fixation on the current market price for energy into an exclusive criterion. For renewable energy, this short-term and one-dimensionally conceived price criterion becomes a murderous argument – no matter what the cost is to society.

The hypocritical debate on energy prices

The price for a product, when it is charged under genuine, non-discriminatory competitive conditions, is regarded as an unerring and precise criterion that compels all economic participants to engage in rational market behaviour. That an actually existing market economy does not function alone according to this standard is proven by the vast sums of money companies spend on product design, advertising, and brand name identification, expenditures meant to stimulate psychological buying incentives. If peoples' behaviour were exclusively oriented around price, it would be entirely sufficient to publish price comparison tables for equivalent products. Any expenditures on buying incentives above and beyond the published price would be a superfluous cost factor. The advertising business would amount to a gigantic reserve that could be rationalized away in the interest of greater efficiency, as would all the professions engaged in product design. Yet every market participant, whether supplier or buyer, knows that, even if market processes functioned according to the principle of supply and demand, there would still be criteria for decision making other than price. If price were everything, we would be dealing with a society that had no culture.

Reducing all questions exclusively to price (taken in isolation from everything else), a simplification that is unrealistic even when we are dealing only with the behaviour of individual participants in the market, is an attitude that acquires even more unreal qualities when it comes to basic questions about society's overall use of energy. It is an attitude that leads to a cost-cutting extremism celebrated as the highest form of rationality even when the consequences turn out to be extremely irrational: obsession with the present, coupled with forgetfulness about the future. This one-dimensionality has, however, become the hallmark of modern economic thinking – promoted by a 'science' of economics which, in its aspiration towards greater exactitude, attempts to monetize all problems and insists on abstract mathematical models, with a message to both society and economy that they should please be so kind as to make this their own orientation; the result is models without any reference to their subjects. For every political goal an artificial attempt is made to define a price so that the goal can be exchanged or bargained on the market. This results in numerous assumptions and concepts that are remote from reality and mock common sense. One attempts to force upon reality isolated 'parameters' that lend their concepts a certain theoretical elegance. Even environmental economics, anxious about obtaining 'scientific' recognition, has (as we shall discuss in the section after the next one) adopted constructs like this as their own.

An energy discussion is bound to be disastrous if, in ignorance of all existing and foreseeable energy problems, it hammers home the point that nothing is more important than the current price of energy. Daily fluctuations in the price of oil testify to that price's incalculability, as well as to the irrationality of a discussion fixed on price. In such a discussion, all the decisive questions about all the other political, social, industrial, and especially ecological costs or advantages of different energy options are turned into secondary questions, or else they are avoided altogether. And this is happening at a time when the question of energy security and the environmental compatibility of energy use becomes more relevant with each passing day. Even investments meant to create something new are turned into 'costs' to be avoided wherever possible. The more long term such investments are conceived, the more they are regarded as inimical to competition. Because their economic impact cannot be precisely calculated, these investments are dropped if there is doubt. As a result, the idea of the market economy degenerates from an economic ordering principle into organized social irresponsibility.

An inalienable part of a competitive order has to be the prevention of monopolies and oligopolies; there should also be limits on economic freedoms for the sake of elementary social interests. The economic function of markets dare not be played off against political goals and concerns of social ethics. Obstructive and unscrupulous competition needs to be ruled out so as to enable 'peaceful competition' rather than 'hostile competitive struggle' – according to Franz Oppenheimer, one of the intellectual fathers of liberal economic doctrine, in his standard work *Theorie reiner und politischer Ökonomie* (Theory of Pure and Political Economy).[11]

Wilhelm Röpke, another intellectual father of the market economy, warned against the kind of 'theoretical perfectionism' that makes competition depend on conditions 'in which it is established a priori that they can hardly be met in reality'. In

Jenseits von Angebot und Nachfrage (English title: *A Humane Economy*), a classic of market economic doctrine, he emphasizes that competition dare not be given more to do than can reasonably be expected of it. For competition is not always able to exercise its ordering function in a market economy, nor can it always, of its own accord, create the 'moral foothold' without which it 'constantly threatens to degenerate'. Market participants need to be 'compelled' by way of political rules into behaviour that takes into account societal concerns, behaviour they would forego if acting solely out of self-interested economic calculation – and whereby they would also force other competitors into 'generally damaging borderline behaviour'. Röpke envisions the necessity of limiting market competition when the supplier's profits and the consumer's price advantage 'are all out of proportion to the expenditure that society as a whole has to bear'. Limits on the principle of competition – in other words, 'exemptions from the order of market transactions' – are therefore also imperative in a market economic order.[12]

Oppenheimer's and Röpke's ideas about the market economic order make it clear how hypocritical are those demands, raised in the name of competition, that renewable energy should prove itself 'in the market'. A minimal precondition for such competition would be equality of opportunity between atomic/fossil and renewable energy in the market-place – and social equivalence for all energy options with reference to environmental damage and future availability. Yet even if all subsidies and privileges for nuclear and fossil energy were immediately done away with, there would still be no equality of opportunity for renewable energy. Only if the suppliers of nuclear and fossil energy were required to pay back all the subsidies they previously received could we talk about microeconomic market equality for renewable energy. But since this is not feasible, the mockery and indignation constantly poured on ambitious political programmes to promote renewable energy (under constant reference to the market) are either sanctimonious or show that the authors of these derisive attitudes have simply not understood the real context. The pure market viewpoint proceeds from an assumption of neutrality among energy forms that simply does not exist and would lead to rebellion were it applied to other products. Should baby food containing harmful substances have the same market access as pollutant-free baby food?

No market equality without equality of opportunity

Elevating market price into an absolute value is ahistoric, apolitical, anti-ecological and, not least of all, anti-market. To put the point sharply: a nuclear and fossil energy supply is ultimately incompatible with a functioning market order. For this reason, the most ardent champions of the market economy as a regulating principle ought to be the ones advocating a rapid shift to renewable energy. Only on this basis is there any possibility of free supply and demand conditions and of productivity competition without (self-)destructive consequences and government intervention along the lines of a planned economy. The precondition for this shift, however, is establishing a market priority for renewable energy, because there is no immediate prospect of market equality with traditional energy suppliers. The market advantages and privileges obtained over decades in a manner that did not conform to market rules cannot be rewound, and even the trillions of dollars in subsidies lovingly bestowed on the traditional energy system cannot be rescinded. An equality of opportunity that would constitute market equality simply does not exist in any way, shape or form. It also cannot be established. Renewable energy can satisfy people's energy needs, but it is a different, and in many respects a more varied, 'product' than is conventional energy. Society also cannot afford to wait until the conventional energy system runs up against its limits without disastrous consequences.

Market equality presupposes market comparability. This, too, does not exist, because (even from a microeconomic perspective) there are different factors for making elementary calculations between conventional energy and the bulk of renewable energy forms. For the former there are blocks of fixed costs for the energy plants and infrastructure for supplying energy; in addition, there are variable costs in the form of fuel costs, energy transport and disposal, as well as high capital costs owing to

relatively late returns on investment because of latent installation times for energy facilities. With renewable energy there are
fixed costs for plant, a quick return on investment, but with the
exception of bio-energy there are no fuel and disposal costs and,
for the most part, the energy delivery costs are either lower or
non-existent. There is no appropriate method for registering
these differences, rendering them comparable, and comparing
them on the market. The longer the calculation period, the more
'external' factors get included, and the more trivial become the
price calculations that refer only to actual costs and are undertaken in isolation.

In any event, the type of price comparison currently upheld
by the energy business, comparison between conventional energy
from amortized old plants and renewable energy from new facilities, lacks any informational value. Just a price comparison with
energy costs from new conventional energy plants yields a different picture. This changes again in favour of renewable energy
when its cost degressions are considered on the basis of technological optimization and the scale effects of productivity
increases. And it changes yet again when one considers how
infrastructure and transport costs can be avoided because of
decentralized energy supply – not to mention the external costs
that are avoided. Renewable energy is about the future, about
leaving behind the disastrous present shaped by traditional
energy.

The illusion of global negotiation solutions

'Think globally, act locally' is the motto of numerous strongly
committed environmental initiatives. But in politics another
leitmotif has prevailed: act globally, and don't implement nationally until an international treaty has been concluded. Since the
major ecological threats are global in nature, it is argued,
solutions can only come from plans conceived by mutual agreement on a global scale. The multilateral principle of
environmental action has become the credo not only of most
governments, but also of many internationally active NGOs.
Multilateralism aims at a harmony of all governments – or at

least of as many as possible – reached in a spirit of partnership bound by treaty. Its opposite is unilateralism, one or several states going it alone; dashing ahead in this way places no high value on other governments' approval and related negotiations.

In Europe especially, unilateralism has been ruled out since the Bush administration used this doctrine not only to torpedo environmental treaties but also to legitimize pre-emptive war strategies. In his book *Of Paradise and Power* (based on an earlier article 'Power and Weakness'), the US security adviser Robert Kagan has written about how unilateralism is an expression of strength emanating from the US while multilateralism, preferred by European countries, is a sign of their weakness.[13]

His argument refers to military capabilities. In the 2003 Iraq war, the US – with the UK and a number of other governments in tow – practised a unilateralism so conceived, conducted without a UN mandate. Since then unilateralism per se has been regarded as a ruthless method of military action undermining world stability.

This was not always the case. Back in the days of the cold war arms race it was, above all, the peace movement that strongly advocated one-sided renunciation of armaments and unilateral disarmament. This attitude was based on the experience of what happened with multilateral negotiations on arms control and disarmament – they took years, were repeatedly interrupted, and barely got off the ground – and when they finally did get started, they were incapable of really stopping the arms race, with its enormous capacity for technological enhancement. It is curious, then, that so many environmental activists coming out of the peace movement are now not more sceptical about multilateral efforts to produce environmental treaties.

Just this comparison between two widely divergent motives for proceeding unilaterally ought to make it clear that evaluating any international approach to action should not be limited by merely formal criteria. Whatever method proves useful should emerge from the substantive goals these methods are meant to pursue, from given circumstances, and from the results these methods may help to achieve. Proceeding unilaterally can even become an urgent imperative when a multilateral method of action proves an evident failure and no satisfactory solution emerges. Unilateral action does, however, need to be legitimized by generally accepted goals.

The practical results of the multilateral approach to global environmental policy are so sobering that is it is well past high time for this method to receive critical scrutiny and no longer be relied on so exclusively. This is especially true when it comes to solving those global problems whose origins lie in the way energy is currently supplied. It is an illusion to think that a worldwide breakthrough to renewable energy can be achieved through global negotiations. All attempts to do this have just proved the point. They even show that global negotiations are more part of the problem than a path towards their solution. The question needs to be asked: have not some routine multi-lateral efforts done more to halt progress than to advance it, and have they not therefore done more harm than good? Does the amount of effort and attention expended stand in any reasonable relation to a realistic, practical result? Do not global negotiations rather tend to serve most participants as a substi-tute for action, as a shunting yard putting problems off to the side, as a cheap excuse for postponing action once again? Are these negotiations not a carte blanche for additional inactivity, since (obviously) little is accomplished when one acts on one's own while others fail to act? And, above all, what might acting unilaterally accomplish, as opposed to all these multilateral negotiations, and where might taking unilateral steps actually constitute an urgent imperative in order to overcome paralysis of action in the energy question?

Neither the 1972 UN Environmental Conference in Stockholm nor the 1990 Our Common Future conference of the UN in Bergen, Norway, nor the now legendary 1992 'Rio Conference' of the UN on the environment and development with its Agenda 21, nor the 2002 UN Conference on Sustainable Development in Johannesburg, together with all these conferences' respective preparatory rounds and commis-sions, prevented fossil energy consumption from escalating like never before, blocked deforestation in the tropics from continu-ing unabated, kept water scarcity from increasing in many regions of the world, hindered poverty from continuing to spread, or stopped the ranks of environmental refugees and those fleeing poverty from continuing to swell. Here it is worth noting that it took a long time before conventional energy use was even discussed in a relevant way as the most important source of global environmental damage. Even at the Rio Conference (and, by implication, also in Agenda 21), the energy question was at best a marginal theme – all the more so for renewable energy. And when the Preparatory Committee for the Johannesburg Conference presented a draft for a final declaration in New York in April 2002, there was still no mention of a key role for renewable energy as part of a strategy of global sustainability. Only after the General Secretariat intervened was a small group invited to New York in order to draft proposals to fill this gap. When the Johannesburg Conference convened in August, renewable energy and water were the topics most discussed. Since then, that is, in the space of just a few years, it has no longer become possible to sustain the decades-long attempt at making renewable energy taboo at global conferences.

Usually at these global conferences, however, the only thing that happened was the establishment of networks, new commissions and follow-up conferences. There were discussions about what 'one' should do, and not about what has to be done immediately – and by whom. A global 'community' – representatives of international governmental and non-governmental organizations, civil servants from the relevant departments of national governments, and scientists – has emerged. The members of this community know and meet each other frequently, develop a common language of expertise, produce yards and yards of papers that align ever more closely with each other, and haggle for months about statements that as many people as possible can approve. The result is a self-referential system, a virtual world that seems to satisfy itself and that confuses its own progress on paper with real progress. The larger these conferences get, the more illusions they produce. They turn into temple celebrations of narcissism in environmental diplomacy. High-sounding declarations are issued, and new hopes are constantly being awakened. Warnings are issued saying that continued postponement can no longer be justified; and then one adjourns yet again. The final declarations are then forgotten more quickly than the time it took to compose them.

The unbridgeable gap between consensus and acceleration

The reasons for this cannot even be directly attributed to (and therefore blamed on) all participants. The working principle and logic of multilateral negotiations is the search for consensus. But there is an unbridgeable contradiction in practice between that working principle and rapid solutions to problems. Where rapid solutions to problems are absolutely necessary, the multi-lateral consensus orientation dare not be the chief formula for action. This orientation is, in any event, only necessary when the goal being pursued is a treaty in international law. But whether such a treaty is really indispensable for solving problems is, in turn, a question that cannot be answered with absolute certainty.

In disarmament and arms control negotiations it was relatively easy to reach a consensus when it came to so-called non-armament treaties – in other words, to renouncing armaments projects that no side had even got around to start-ing yet. This is how the Outer Space Treaty and the ban on biological weapons came about. Similar efforts to stop nuclear weapons, like the so-called Baruch Plan of 1946, came too late. The Nuclear Non-Proliferation Treaty (discussed earlier) is above all a non-proliferation treaty for those countries that still do not possess any nuclear weapons. It was much more difficult to achieve a consensus when it came to limiting already existing weapons. The precondition for success was always to focus negotiations on one problem segment, such as the Limited Test Ban Treaty of 1963 that banned nuclear tests in the atmosphere and underwater (while excluding underground tests, which are still not forbidden), or on the treaties limiting the numbers of 'strategic nuclear missiles'. These kinds of treaties can even lead to intensifying the arms race – as 'compensation' – in other armament sectors. These were 'one-point' negotiations that never dealt with the structural problem. In his 1982 book *The Nuclear Delusion*, the US diplomat George F. Kennan, a seasoned observer of this development for decades, posed the fundamen-tal question about these negotiations, namely whether they should be allowed to continue concerning themselves only with precisely balanced cutbacks. This kind of thinking always ended 'on the same old fateful track that has brought us where we are today. Whatever the precise results of such a reduction, there would still be plenty of overkill left.'[14] Kennan's critique does not refer to negotiations in general, but to how they will not have the desired effect when the strategies and structures developed for these strategies remain unchanged – and it is also a warning that one should not make everything one could do on one's own initiative to end the arms spiral depend upon negotiations. When it came time for the Strategic Arms Reduction Treaty (START) in 1987, one of the politically most important arms control steps ever taken in Europe, it was not about counting missiles, it was about changing structures. START was preceded by a fundamental political decision that was anchored in the treaty.

If parallels are being drawn here between yesterday's negotiations for disarmament (or arms control) and today's global environmental negotiations, then this is being done for two reasons: first, the latter is also about dismantling overkill capacities, and second, the objects of negotiation involve quite similar problems in each case. Results were easier to obtain when governments were able to agree on avoiding resource exploitation that nobody had actually yet begun. A good example is the Antarctic Treaty. At the time it was negotiated no influential industrial interests had yet lined up around the Antarctic. Talks always became more difficult when they involved withdrawing some dangerous product from worldwide circulation – as in the case of the Montreal Protocol for the protection of the ozone layer, which affects the use of chlorofluorocarbons (CFCs). This treaty is cited by the advocates of multilateral environmental policy as a great success story. Yet it was still relatively easy for negotiations to achieve results because the subject was quite selective and no broad-based structural interests were affected. It was simply a matter of substituting one material for another by the same producers. Nonetheless, it took a long time before this protocol came to fruition.

During global climate negotiations, by contrast, it is energy consumption on the whole that is up for grabs; these negotiations address a structural problem with an all-encompassing broad effect. There is a total absence of the prerequisites giving everyone an equal start and equivalent duties. The differences in energy consumption, which mirror different levels of economic and technological development, are crass. There are energy exporting countries and energy importing countries, climatic differences, differences in how strongly interests are organized both nationally and internationally. The result of these negotiations that dragged on for years – between 1995 and 2002 there was a total of ten global climate conferences – is celebrated as an international success story. The only problem people still complain about is that the US, by far the greatest emitter of greenhouse gases, is refusing to participate. In fact the Kyoto Protocol – for reasons completely different from those put forward by the US – is not only a construct that is miles behind what the world needs to do and is capable of doing (a subject we shall examine more closely in this chapter's next section). Lurking behind the treaty's one-dimensionality – a narrowness that is determined by 'negotiation technique' and unsuitable for stimulating the kind of far-reaching dynamic that might facilitate the emergence of a shift to renewable energy – there lies a prejudice about how this development would represent an economic burden for everyone. But since the opposite of this 'burden premise' is true – meaning that mobilizing for renewable energy and for higher energy productivity will bring substantial social and even economic advantages – the very meaning of such strategies must be called into question. Whoever recognizes these prejudices will have to seize the initiative without relying on any international consensus or treaty obligations.

No technological revolution in economic history that achieved a broad impact worldwide ever happened because of international negotiations resulting in the introduction of obligatory new quotas and joint accounting regulations. Most technological revolutions also were not started by governments; rather, they were founded on private initiative. Imagine how those at the forefront of the most recent technological revolution in information technology would have reacted if, at the outset, governments had put a stop to this initiative with the argument that the information technology boom would prove too burdensome because old industries would fall away, lots of traditional jobs would be lost, and so information technologies should only be introduced 'in international consonance' with at least all of the industrial nations and on the basis of an international agreement using fixed quotas to introduce the new technologies. A demand like this would have been ridiculed, and quite rightly. In every other technological field, the word is: be faster than all the others because this helps competitiveness. Only when it comes to renewable energy technologies is this inapplicable. This static kind of thinking is unique in economic and technological history, and it demonstrates the kind of twisted standards that are used to evaluate renewable energy. All the evidence points towards the need to use unilateral initiatives as a way of pushing ahead with the shift to renewable energy; this can also happen when well-meaning governments undertake immediate joint initiatives on their own instead of waiting for the day when they can rally every last ill-intentioned government to their side.

Multilateral 'collectivization' of each country's own political responsibility is thus the most inappropriate of all methods for taking action on the shift to renewable energy. This does not mean that multilateral treaty negotiations are pointless from the start. But they are only promising when they relate to isolated subjects that can facilitate a major step forward, and when the negotiating partners want to move in the same direction. They are justified when they help governments accelerate a necessary development. They have a perverse effect when they end up justifying delays where there is no longer any objective reason to permit a delay. It is self-evident that treaty negotiations require striving for a consensus. The stipulation (it may be stated by way of provisional summary) is that treaties should not be used either as a substitute for or barrier to more far-reaching programmes by participating countries.

When the creation of an international legal order – say, the establishment of an international environmental court – is at stake, there is no alternative to consensus-oriented international negotiations. But when it comes to implementing path-breaking technologies, treaty negotiations are an inappropriate instrument. This is even more true when it comes to global UN conferences, which are not treaty negotiations of any kind and also have no mandate for generally binding resolutions. The rationale is that these conferences' non-binding character makes their outcomes even more dependent on consensus, so that at least their penetrating power is enhanced. Instead of polishing consensual statements, there should be an agenda shaped by completely different themes. not just general discussions about global dangers, but also a frankly undiplomatic identification of their causes and authors, an unvarnished evaluation of strategies, and especially an accounting of the work done by international organizations – which means looking at the question of what these organizations can actually contribute to solving problems and how they can overcome their own, often mutually reinforcing, contradictions, what priorities they should have, and the kind of equipment they need to do the job. Yet these objectives are blocked both by diplomatic niceties and an unwillingness by most of the UN's and World Bank's agenda-setting organizations to subject themselves to critical discussion about their own actions. That is why it is part of the character of these conferences to remain at a very general level of fundamental principles, in other words, to beat around the bush. It is a measure of some small progress that the UN Conference on Sustainable Development in the summer of 2002 addressed this very problem itself. That conference's final declaration warns:

> We risk the entrenchment of these global disparities and unless we act in a manner that fundamentally changes their lives the poor of the world may lose confidence in their representatives and the democratic systems to which we remain committed, seeing their representatives as nothing more than sounding brass or tinkling cymbals.[15]

Is this an admission with practical consequences or just a rhetorical ploy of engaging in criticism while continuing business as usual?

The squandered opportunity of Renewables 2004

A remedy was supposed to come from two initiatives that were introduced at the conference in Johannesburg. One was the German government's invitation for all governments to attend the Renewables 2004 conference in Bonn, in order to go beyond the narrow consensual framework of UN conferences and to generate international initiatives. The proposal to invite governments who shared this ambition to an international conference was something I had already suggested to Chancellor Schoeder in July 2001. Among other things, this was intended to motivate other governments to participate in founding an international agency for renewable energy. The second initiative was the declaration, initiated by the EU Commission in a statement signed by over 80 governments, to form a 'Johannesburg Renewable Energy Coalition' (JREC). It should have been obvious from the outset that the latter was not meant to be taken seriously; many governments that signed the declaration had not undertaken any initiatives worth mentioning on behalf of renewable energy, neither beforehand nor afterwards. Apart from JREC holding a few meetings, which the majority of countries officially supporting the coalition did not even bother to attend, and aside from publishing some official 'targets', nothing much was accomplished; there was not even any discussion as to whether the coalition's goals can be achieved with the measures taken in each case. What little practical value 'targets' have if they are not made more concrete by related political actions is something that has been demonstrated by the sorry affair of that 35-year-old call repeatedly issued at UN conferences for the 'Western' industrial countries to devote 0.7 per cent of their GNP to development aid. Only three countries have fulfilled this demand, while the others remain far away from meeting the quota; most countries, in fact, are even further away than they were when the 0.7 per cent target was first announced.

But Renewables 2004 also stayed stuck — contrary to its underlying intention — on the well-worn tracks of international environmental diplomacy. At the international governmental level, to be sure, the conference made the greatest contribution of any organization thus far to dismantling mental barriers against renewable energy — simply by virtue of the fact that it took place at all. It would, therefore, not even have been necessary to simulate a consensus following the UN pattern, mixing the wheat with the chaff. Instead, in the Political Declaration, an effort is made to please all the participants as a way of feigning unanimity – even with the Bush administration's delegation or with the representatives of the OPEC countries. The text is correspondingly meaningless, full of talk in which it is 'acknowledged' that 'renewable energies ... can significantly contribute' to sustainable development and invoking 'cooperation' to that end. The conference, meant to point the way beyond Rio and Johannesburg, has government ministers saying they 'agree' to 'reaffirm' its results for renewable energy. Governments say they would 'take note' that there are countries that did not establish goals for the expansion of renewable energy. You can't get more cautious-sounding than that. The declaration 'supports' the expansion of institutional capacities for renewable energy without saying which forms of renewable energy these might be, and the participants 'emphasize' the need for additional R&D goals – a throwaway statement that is empty because it is always correct. And the delegates 'agree' to form an 'informal' and 'global policy network' including parliaments, local and regional authorities, the academic and the private sector, international institutions and industrial associations, consumers, civil society, women's groups and 'relevant partnerships worldwide' – in other words, everyone. Finally, this conference's intention to overcome the paraplegia of consensus-bound UN global conferences was officially filed away for good: 'Measurable steps' should be reported to the UN Commission on Sustainable Development (CSD) – which undertook to deal with energy problems by 2006/07 (!), and then a 'follow-up' is promised. Everybody could agree to this without thereby contradicting their continued inactivity. So was everything the same as before?

Tacked onto the declaration were the 'policy recommendations' mentioned at the outset, which are not much more than an insubstantial collection of arbitrary approaches to action ('a menu of options to decision makers'), as if the problem were that governments previously lacked access to this kind of information. Renewables 2004 became a kind of 'UN conference lite'– since the governments invited to the conference seemed to lack the courage of their convictions. The International Action Programme presented at the conclusion was lauded as the genuine novelty of the conference. In fact it was merely a compilation of the different countries' initiatives, either current or planned, which they had listed on a form distributed for this purpose. In other words, the programme was the product of a survey of conference participants, from China's announcement that it would cover 17 per cent of its energy supply by the year 2020 with renewable energy to other countries' announcements that they would conduct seminars on renewable energy and compile documentation. This 'programme' was passed unanimously. But why should any country's delegation even want to vote against what other countries were doing on their own (or announcing they would do)? Only 58 of the 154 participating countries filled out the form. Almost two-thirds of the country delegations left the conference without committing themselves to any specific action of their own.

Mammoth international conferences are banking on a psychological effect that is supposed to come from having a large number of participants. Because the impression is created that something substantial is going to happen, there is a mass urge to make sure nobody misses anything. The more participants there are, the greater the hope. In fact, however, the size of the conference is in inverse proportion to its level of efficiency. In order not to cast a cloud over the conference atmosphere, it is good form to attest that everyone is full of good will. This etiquette disguises every problem, for it is impossible to get to the bottom of any problem without unmasking those who are in charge and may be culpable and without criticizing those who act hypocritically – except that they are all present at the conference. Even NGOs, who have been integrated into these UN conferences since the Rio Conference of 1992, hardly every violate these proper manners. Those who are officially invited feel as if they have been privileged; participation is more important than arguing.

The discussion forum for the NGOs is the 'Multi-Stakeholder Dialogue,' which has gone on to become a permanent component of the ritual at UN global conferences, a rite also conducted in exemplary fashion at the Renewables 2004 conference. Even powerful economic interest groups take part in the dialogue because, according to UN rules, they are all

NGOs, from Greenpeace to the World Energy Council, which represents the 'hard-core' interests of the nuclear and fossil energy business. At this forum, fundamental differences are reduced to simple differences of opinion – as if there were unity in principle about the desirable goal, just not about the steps that need to be taken and the instruments to be used. In the 'Conclusions of the Multi-Stakeholder Dialogue' submitted to the Renewables 2004 conference it says:

> *There was strong consensus among stakeholders over many issues and well articulated concerns were highlighted on a number of others... As the dialogue progressed it became clear that there was considerable convergence and widespread agreement on the principal themes of the conference. The degree of concurrence was remarkable given the diversity of stakeholders in the discussion. This concurrence supported by apparently widespread political will should equate to substantial and rapid progress but there seems to be a problem over the capacity to act.*[16]

Seemingly, all those ubiquitous conflicts about renewable energy have simply vanished into thin air – albeit only during the hours spent in dialogue, as may be seen by the presence of these conflicts before and after.

Conferences arranged this way keep turning around in circles; they become ends in themselves. The Renewables 2004 conference was made 'UN-compatible', which is why it could not succeed in going beyond the general pattern of UN conferences. Since, in contrast to the latter, the participation of governments was not obligatory and there was an effort not to frighten anyone, the consensual principle was even stronger than at regular UN conferences, so that the Political Declaration was not one bit more specific than the implementation plan passed at the 2002 Johannesburg Conference for the promotion of renewable energy. Indeed, the Renewables declaration represented something of a relapse compared to the 1981 UN Conference on renewable energy at Nairobi, which had recommended the establishment of a separate UN institution for promoting renewable energy. This can be seen in the synopsis of the conference resolutions in Table 5. For the sake of broad participation by as many governments as possible, the conference organizers shied away from emphasizing anything new. They would have had substantive legitimation for doing so, because the political initiatives introduced in Germany have an internationally recognized and model character. For a leading role it is necessary to forge a 'coalition of the willing' instead of trying to create a bland consensus that pleases everyone but where the real problems and conflicts are hushed up. At a conference with a real strategic profile, there would have been fewer participating governments, and in return the impetus would have been all the more stimulating.

That it is possible for an international conference at the level of political institutions to be conducted differently has been shown by the International Parliamentary Forum on Renewable Energy, which took place parallel to the Renewables 2004 conference.[17] Germany's Bundestag had issued the invitations to this conference and prepared for it by appointing a group made up of members from all the different parliamentary parties. 350 representatives from 70 different national parliaments took part. From the outset no effort was made to seek an all-encompassing consensus. To be sure, the participants were presented with a draft resolution to which they could make supplementary proposals. But the only proposals to be incorporated with the help of an editorial committee were those that enriched the text rather than diluted it. Afterwards it was open to every participant as to whether they wanted to sign the resolution. Some legislators did not sign, but in exchange there was a recommendation for action that established clear new emphases. And there was a political discussion that did not ignore conflicts about renewable energy and that candidly mentioned sources of resistance by name and without diplomatic circumlocutions. Thus, for example, the UK MP Desmond Turner stated:

I am a member of the governing party in the United Kingdom. There is nothing that would be more justified than promoting renewable energy. I stand here as the representative of a country that could have made a wonderful contribution to this. The technology is there, but the problem is that politics is not taking

Table 5 *Synopsis of political demands in the resolutions of international conferences in the area of renewable energy*

	UN Conference on New and Renewable Energies *Nairobi, 21 August 1981*	**World Summit on Sustainable Development 2002** *Johannesburg, 5 September 2002*	*Renewables 2004* *Bonn, 4 June 2004*
International institutional measures	Establishment of an inter-governmental organ to accompany implementation of the Nairobi action programme Implementation reports to ECOSOC and UN General Assembly	Construction of a network of relationships between centres of authority and expertise Take measures within framework of CSD-9 Support for international financing institutions to create equal starting conditions	Formation of an informal 'Global Policy Network' Report/monitoring about quantifiable steps to the UN CSD
New international treaty goals	Concerted actions in the areas of capacity building, R&D, information dissemination and technology transfer		

International Parliamentary Forum on Renewable Energy	World Council for Renewable Energy Forum	Energy for Development Conference	
Bonn, 2 June 2004	Bonn, 31 May 2004	Noordwijk, 14 December 2004	
International Agency for Renewable Energy to promote non-commercial technology transfer of renewable energy and efficiency technologies in developing countries	International Agency for Renewable Energy as international government organization on basis of voluntary membership	Follow-up group with meetings twice a year Progress reports on individual areas submitted to CSD-14/15	**International institutional measures**
Continuous parliamentary exchange of experiences in the framework of the parliamentary network of the WCRE and 'e parliament'	Establishment of an international university for renewable energy with emphasis on post-graduate training		
Continuation of the International Parliamentary Forum			
Energy and efficiency technologies at low tariffs or tariff-free in the framework of the World Trade Organization (WTO)	Renewable Energy Proliferation Treaty as supplement to Nuclear Non Proliferation Treaty		**New international treaty goals**
Global industrial norms and standards for renewable energy technologies	Abolition of trade barriers for renewable energy and efficiency technologies in framework of WTO		
Provision for all emissions in the entire energy supply chain	Global industrial norms and standards for renewable energy technologies		
	Take into consideration energy emissions for the entire energy supply chain in the machinery of the Kyoto Protocol and in emissions trading		

Table 5 *continued*

	UN Conference on New and Renewable Energies	World Summit on Sustainable Development 2002	Renewables 2004
	Nairobi, 21 August 1981	Johannesburg, 5 September 2002	Bonn, 4 June 2004
Political recommendations for action at the national level	Development of parameters for promoting renewable energy Information about renewable energy potentials Establishment/ strengthening of national renewable energy institutions Strengthening of R&D work Creation of training programmes Political incentives for renewable energy investments	Dismantling market distortions Step-by-step removal of damaging subsidies; tax restructuring Promotion of educational work in the energy field Dialogue forums between energy producers and consumers Intensifying R&D work	Coherent political parameters for renewable energy Formation of export promotion agencies Expansion of personal and institutional capacities for renewable energy New goals for R&D
Financing for renewable energy	Providing additional funds through the World Bank, UN, international financial institutions and other organizations Supporting investments in developing countries (in both financial and non-financial manner) International support for South–South trade	Utilization of Global Environmental Facility Financial assistance (in part for individual programmes)	Extension of credit lines with the World Bank and regional development banks for renewable energy

International Parliamentary Forum on Renewable Energy	World Council for Renewable Energy Forum	Energy for Development Conference	
Bonn, 2 June 2004	*Bonn, 31 May 2004*	*Noordwijk, 14 December 2004*	
Political priority for renewable energy Legal obligations to renewable energy and energy efficiency increase in the areas of education, R&D, construction, agriculture, and development assistance	Orientation to Renewable Energy Sources Act for renewable energy policy fields Tax exemption for bio-fuels Obligation to use renewable energy in buildings Incentives for agriculture in for energy and raw direction of biomass materials Rededicating fossil and nuclear energy subsidies into promotional programmes for renewable energy Broad training offensive at all levels Dismantling nuclear and fossil energy subsidies	Integration of different policy fields Parameters for rural energy supply for private energy service providers Strengthening cooperation with energy supply companies Development of programmes for utilization of local renewable energy Internalization of external costs and benefits Subsidizing of public welfare-oriented components of energy services	**Political recommend-ations for action at the national level**
Orientation of credit programmes of national and international development banks towards renewable energy, especially towards micro-credits	Orientation of credit programmes of all development banks towards renewable energy Certification of renewable energy project sponsors for development assistance with efficient use of funds Growing obligatory share (to be determined) of renewable energy in development budgets	Expanding public and private investments in energy field Utilization of export credits Support for local institutions to develop micro-credit programmes	**Financing for renewable energy**

it into account. Previously we have only shown that we are timid, and how not to reach the goal.

The Luxembourg MEP Claude Turmes said it had become:

Europe's biggest problem that we have seven electricity producers who control 60 per cent of production, 70 per cent of the entire European network, and 95 per cent of compensation of current in Europe. The people who sit on coal and nuclear power plants will simply not allow a shift to renewable energy.

The German MP Michaele Hustedt addressed the issue of how the many different UN organizations 'promoting renewable energy are not strong enough in the aggregate to apply pressure against the powerful lobby of oil, nuclear and fossil energy providers'. The Japanese member of his country's lower house, Taro Kono, who is a member of the governing Liberal Democratic Party, bluntly stated:

Corrupt politicians, shameless bureaucrats, and dirty supply companies form an iron nuclear triangle. Every attempt to increase the share of renewable energy is seen as a danger to what is regarded as in our own best interest: promoting the nuclear industry.

The Swiss National Council member Rudolf Rechsteiner recommended that politicians 'start out by separating themselves from false advisers'; he also said that the International Energy Agency should be 'abolished because it is showing us the wrong way'. And Brazilian Congress member Fernando Paolo Gabeira said that he perceives 'a dream of humanity' behind renewable energy – the 'dream of political independence'. That is a different political tune.

The IRENA controversy as a litmus test of international policy on renewable energy

The Parliamentary Forum's resolution corresponds on many points to the demands of the World Renewable Energy Agenda.

This had been submitted by the World Council for Renewable Energy, which held its world forum immediately prior to the Renewables 2004 conference. Its centrepiece was especially pertinent – the demand for an International Renewable Energy Agency (IRENA). Setting up this agency was supposed to be an approach to action bringing about a new international quality. An elaborate proposal to this end had already been presented in 1990 by EUROSOLAR. A working group established at the time by UN Secretary-General Perez de Cuellar – the United Nations Solar Energy Group on Environment and Development, under the chairmanship of the Swedish energy and environmental economist Thomas Johannson – proposed in 1992 that the Rio Conference install this group. This had already been rejected by the preparatory committee in the run-up to the conference – with reference to the work being done by existing UN organizations, of whom it was said that they were keeping the promotion of renewable energy in the best of hands. In 2001 EUROSOLAR, against the background of completely inadequate international efforts on behalf of renewable energy, initiated a second attempt and sponsored an international conference in Berlin to give the initiative some impetus. In 2002, when Germany's government of Social Democrats and Greens was re-elected, the two parties' coalition agreement for their second term in office included a call to seize upon this initiative, and it was also called for in several Bundestag resolutions.

Yet in the preparatory phase for the Renewables 2004 conference, care was taken to avoid even mentioning the subject. This, more than anything else, shows why this conference was ultimately a missed opportunity. Nobody had the courage to assume a genuine leadership role. Anything had to be omitted that might encounter resistance, disturb consensus and aggravate cooperation with UN organizations and the World Bank. These organizations are opposed to any agency like IRENA, simply on grounds of institutional competition. Just calling for such an agency is viewed as criticism of their own work. Hence IRENA remained unmentioned in all the conference papers given at Renewables 2004, even though German Development Minister Heidemarie Wieczorek-Zeul had publicly embraced the proposed new agency several times and German Chancellor

Gerhard Schroeder had emphasized in his speech at the conference that he regarded the call for IRENA, taken over from the Parliamentary Forum, as an 'important impulse'. German Environment Minister Juergen Trittin, however, refused to issue this call, and even some NGOs from the environmental spectrum came out decisively against it, canvassing instead for an international 'informal network'. But to view such a network as an alternative to an international governmental organization is just as absurd as calling for one of the existing UN organizations to be replaced by an informal network.

Organizations like IAEA and IEA are constant reminders of the value an international agency has. The IAEA is the stronghold of the international 'nuclear community'. It annually conducts hundreds of conferences and workshops, canvasses for nuclear energy worldwide with the authority of an international office and the capacity of a staff and contractual partners numbering in the thousands, helps governments construct nuclear energy programmes – and advises these governments that renewable energy will never amount to a real alternative. Without the IAEA there would be no worldwide campaign for the renaissance of nuclear energy. And the IEA also leaves no stone unturned when it comes to emphasizing the long-term indispensability of nuclear and fossil energy. Its recommendations for expanding fossil energy use go so far as to thwart the goals of the Kyoto Protocol that are supported by most of its member governments. Both agencies are heavyweights in the international energy debate and shape opinion in UN organizations, development banks, governments and the public. So long as there is no countervailing power in the form of an organization like IRENA, it is no wonder that renewable energy is viewed and treated as little more than an accessory.

The reasons why the call to establish a government-level International Renewable Energy Agency is greeted with indifference, and even with open rejection by environmental NGOs like the World Wide Fund for Nature (WWF), have to do with the downright apolitical underestimation of such an institution's value (a value comparable to what has been demonstrated for nuclear and fossil energy by the IAEA and IEA). In addition, there is the NGOs' own overestimation of themselves when they imagine they could accomplish what only an agency like this can really do. Also playing a role, certainly, is the way the NGOs have adjusted to international environmental diplomacy's habit of demanding only what they regard as capable of commanding a consensus. It would indeed have been unrealistic to seek a consensual resolution at the Renewables 2004 conference about setting up an organization like IRENA. But it would have been important at this conference to address openly the need for such an agency and to mention the reasons why Germany's governing parties passed resolutions in their party programmes to seize the initiative for IRENA and then buttressed this call with a Bundestag resolution. Where else, if not at the Renewables 2004 conference, should this have been articulated? The major reason why Germany as the host government – especially at the instigation of the Environment Minister – did the opposite and remained silent about IRENA during the conference is Germany's habit of clinging to the premises of an all-around multilateralism and to the kind of 'business as usual' practised by UN organizations. The notion that there might or should be unilateral international initiatives is regarded from the outset as misplaced, even if it were open to everyone to join such an agency sooner or later – and in spite of the fact that there are plenty of international governmental organizations in other fields, ranging from economic organizations to military alliances, that are not UN organizations. For the Lords Privy Seal of multilateral environmental diplomacy, internationally mobilizing renewable energy by way of a unilateral initiative lies outside the realm of the thinkable and doable.

The Kyoto Syndrome and the misery of modern energy and environmental economics

When the Kyoto Protocol went into effect on 16 February 2005, it was effusively celebrated, especially by environmental politicians, organizations and scholars. Again it was said that 'a new era' had begun. Newspaper ads put out by Germany's federal government proclaimed that 'Siberia will stay cold' – as if the world's climate had already been saved. The parliamentary party of the Greens in the German Bundestag called the Kyoto

Protocol a 'milestone for international climate protection', and Environment Minister Trittin characterized it as the 'most important and most proper step towards climate protection'. The headline in the left-wing alternative daily *tageszeitung*, whose self-image includes journalistic commitment to environmental questions, said: 'A giant step, but only a small step for the climate'. This headline, whose two half-sentences contradict each other, articulates the dilemma of the Kyoto Protocol: everyone knows that it is completely inadequate for global climate protection. This is a dilemma that is also expressed in a statement by German climate researchers: the Protocol, they said, was 'a gigantic gain, but ultimately there's no pay-off'.

The general tenor goes that what really matters for the future is to dissuade the US from its refusal to participate and to draw as many countries as possible, especially China, into a commitment to reduce greenhouse gas emissions; in addition – in the next step – to increase the size of these countries' obligatory quotas. After all, according to the worldwide chorus that greeted the Kyoto Protocol, the treaty succeeded in initiating a common order for making fundamental decisions about energy – and even in doing so with market mechanisms. These are lauded as an exemplary, universally applicable strategic concept for introducing a fundamental shift in energy use. Only a few people expressed any criticisms on 'Kyoto Day' as forcefully as did Klaus Töpfer, the Director of the UN Environmental Programme, who called for 'new solutions, as soon as possible'.

The Kyoto Protocol does not deserve these paeans, and not just because of the minimal obligatory quotas it contains. It contains all the elements that misdirect, cripple and restrict political and economic action on behalf of a global shift in energy use, elements that were described in the previous sections: the monomaniacal fixation on a consensual global solution and on 'market mechanisms' that attempt to compare the incommensurate and that congeal the structures of traditional energy supply. It is a dubious construct of 'neoliberal' thinking about energy, whose implementation nevertheless requires a growing bureaucratic effort.

When, at the insistence of the US, a highly diluted draft for the Protocol was presented at the end of 2000 in a round of negotiations in Den Haag, Clinton was still president. When the draft was rejected by the European governments, the NGOs greeted this failure with the statement: 'better no agreement than a bad one'. In the next negotiating round in July 2001, however, when the agreement that was now going into effect was concluded, it was diluted again in order to facilitate the US possibly joining later. Once again the accord was praised to the skies with the statement: 'better a bad agreement than none at all'. Even the NGO representatives present rejoiced.

Since then, the prevailing view has been an uncritical attitude towards the Kyoto Protocol lending a false sense of reassurance that everything is on the right path.

Because of the rejection of the agreement by the US government and the US Senate, Kyoto has become a symbol for a political disposition in favour of active global climate protection – a mark of distinction between good and evil. Once something becomes a symbol, it is usually viewed uncritically. Had the US agreed to the Protocol, we would probably have been treated a long time ago to broad and critical debate about the treaty's seamy side. That is why the US rejection has been damaging in two ways: it prevents the negligible positive effect of the Protocol from taking effect, but it also prevents its negative effects from being perceived. The treaty's enormous complexity is an additional factor impeding broad public discussion. And many people shy away from any criticism so as not to receive 'false applause' from those who are generally opposed to climate protection policy. What are the treaty's problematic points?

The minimum as maximum

The Protocol commits the industrial countries to reduce their greenhouse gas emissions by 2012 by an average of 5.2 per cent compared to their 1990 levels. Yet the IPCC, in which all countries' climate scientists cooperate, regards a 60 per cent reduction by 2050 as urgent. But if nothing decisive happens that goes way beyond the Protocol by 2012, there will be about 50 per cent more greenhouse gases worldwide, and 11 per cent in the industrial countries. This is according to calculations by the Secretariat of the Protocol and by Hans-Joachim Luhmann, a climate expert from Germany's Wuppertal Institute.[18] These figures assume that the Kyoto Protocol will actually be implemented – though that is highly dubious. Where do all those who imagine that only the Kyoto process provides a framework for more far-reaching solutions get their optimism about even remotely reaching the reduction goals required by the IPCC for the period after 2012 if they proceed this way? In December of 2004, when the negotiations for 'Kyoto II'were started in Buenos Aires, the same time-honoured arduous haggling could be observed.

The countries that joined the Protocol are broken up into three groups: industrial countries ('Annex I Parties'), with roughly equal reduction commitments; emerging industrial countries ('Annex B Parties'), including most of the former Soviet bloc countries, which have been granted different upper limits for greenhouse gas emissions (in a spectrum from 8 per cent to over 10 per cent compared to the reference year 1990); and developing countries ('Non-Annex I Parties'), which are not subject to any obligatory limits. To the extent that the Protocol contains obligations, they are directed towards states. It is up to these governments to determine how they fulfil their commitments. Had the Kyoto Protocol settled for this commitment goal, there would have been some justification to the assessment that even a minimal compromise is better than none at all. Every obligated country would then have had to develop its own implementation plan. More problem-conscious governments and legislatures would have pushed to go beyond their international obligation (also for reasons other than those having to do with the climate), and environmental movements would have pushed for this. There would have been a competition for plans to implement Kyoto that could have had a mutually stimulating effect.

But, in addition, the Protocol contains a supplementary provision consisting of three so-called 'flexible instruments'. First is trade with emission rights – every state has 'emission rights' in the amount of its obligatory target, for which it receives certificates (a certificate per metric ton of CO_2 or the equivalent amount for other greenhouse gases like methane), which it sells to other states if it decides not to use them itself. If it emits more than it is entitled to emit, it can purchase 'rights' from other states that are emitting less than they are allowed. Every state can also, according to a procedure to be determined, allot emission rights to private plant operators on its sovereign territory in the form of tradeable certificates. Whichever one of these has not, in turn, fully exhausted its rights on its own initiative can then sell them to those plant operators who prefer purchasing additional emission rights as a substitute for making more investments in emissions reduction.

The second flexible instrument is Joint Implementation (JI), and the third is the Clean Development Mechanism (CDM). With the JI instrument, states bound to the treaty, or companies from these countries, can acquire from other treaty-obligated states an emissions certificate that can be traded again. With the CDM instrument it is possible to acquire certificates through projects in developing countries that are not committed to any reduction.

Officially, adopting these 'flexible instruments' is voluntary. But since they offer international accounting opportunities that states and their companies can use to buy themselves free of their obligations, no state will be able to (or will want to) avoid adopting these instruments as part of its policy rules. Companies will push for these flexible instruments, and no industrial country will give up the opportunity to credit relevant projects from its development assistance programme.

The Kyoto Protocol has garnered praise because of these 'flexible instruments'. In fact, however, they are actually the problem. Instead of resulting in market solutions, these instruments lead — as will be shown — to a bureaucratized and correspondingly inflexible system of investment controls. Instead of producing cost-effective solutions, these instruments will tend to drive costs up, since they will increase the number of lodgers and boarders in the energy system. Instead of easing the reorientation to renewable energy, these instruments are already being employed as battleaxes against those political instruments that some countries have used to initiate a breakthrough to renewable energy. They harden the structures of the traditional energy business and help them expand even further, including into developing countries; in this way they contribute to delaying a global reorientation to renewable energy.

By way of these 'flexible instruments', the Kyoto Protocol's minimal compromise is turned into a de facto upper limit for CO_2 reductions that are supposed to take place by 2012. They amount to an indirect economic incentive to avoid going beyond the obligatory quota of 5.2 per cent on average. The result is that initiatives going beyond current obligations get postponed to the time period after 2012. Calls within countries obligated under the treaty to go beyond the minimal goal are, in any event, often met with resistance by those who claim that all this does is subject the country to a self-inflicted wound. If no financial bonus for overfilling quotas beckons, this kind of resistance acquires additional 'Kyoto-logical' importance. The mechanism to make emission rights internationally tradeable, therefore, leads to a situation where no more emissions are reduced than what the Protocol requires. The mechanisms are more related to the 'efficiency' of the Kyoto Protocol than to effective CO_2 reduction. Measured against actual climate dangers, therefore, this instrument is irresponsible. As a practical matter, it turns the minimum into the maximum. This proves that it would have been better to restrict the Protocol to a commitment to reducing 'greenhouse gases' and to dispense with the 'flexible instruments' so that every country can go its own way towards fulfilling these obligations.

More bureaucracy than market, more emissions trading than reduction

In Germany, the trading in 'emissions rights' that was introduced in 2005 comprises 1200 companies with 1849 plants. For a three-year period these companies were allotted (by the emissions trading office set up for this purpose, which is already employing 120 staff members) 495 million metric tons of CO_2, which will have a value of five euros per ton. Their annual trade value, therefore, is around 2.5 billion euros. The price is determined on the market and can be expected to fluctuate to a greater or lesser extent. Nobody can say how many companies will be stimulated to invest in measures of their own or to buying back emission rights instead. The allocation of 'emission rights' took place according to the state of technology and in line with earlier efforts at reducing emissions. In 799 out of 1849 issued allotments, appeals were entered, opening up a big market for lawyers – alongside the market for institutes specializing in certification.

Power plant-related CO_2 calculations, however, have their pitfalls. For they do not speak the whole truth about emissions, since (after all) emissions also occur when fuels are being transported. If this is not taken into account, every emissions measurement that is only plant-related leads to self-deception in climate policy. Take the example of a German coal-fired power plant that gets credit for reducing its CO_2 emissions but at no time draws its coal from a nearby German coal mine. If, in the following years, it buys its coal from Australia, there will be additional transport emissions, meaning more CO_2 emissions. In Germany, according to the new emissions trading law, it is possible to take this change into account. There is an annual reporting obligation, and according to the so-called GEMIS methodology – which uses the entire fuel flow as its point of reference – the plant's CO_2 accounting changes accordingly. Yet, inevitably, the data situation for this is incomplete. This method, furthermore, is hardly practised in all countries, so that in comparable cases a coal-fired power plant can become a polluter causing more emissions while still receiving its reduction bonus.

With the JI and CDM mechanisms, it is even possible to undermine real global CO_2 reductions if one proceeds from the status quo of current emissions. Russia, as a result of its economic situation, currently has about a billion metric tons fewer CO_2 emissions than were granted it by the Protocol, and the Ukraine over 400 million tons less. Since it can hardly be expected that the next several years are going to bring the kind of economic growth that will entail an exhaustion of these 'rights' in each of these countries, both countries will be able to sell gigantic quantities of emissions certificates. If Russia sells only 500 million metric tons, it might be able in exchange to redeem (with sales proceeds of US$7 per ton of CO_2 emissions on average) US$3.5 billion annually through 2012. There is no reason to assume that Russia and the Ukraine will let this business transaction escape their notice. Just by way of emissions transactions with these two countries, other countries would be able to ransom their way out of most (if not all) of their commitments without a single ton of CO_2 being reduced; an accounting entry made out of thin air in spite of technically living up to the Kyoto Protocol. Sellers have between 2008 and 2012 to offer up their potential emissions rights. Even before 2008 countries can secure equivalent buying options – and some are already on a shopping tour, such as Japan, Italy, The Netherlands and the UK. The JI instrument is also serving as a means for enticing the US into possibly joining Kyoto before 2008 – in the hope that energy conglomerates and banks interested in emissions trading will push the US government and Senate to take this step.

And what about the CDM mechanism? Assume that a new fossil fuel power plant is built in India that has significantly fewer CO_2 emissions than the 'reference power plant' defined by the CDM Board as the basis for calculation. When this power plant is built by a German corporation that is itself obligated to reduce emissions, the company can receive a credit voucher that takes pressure off its own CO_2 account. If the new power plant replaces an inefficient old one, a real CO_2 reduction will have been achieved. If this is an additional plant built to satisfy a growing energy demand, however, then CO_2 emissions will increase – but the German power plant manufacturer still gets the bonus. The foreign investor has to register the project with the CDM Board. The investor is required to transfer 2 per cent of his profits to the government at the site of the project. India has decided to use this income for renewable energy – but simultaneously to reduce the funds it previously dedicated to promoting renewable energy by the same amount. The CDM instrument is giving governments in developing countries an incentive to continue making the construction of large fossil fuel power plants or dam projects a priority, instead of banking on decentralized renewable energy.

For investors from an industrial country with treaty obligations, the CDM instrument creates a competitive advantage because these countries can use their credit vouchers to improve their supply financially. There will also be a tilt in favour of large power plant projects because of the big administrative and financial expense required to stay active within the framework of the CDM. The procedure is unavoidably bureaucratic, so as to prevent abuse.

The Executive Board, which consists of ten members, oversees the procedure with an apparatus whose size grows with the number of registered projects. Project proposals need to be directed to the Designated Operational Entity (DOE). This body compares each proposal against the criteria of the CDM. If the criteria are met, the project is registered with the Executive Board and then examined by experts – specialized consulting firms, engineering firms, environmental institutes and NGOs – using methodologies recognized by the Executive Board. This procedure is protracted and tends to inhibit investment because the first thing people try to do is attempt to get a credit voucher.

As a result of all the bureaucratic effort and expense, the financial expenditure is also high, which amplifies the trend to giant projects. The bigger the project, the lower the share of so-called 'transaction costs' required for examinations. According to information from those already active obtaining certification, the transaction costs for each project are around US$250,000. As a result, smaller projects – like a 2-megawatt power plant for biomass – can have a transaction cost share amounting to more than 20 per cent of total costs, whereas these costs sink with larger projects. Among those earning off the system, moreover, are the emissions traders, who get 10 per cent for their broker-age work.

Traders in 'emissions rights' are interested in high prices because this increases their commissions, and the certification experts are interested in a huge effort and expenditure for exami-nation because this expands their business. The more Kyoto's 'flexible instruments' are utilized and the more spot checks are necessary for the sake of ongoing control of national registers and projects, the better things are for these participants. Thus arises a flourishing new branch of business. All this makes it incomprehensible as to how the kind of 'cost-efficient' climate protection promised by Kyoto is supposed to be achieved with so many new boarders being added to the lodgers already involved in the energy business. As the old saying goes: 'No matter how small the trade may be, its still brings in more work'.*

At the same time, most climate specialists become tightly integrated into the implementation of the 'flexible instruments' and profit from it. They form an army of promoters advocating this kind of Kyoto Protocol. This helps explain why, so far, there has been no broad, critical debate about the more dubious aspects of the 'flexible instruments'.

In case an industrial country does not meet its obligations by 2012, there are provisions for financial sanctions. For the period that follows, its obligations are then supposed to go up by a factor of 1.3. Yet this sanction is hardly worth the paper on which it is printed. Broad agreement will also be necessary for the next round of commitments. It is as clear as daylight that the political price for the next round is going to be an amnesty for treaty violators.

The cheap answer to critics of the Kyoto Protocol and its instruments is that all of the treaty's defects will be overcome in future negotiations, not only by increasing commitments after 2012, but also by including every country without exception. Each state would then receive an 'emissions right' based on its population. The only way to guarantee a willingness to participate will be if the allocation of country quotas does not codify in stone the extreme divergence in energy consumption between industrial and developing countries. A 'Kyoto II' that grants the industrial countries multiple 'emission rights' would be a 'two-class treaty'. Thus, a principle of equality would somehow have to be observed so that all countries might converge towards a medium-range spectrum – which would lead to the developing countries being allocated a great many more 'emission rights' than the number of emissions they actually have, as is currently the case with Russia. The expected result is then – as always – that there will be a dramatic increase in the number of accounting entries capable of earning commissions and certificates but based entirely on thin air. Because of these 'flexible instruments',

---

* Translator's note: In German, the saying is 'Und ist der Handel noch so klein, bringt er doch mehr als Arbeit ein'. A rhyming English equivalent would be 'And if the trade be e'er so small, it brings in more than work withal'.

it will continue to be the case that the global reduction quota – which is the lowest consensual denominator anyhow – will not be exceeded even in the next commitment period. There will be an attempt, furthermore, to keep polishing the 'flexible instruments' so that their weak points, no longer capable of being ignored, can be remedied. But every bit of polishing simply increases the bureaucratic effort and financial expense, so that it leads to an 'improvement for the worse'; maybe it will lead to including smaller energy projects – or perhaps even all energy projects – with the result that there will be complete global coverage and comprehensive registration of every single project and investment everywhere. When every tiny investment is embedded into a registration and examination procedure, the result will be a total bureaucratization of all global energy activities, making a mockery of any kind of economic dynamism and putting decentralized energy technologies at a special disadvantage. One of the reasons why the World Bank favours financing large projects in its lending practices is the lower share of administrative costs per amount of credit; these costs grow automatically when, for example, a credit amount of US$1 billion is allocated to a hundred or a thousand smaller projects instead of one large one. This principle of business economics is no different from the one applied to the practice of 'flexible instruments'.

The world's climate is hardly going to gain much from the Kyoto Protocol. Major energy consumers enjoy loopholes that have been officially legitimized. Energy conglomerates receive additional development opportunities. The winners will include those countries who can sell lots of certificates because their economies are in miserable shape. Let us not begrudge their advantage. It is another question what they do with it. There is no guarantee whatsoever for the ideal notion that they will use this income to finance their own ecological initiatives. If, in the future, the attempt is made to impose such practices on them, this will not further their willingness to agree that Kyoto's commitments ought to be expanded.

'Emission rights' that legitimize emissions

The concept of an 'emissions right' transforms what had been a legally tolerated emission into one that is publicly legitimized. Tolerating emissions was always justified by saying that there was no alternative and that energy is simply indispensable. Legal history shows that no legal framework can be maintained over the long run if it is no longer regarded as legitimate. Not everything that is legal is also legitimate. Fossil energy loses its legitimacy with the recognition that renewable energy provides an opportunity for an emissions-free energy supply. When there is a tradeable quota of 'emissions rights' anchored in international law, however, only outlawed emissions appear illegitimate. Those in possession of 'emissions rights' are lent a higher consecration anointing them as part (an indispensable part) of an attempt to save the world. The psychological effect of legitimizing an unsustainable condition – in this case, moral justification for emissions that damage many people even though they could be completely avoided by shifting to renewable energy – is not something one notices right away, as a rule. It leads to a values shift in society.

This is easiest to illustrate with a comparison. In most countries it is illegal to produce and trade hard drugs, and these activities are also overwhelmingly regarded as illegitimate. What would happen if, instead of generally forbidding both, a different approach were taken for the sake of containing them 'more effectively'? What if drug production were to be reduced by 5 per cent by 2012, and if certified and tradeable production rights were handed out – among other reasons, in order to give producers an economic incentive to cooperate? This could also be justified by saying that the drug business could then take place under controlled conditions with a regulated labour market, and to the benefit of the public purse, which would take in taxes because an official market could come out of the shadows. Pragmatically, all this could be justified – but what would be the consequences?

The unholy economistic alliance

To be sure, there will also be renewable energy projects that come about by way of these 'flexible mechanisms'. The diverse motives for doing these projects, however, get reduced to just one. Other motives – such as long-term energy security, saving on foreign currency by reducing energy imports, avoiding health defects, conserving water – fade into the background. Because measures to reduce CO_2 emissions are monetized according to a uniform pattern – something that is hardly possible with other ecological initiatives – the latter remain out of view and are excluded as decision-making criteria. 'Flexible instruments' favour short-term CO_2 reductions by increasing the efficiency of traditional energy supplies, in contrast to the more permanent and comprehensive avoidance of emissions that comes from using renewable energy. This is simply a consequence of the period designated for making calculations, which the Protocol itself, in the interest of easy comprehensibility, has oriented towards shorter rather than lengthy periods.

Through the installation of a global 'emissions business', the energy problem, which is multi-dimensional, is turned into something that is one-dimensional. The many motives for shifting to renewable energy are reduced to a single motive, and in this way many approaches to action are reduced to the single approach of the 'flexible instruments', which are turned into a single programmatic guideline. The impression is encouraged that the world would not have any serious problems with its current way of supplying energy if only there were fewer greenhouse gases. All the global crises surrounding energy are turned into a 'one-point programme' for which a 'one-point strategy' is offered as a solution.

The rationale for 'flexible instruments' in terms of energy economics is that these instruments would steer investments to where the desired effect can be achieved with the smallest possible financial expenditure. This notion derives from the 'market economy' reductionism already described, which says that everything has to revolve around cost reduction. It is a notion that appeals to a seemingly unerring economic rationality in which any kind of structural or social welfare question is suppressed.

The rationale in terms of environmental economics is that it is a matter of indifference, as far as climate protection is concerned, where on the globe greenhouse gases are reduced. Hence the fastest way to achieve climate protection is to have investments made where the greatest success in reducing emissions can be achieved. This concept leaves no room for structural problems either; any recurring consequences of traditional energy supply apart from ones related to climate protection are left out of the picture.

The one-dimensional environmental economics rationale is, at its core, identical with the one-dimensional energy economics rationale. Both go down well with the same economistic (that is, ripped out of its real economic context) concept. Not least of all, this is why the principle of 'flexible mechanisms' is so uncontroversial – including among those in the US who reject the Kyoto Protocol.

It has apparently been forgotten who the actual authors of this basic idea are. This can be gleaned from the book *Global Spin* by Sharon Beder.[19] In the 1980s, the think-tanks of the US neoconservatives were looking for an approach to thwart environmental policy and counter the environmental movement. The neoconservatives recognized that they needed to present supposedly better concepts for environmental protection if they wanted to avoid being regarded as ignoramuses. Their pithy recipe became 'free market environmentalism', which they opposed to an alleged 'command-and-control' environmental policy. Environmental problems were to be seen as resulting solely from market imperfections because environmental goods did not have a price tag. The solution would be tradeable pollution rights. All other approaches to action aimed at making energy supply more ecological – higher energy taxes, energy savings laws, investment programmes and laws promoting renewable energy – were condemned as absurd. Because President Clinton and Vice-President Gore had no chance of getting their way with climate protection initiatives in the Senate, they adopted the recipes of the neoconservatives in order to strike at them with their own weapons. The Clinton administration hoped, in this way, to gain approval for an international climate protection accord from those neoconservatives for whom trading in pollution rights is more than a pretext to prevent climate protection initiatives and who actually believe in this concept's effectiveness. And since people at global climate conferences knew that a treaty without the US makes little sense, there was an early and influential trend to making trade in emissions rights the major guideline and to stop pursuing other approaches — such as abolishing the worldwide tax-exempt status for especially damaging pollutants like jet fuel. In this fashion a neoconservative concept took charge that dresses itself up as neoliberal but is really all about making sure that established big business interests remain as undisturbed as possible.

This motive certainly cannot be imputed to the environmental economics school of thought that swears by 'flexible instruments'. There are other reasons why this concept went down well with them. They have to do with the environmental economics school's attempts to refute the disreputable accusations that environmental protection is incompatible with market principles and that it constitutes a prohibitive cost burden on 'the economy'. This led to efforts at coming up with theoretical concepts that could be recognized or labelled as 'market'-based and calculated as particularly 'cost-effective'. In this way environmentalists let themselves go in for isolated perspectives — so that they end up, unexpectedly but not accidentally, in the 'neoliberal' camp. Also playing a role was the hope that they might demonstrate their 'economic competence' in the dominant economic ideology. The 'neoliberal' environmental economics school is so fixated on one-dimensional models for 'cost-effective' climate protection in line with the Kyoto Protocol that it is helping provide catchwords for a roll-back against renewable energy. One hears constantly that investments to reduce CO_2 emissions from the traditional structures of fossil energy supply and consumption would accomplish more than investments in renewable energy — especially when the CO_2 reductions take place in developing countries.

The abuse of the Kyoto Protocol as a tool against renewable energy

The most prominent example of this is the report on renewable energy submitted by the German Bundestag's Scientific Advisory Council in January 2004. According to this report the Renewable Energy Sources Act, 'in the interest of economic rationality and ecological reason, [should] be abolished' in favour of a scheme for trading in fossil emission rights. Prices for renewable energy, the report said, were 'not in line with the market'. There is not a word in the report about past and present conventional energy subsidies, not a word about their damaging social consequences, or about dwindling resources. The report, with an attitude towards renewable energy seeming to favour wholesale demolition, is fixated exclusively and to the point of absurdity on CO_2 reductions, regardless of the reasons that argue for a shift to renewable energy.

The Renewable Energy Sources Act, with its special market framework for renewable energy, is declared to be 'unreasonable' because it offers protection against 'all too intense competition'. It is illegitimate, according to the report, to make a political choice between different energy options because there are 'numerous other procedures' that 'do not fall under the rubric of renewable energy and that conceivably contribute much more effectively and quickly to a reduction of CO_2 emissions'. The report glosses over the fact that the Renewable Energy Sources Act is not exclusively concerned with CO_2 reduction. Also overlooked is how the law opens up a market space for renewable energy technologies and their industrial profile. The technology market opened up by the law, however, is not a protected market by any means. Opportunities are open to all suppliers of renewable energy technologies anywhere in the world within the ambit of Germany's Renewable Energy Sources Act. The Renewable Energy Sources Act contains clear market-based productivity incentives; the more productive the technology employed, the higher the economic returns to the plant operators. The law has undoubtedly done more to impel the rapid development of renewable energy technologies worldwide than had ever been the case before. The standard arguments against protected markets are therefore wholly inapplicable to the Renewable Energy Sources Act. It is not the needs of consumers – who (as surveys show) overwhelmingly accept the additional costs that the Renewable Energy Sources Act imposes on electricity prices – that are decisive for the authors of this report; rather, the decisive question for them is whether the law is compatible with their own one-sided market theory, which is focused exclusively on the energy market. It is the energy market that they believe should dictate what needs people should have.

In a veritable somersault of economic dogmatism, the Economics Advisory Council to the Environment Ministry contrasts the Renewable Energy Sources Act with a climate protection proposal whose realization would require a rigorous and globally planned economy: 'The modernization and expansion of China's power plants present a gigantic potential for reducing and avoiding CO_2 emissions', supposedly 'at costs that are 30 to 50 times more favourable than the savings effects of the Renewable Energy Sources Act's methods'. In other words, instead of directing investments to plants stimulated by the Renewable Energy Sources Act here, it would be better to direct them to China or similar countries. Quite apart from the fact that this cost accounting has never been proven, the proposal is doubly absurd.

On the one hand, this deals a blow to practically every investment in an industrial country's CO_2 reduction. For, by using this argument, every investment in an industrial country's environmental good can be branded as economic and ecological nonsense, since it would always be possible, theoretically, to achieve greater CO_2 reductions by investing the same amount in a developing country. In other words, the public should just gratefully continue to accept environmental damage from fossil energy use (which is creating not only global climate change, but also local and regional damage to the air, water, soil and forests), since the funds that might be invested in preventing this at home would be more effectively employed to reduce environmental damage in Africa or Asia. By this line of argument, it is even possible to denounce any local self-interest in clean energy if it applies to an industrial country; it would be deemed irresponsible as a matter of environmental ethics.

On the other hand, the only practical way to implement the Council's proposal would be under conditions of direct government control over all domestic energy investments in the developing countries. The funds that a private investor is willing to employ for a photovoltaic, wind, biomass or hydropower plant are not necessarily going to be put into China or another country if the Renewable Energy Sources Act is abolished in Germany. This would only be possible if a clairvoyant were around to investigate who might want to invest in a future renewable energy plant (should the Renewable Energy Sources Act still be on the books); afterwards the government would have to confiscate from the investor the sum originally intended for use in Europe and transfer it to China for power plant modernization there. But this would be tantamount to a pure-bred planned economy for energy on a global scale, an Orwellian scenario based on some non-existent parapsychological investigation technique.

The actual upshot of abolishing the Renewable Energy Sources Act would be that potential investors would put their money into all manner of possible projects, just not for any investment in China. The Council's theoretical cost accounting example does something that the market economy theorist Wilhelm Röpke had insistently warned against: 'making theoretical perfectionism depend on conditions for which it is a foregone conclusion that they can hardly ever be met in economic reality'.[20] In brief, it is analytical junk, the product of tinkering in a workshop with 'market economy' models and of ideological delusion. Yet the economists' report does nothing more than take the logic of 'flexible instruments' (along with their premises) and think them through to their logical conclusion; the report simply leads these instruments and premises to their absurd end point in a way that is completely consistent with the theoretical model.

In a report by Germany's Federal Environmental Office about the 'environmental compatibility of small hydropower plants' it says that 'too much expense is tolerated in order to avoid carbon dioxide emissions' when hydropower facilities are built.[21] As if the investor who is refused permission to build a hydropower facility will then instead pass on his own funds to a coal-fired power plant operator so that this operator will reduce CO_2 emissions there! Numerous studies by environmental institutes end up making the boilerplate statement that, for the sake of a more cost-effective CO_2 reduction, money should be used for energy savings initiatives instead of renewable energy. When a private person invests money in energy-saving devices at home instead of in a solar installation on the roof, that person is able to do something with this recommendation. He or she has freedom of choice about a self-determined goal and control over the use of funds. That person also has the freedom to install the solar device out of other motives than mere CO_2 reduction. Should this individual investor, instead, allocate his money for a solar facility in Madagascar or an energy-saving investment in the Philippines, he would be giving the finger to advisers like that. Yet statements drawing conclusions like this may be found in numerous reports by energy and environmental economists. Lurking behind all of these pronouncements is the unarticulated and unreal notion of some entity that initiates all energy investments, regardless of where in the world one might be – a kind of global agency for energy investments that selects the optimal site for investment and picks the optimal technology. 'Flexible instruments' are the substitute for this global agency. Ideas like this are not sustainable from the standpoint of economic sociology; they arrogantly ignore the diversity of human motives and ultimately they endorse a total separation between investor and investments. Such otherwise highly vaunted market virtues as personal responsibility, self-determined action, integrated thinking and the willingness to make bold investments in the future – these virtues all fall flat, giving way to dirigiste economic concepts.

It should come as no surprise that there is a growing call – on the part of governments as well as among energy corporations, in conventional energy study institutes as well as among environmental institutes – for a national and international *Gleichschaltung* bringing all energy-related policy instruments into line with the pattern established by the Kyoto Protocol's 'flexible instruments'. Those who call for this total coordination around a single policy mechanism want all other approaches to be invalidated.

With the use of 'flexible instruments' in which everything is meant to be 'harmonized', it is not just climate protection that mutates into climate business. Also fused into these instruments of climate business are the one-dimensional approaches of neoliberal energy and environmental economics. Whenever strategies for renewable energy are brought into line with these neoliberal approaches, there is a danger of setbacks even in areas where breakthroughs have already occurred; and the result is simply that more years will have been wasted all over the world.

When Germany's parliament – in the wake of the Kyoto Protocol and the EU implementation guideline based on that treaty – passed the Greenhouse Gas Emissions Trading Law (Treibhausgas-Emissionshandelsgesetz or TEHG), at least it was explicitly stated that this law was not meant to be a substitute for other policy instruments like the energy tax and the laws promoting renewable energy. Instead, the law on emissions trading was simply to be there alongside these other instruments. Facilities for renewable energy built within the framework of the EEG are therefore also not at the disposal of emissions trading. Because of the EEG, direct CO_2 reductions of approximately 35 million metric tons have already been achieved, 25 million tons of these in just five years. By way of comparison, the emissions reduction target sought by the TEHG is 10 million fewer tons by the year 2012 (down to 495 million from the current level of 505 million). But that means, in order to fulfil Germany's reduction obligations, the TEHG would not even be required. Simply continuing the EEG would bring additional real CO_2 emissions reductions of at least 15 million metric tons, along with many other ecological, economic and political effects. With the EEG this all takes place without any emissions trading bureaucracy and without all the costs of certification and brokerage.

Germany's energy business initially resisted the TEHG. After the law went into effect, the energy business attempted to turn the Kyoto instruments against political initiatives favouring renewable energy. Everywhere, not just in Germany, the protagonists of renewable energy are confronted with this energy business abuse of Kyoto. For renewable energy advocates, therefore, the Kyoto Protocol has turned into a Kyoto Syndrome. To be sure, there will be a number of projects for renewable energy that are going to be financed with the aid of Kyoto-like flexible instruments, especially in the field of larger facilities for biomass usage. That is better than nothing at all. For those countries in which there are no political parameters and financial incentives at all for renewable energy, the Kyoto instruments are a welcome aid. But that should not distract from the fact that there are decidedly less bureaucratic, more effective and more flexible strategies for emissions reductions (not to mention for making renewable energy more dynamic) than Kyoto's – and Kyoto should not prevent anyone from pursuing these alternatives as a matter of priority.

Sand or oil jamming up the works? The lost innocence of the environmental movement

The concept of a 'movement' inside society is iridescent. Usually it involves a number of organizations and individuals, both large and small, that get together in order to advocate their goals more effectively. Movements also form outside political institutions that are accused of failure to deal with some fundamental problem, or which are even seen as part of that problem. They have fluid boundaries, there is no formal way to join or leave, new members affiliate or go off on their own. It is just as easy for them to grow as to shrink, to go from being a small group to a mass movement and then become hopelessly splintered again. A movement is, nevertheless, a 'societal unit', and as such – as the political sociologist Amitai Etzioni writes – it is 'for society what psychoanalysis is for the individual. It is an attempt to pry open associations that have formed under the pressure of past events in order to resolve accumulated malfunctions.'[22] It usually becomes a mass movement by way of special triggering events that stir up a lot of people. For the environmental movement, these included the spectacular conflicts over nuclear power plants, such as the near catastrophe of Three Mile Island in 1978 and, above all, the Chernobyl reactor disaster of 1986. It was no longer possible to see these events as accidental or isolated cases, and they prompted fundamental questions about the dominant philosophy of growth and the dangers of large-scale technologies.

A movement is initially a 'negative coalition'. Its 'unity' arises from whatever is jointly rejected. But this conceals a variety of motives that make it hard or even impossible to create a 'positive coalition' with a consistent alternative programme. The variety of motives among the environmental movement's comrades-in-arms reaches all the way from well thought-out critiques of individual technologies to diffuse reservations about technology in general; from a critique of the ecologically negative consequences of growth all the way to a critique of growth in general; from a paramount orientation towards local nature preservation to the struggle against global environmental destruction. Yet a movement that came together because of a joint series of 'nos' tends to let the different positions arising from these diverse motives simply rest. This guarantees successful mobilization, but it eventually leads to growing contradictions and signs of paralysis. Contentious views are readily played down so that the 'social unity' of the movement is not jeopardized. This is reflected in the way that a movement is often strong when it comes to criticizing but weak when it comes to demanding alternatives, either because it never goes beyond formulating some very general goals or because it restricts itself to the smallest common denominator.

The environmental movement has undoubtedly had a major impact. It has sensitized the public to environmental problems and triggered legislation to match. It has stimulated greater attentiveness to environmental questions on the part of the scientific community, which has been reflected in the establishment of numerous environmental institutes. Businesses and a market for natural products have emerged from the environmental movement, along with numerous initiatives for ecological farming. Without this movement the industrial democracies' Green parties would never have been established. With regard to energy problems, the movement has popularized concepts like the eco-tax, helped to prevent nuclear technology from making a clean sweep, and contributed in many countries to decoupling economic growth from growth in energy consumption. But the power machinery of the fossil energy business was never really arrested by these partial successes.

In the energy sector, the counter-proposals of the environmental movement were not primarily aimed at the implementation of renewable energy. Instead, their central demand was energy conservation, undoubtedly an important goal. This only becomes a problem when this approach to action is played off against renewable energy and even used to misconstrue its importance. Thus, the oft-cited statement, 'the greatest energy source is energy conservation', is wrong on two counts: first, energy conservation is not an energy source but instead simply reduces the demand for energy; and second, with non-renewable energy the potential for energy conservation is always smaller than the amount of non-renewable energy's total consumption, since there is no such thing as a perpetual motion machine. 'Negawatt instead of megawatt' is how another slogan goes. In other words, try to avoid using energy as much as possible. Well into the 1990s, environmental organizations and institutes issued energy policy recommendations in which renewable energy was not even mentioned as an active option. To be sure, decentralizing energy supplies was called for, but proponents were mostly thinking about combined heat and power cogeneration and its – considerable – potential.

As late as the 1970s there were still good reasons for setting priorities this way. At this time the development of renewable energy technologies had been so neglected that only a little practical 'evidence' could have been presented on behalf of a reorientation. Energy conservation initiatives, by contrast, can be implemented quickly and cost-effectively, especially since it is easier to appeal directly to energy consumers within the existing energy system this way.

Yet in addition to these kinds of understandable reasons, there have been unacceptable grounds for the neglect of renewable energy by the environmental movement, environmental institutes and, not least of all, many environmental policy makers. Thus, for example, there is a barrage of reservations made against building small hydropower plants and setting up wind power facilities – provisos employing a vocabulary that recalls, in part, the resistance to building nuclear power plants.

Many environmental protection authorities go into a rage against these kinds of facilities when they come up for licensing. Nor should one forget the widespread reservations held against bio-energy, to which an inevitable across-the-board competition with nutritional cultivation is imputed, and which is also accused of inevitably and compulsively leading to damaging monocultures. Bio-energy is also repeatedly accused of standing in the way of expanding nature preserves. For a long time there has hardly been any discussion about whether these objections are justified in the generalized way they are articulated, or about whether they might turn out to be unfounded, without losing sight of the larger goal – the need for an energy shift. To this day, overwhelmingly, such a discussion has been conducted in a superficial way.

Environmental protection without a hierarchy of problems and threats

Such persistent objections help to confirm many people in their diffident, wait-and-see attitude towards renewable energy. To the traditional energy business, their scepticism is highly welcome. Every blocked initiative helps keep the market position of 'old energy' untouched – with all the environmental conse-quences that ensue. The draft to amend the Renewable Energy Sources Act put forward by Germany's Environment Minister in August 2003 envisioned (to the applause of some environ-mental associations) an end to having the law promote new small hydropower plants and restrictions on the expansion of domes-tic wind power facilities. This led to months of debate between renewable energy organizations and some environmental associ-ations about different ideas for environmental protection, but it also led to debate within these organizations themselves and in the Environmental Committee of the Bundestag.

Apparently there is a lack of consciousness about how to estab-lish hierarchies of real ecological problems and threats. This leads to lopsided assessments, to exaggerating micro-problems at the same time that macro-problems are shrugged off. Setting up reser-voirs in flowing waters for small hydropower plants is rejected wholesale on grounds of water pollution control, although it certainly cannot be ascertained what the fundamental distinction is between an intelligently constructed artificial reservoir with a fish ladder and one created by nature. But even if it would make a difference in terms of nature conservation, it should be remembered that this type of small power plant contributes, through its emissions-free electricity production, to cutting back on the production of fossil-based electricity, whose emissions are 'responsible' for dying forests along the river banks and excess acidity in the water — as well as for climate changes that might lead to drought in entire regions and to rivers drying out.

Weighing these kinds of trade-offs is not even something that comes up in the campaigns against the 'blights on the landscape' allegedly caused by wind power facilities, of which there are currently 15,000 in Germany. By contrast, the more than 200,000 high-voltage pylons and their transmission lines are hardly ever a subject for discussion, even though wind power facilities could easily hold their own in a beauty contest against power cable towers. There is an Argus-eyed vigil over the possibility that birds might collide with the wind turbines' rotors and die, although there are entire mega-cities and industrial regions in which, owing to air pollution and a lack of animal nutrition, no avian fauna can even be found any more. In the Naturpark Wattenmeer (Mudflats Nature Park) on Germany's North Sea coast, including its offshore vacation islands, the installation of wind power facilities has been rejected point-blank, even though we can rest assured that this countryside is going to be flooded in a few decades if global warming caused by fossil energy emissions keeps up — and although a very lively ship traffic keeps leaving behind oil slicks that pollute the nature park much more intensively than any windmills ever could.

Misleading comparisons are the order of the day. But looking at a specific landscape with or without a wind power facility is not the appropriate comparison to make; rather, one needs to compare the stress on the landscape that comes from wind power facilities to the environmental stress from traditional energy supply — from the mine to the power plant, from industrial coal heaps, polluted waters and lengthy conveyer pipelines. Without a doubt, wind power facilities are less of a strain on the landscape, and talk about wholesale 'destruction of the landscape' is ridiculous.

The rejection of wind power on grounds of 'aesthetic landscape pollution' is an extreme case of standards gone awry. Nobody who finds the sight of wind power facilities disturbing or views them as a stain on the landscape can be talked out of this perception. Some people find skyscrapers attractive and impressive, while they strike others as repulsive and eerie. One might find a wind power facility beautiful and still not be an advocate of wind energy. One can also find them disturbing to look at yet be in favour of them because one sees the necessity of emissions-free energy production. Let there be no misunderstanding: this has to do with individual standards, not societal evaluations. It is appropriate and advisable, of course, to erect wind turbines in a way that harmonizes with the topography in each instance. This is a cultural service that one also expects developers and architects to perform in a building, and often enough it is not done satisfactorily. Seldom is approval unanimous, because there is not a single 'aesthetic consensus' to which everyone subscribes. To make such a non-existent consensus into a criterion for approval, however, simply leads to the bureaucratization of aesthetics according to the predilections of public authorities. An evaluative arbitrariness would then determine what happens, with standards that – should they be generally applied – would inevitably lead to the immediate cessation of nearly all building activity.

In many places, however, these are the conclusions people draw about wind power. While there is hardly any public discussion about how all conventional forms of energy are awarded privileges to plan and build outside residential areas, any such rights are frequently disputed when it comes to wind power or even biomass facilities. This double standard is treacherous because it expresses the view that renewable energy facilities, in contrast to conventional power plants and transmission lines, are actually unnecessary. How far this schizophrenia can go is demonstrated by a statement made by the Swiss Professor Hans-Christoph Binswanger, who was one of the early advocates of an eco-tax and for many years an author and speaker much in demand in the environmental movement:

> *In the interest of a sustainable way of doing business, wind energy, with its destructive effects on the landscape, should not be advocated or even tolerated. Otherwise one loses any right to defend oneself against additional assaults that ravage nature and the countryside, for example against sprawl, against highways, against brown coal mining. All these intrusions are downright harmless compared to the fields of wind power plants dotting the entire countryside.[23]*

People keep looking for the last little hair in the soup, whereas the pollutants caused by fossil energy continue getting permission to wreak their global destruction, even (in the meantime, and as if this were perfectly natural) with the assistance of 'emission rights'. What some environmentalists seem to be demanding is a 99 per cent purism about ecological projects, which brings to mind that proverb that 'the perfect is the enemy of the good'. Desirable new goals are subjected to more stringent demands than are old ways that have become intolerable, which is simply a way of granting the latter a stock guarantee on continued existence. This perspective leads to placing an absolute value on particularistic outlooks, to a kind of tunnel vision that obscures the larger picture.

Optimal environmental protection would be leaving nature completely alone. Yet intrusions into nature are unavoidable because human life is unthinkable without using natural resources. The landscape of industrial societies is overwhelmingly human-made. The Black Forest, one of the largest German woodland areas, is a forestation project – for the most part one made up of monocultures. In the development of civilization there have even been times when entire woodlands were deforested because they were regarded as threatening. Intrusions into nature need to be evaluated according to whether they are grave and even irreversible or – as far as nature as a whole is concerned – unproblematic and perhaps even helpful. An unrestricted right to the exploitation of nature cannot be seriously advocated – although there are many (including, not least of all, the global fossil energy business) who act as if this right does exist. To counter them with an argument about the 'right of nature' is difficult if only because nature cannot sue for any rights. To this end, nature needs 'trustees', as the legal scholar Klaus Bosselmann insists in his book *Im Namen der Natur* (In the Name of Nature).[24] These have to be trustees whose ideas are not one-dimensional. Nature's only choices are to tolerate quietly the merciless treatment it receives or to become unpredictable and then 'strike back'.

The compromise reached between these two extremes – arbitrary exploitation of nature or leaving nature completely alone – was coexistence between the industrial use of nature and maintaining nature sanctuaries. But this coexistence remains an unattainable goal for as long as fossil and nuclear energy use, with its emissions and dangerous radiation, continues to exist. These do not exactly give a wide berth to unspoilt natural spaces. Energy emissions no longer leave so much as a square metre of the Earth's surface untouched, as melting glaciers in the Alps or melting icebergs in the Arctic and Antarctic attest. The simplest and most effective measure for protecting nature and the landscape, therefore, is to make a thoroughgoing shift to renewable energy, so as to protect nature from emissions. The right synthesis between using and preserving nature is finding a way of doing business that is integrated with nature, something that is only possible with renewable energy and natural materials. In doing business this way, there is nothing to be said against agricultural operations even if they are conducted inside nature sanctuaries, and there is also nothing to be said against wind power plants set up there.

Avoiding emissions is a more realistic and less ambiguous goal than that of 'energy avoidance'. Focusing on the latter makes it look as if the many grave differences between types of energy are a secondary matter. That oversight leads directly to the kind of policy just described, in which concrete initiatives for avoiding emissions are blocked with reference to abstract initiatives undertaken somewhere else by anonymous third parties. The message is, don't act here and in this manner, but somewhere else and differently.

In the hierarchy of environmental threats, conventional energy consumption occupies first place, which is what justifies the priority of shifting to renewable energy in the practical world of environmental protection. Saving energy and increasing

efficiency constitute a complementary goal. Environmental legislation, however, is still a long way from weighing trade-offs like
these, as are environmental administrators, environmental scientists and many conservation activists. The demand for 'harvest
acreage' for renewable energy should not be confused with
'acreage consumption', as this is superficially called (as if a wind
power plant in the middle of a pasture or a wheat field is equivalent to overbuilding or sealing off some country acreage). When
efforts at preserving the countryside are especially directed
against the shift to renewable energy, they become counter-
productive, even in terms of their original goals. To take the
energy shift we need as seriously as the energy crises seem to
demand can only mean that we must expand renewable energy as
widely as possible. In plain language, this can only mean the
following: wind power plants as a natural, integrated component of the future landscape, and not just crammed together in
a few wind parks; solar facilities as a self-evident element of
entire building landscapes, the way roof tiles and glass facades
are today; also new pump storage works in mountainous
landscapes, small weirs in water landscapes, or the construction
of many regional bio-refineries. The current energy system
already shapes and delineates the landscape. Renewable energy
will shape the landscape in its own way. With this new kind of
shaping, the old kind will disappear. A structural change in the
landscape will take place. Not wanting to pay this 'price' in the
name of nature conservation and environmental protection
means not being able to stop wide-scale environmental and
natural devastation. It also means risking the not too distant
day when even people in industrial societies, blinded by sheer
desperation for energy, will increasingly resort to cutting down
every tree within reach in order to satisfy their daily energy
needs, just as it was in German cities after the Second World
War and is still the case in many developing countries today.

Since conventional power plants and electric transmission
lines are, for the most part, already there, landscape preservationists' resistance is mostly directed against new energy
facilities. Whatever has already been built benefits from a kind
of mental habit protection. This makes anyone who thought-
lessly refuses to make sites available for renewable energy

facilities into a reactionary groundskeeper for the energy business. People with this attitude are losing their virginity to real-world environmental devastation. By way of analogy, it is as if one refused permission for any new shops in a city so that already existing supermarkets can continue to be used to capacity. In this way countless projects using renewable energy have been prevented in the name of nature and landscape preservation. In many regions the introduction of wind power was already nipped in the bud this way. But there is an indirect effect that is even more serious, in two respects. At any location where one facility was meant to be built but not approved, it usually takes a number of years before another attempt is made. Many people are so intimidated at the outset because of the petty wars they have to fight with officials and local initiatives that they refrain from even trying. But the worst effect of this fatal situation, which in no way corresponds to majority will, is the way it nurtures the view that, since renewable energy is subject to so many restrictions, the traditional way of supplying energy is going to remain indispensable for a long time to come.

The particularization of holistic environment thinking

Ecological thinking needs to be holistic so that its impact can be understood in context. Ignoring these contexts – proceeding from that particularistic concept of science that has become dominant in modern natural science – is a profound cause of the ruthless way that industrial growth societies have dealt with natural goods. Specializing in the particular has been carried forward from the natural and technical sciences onto an ever-growing number of scholarly fields. A particularistic understanding of science shapes teaching and occupational training, and it promotes the increasingly frayed specialization of professions. Weighing trade-offs between a number of factors is becoming harder, as is the evaluation of their relative significance. By contrast, the capacity for a holistic view of strategy against environmental crises is indispensable. Yet it is a tortuous path from these imperatives of thinking and acting to heeding what they tell us to do.

'Any new interpretation of nature', according to the physicist, philosopher and historian of science Thomas S. Kuhn in his book *The Structure of Scientific Revolutions*:[25]

> *emerges first in the mind of one or a few individuals. It is they who first learn to see science and the world differently, and their ability to make the transition is facilitated by two circumstances that are not common to most other members of their profession. Invariably their attention has been intensely concentrated upon the crisis-provoking problems; usually, in addition, they are men so young or so new to the crisis-ridden field that practice has committed them less deeply than most of their contemporaries to the world view and rules determined by the old paradigm... [At first] a new candidate for paradigm may have few supporters (and the motives of the supporters may be suspect). If the supporters are competent, they will improve the paradigm, explore its possibilities, and show what it would be like to belong to the community guided by it. For the paradigm destined to win, the number and strength of the persuasive arguments in its favour will increase. As more and more scientists are converted, exploration increases. The number of experiments, instruments, articles, and books based on the paradigm will multiply. More scientists, convinced of the new view's fruitfulness, will adopt the new mode of practising normal science, until only a few elderly holdouts remain.*

So far, however, the scientific revolution leading to a holistic ecological approach has remained bogged down. Renewable energy, which is the natural linchpin of the new paradigm from a holistic perspective, has hardly gone beyond the candidate role, in spite of enormous interest on the part of younger scientists.

Specialized disciplines dominate the world of science so much that they have succeeded in subordinating holistic efforts. There are quite normal reasons for this, having to do with inertia inside the world of science itself, a system that is not eager to rewrite its textbooks, and whose exam regimens and careers are oriented around specialized disciplines. Instead of a new holistic approach, often nothing more is ventured than a summation of specialized perspectives that empty out into a sea of 'complexity'. This goes along with a refusal to recognize just one parameter — in our case, renewable energy — as the key factor, and not just for overcoming a single problem, but for overcoming several. To the representatives of the particularistic scientific establishment, this seems too monocausal, although it cannot be disputed that the central cause of most environmental problems is fossil energy consumption, which is why the central solution — which will enable many other problems to be solved simultaneously — can only lie in a shift to renewable energy. But the moments of inertia in today's specialized culture of science are not the only impediments to a holistic perspective; equally obstructive are the economic interests and dependence relations of scientific training institutes.

Even environmental policy, although it is a classic case of a problem that cries out for a comprehensive approach, became enmeshed in a political decision-making operation that was also organized in a particularistic way; environmental policy became just one department among many. This started with the instal-lation of environmental ministries. Their job, to be sure, is championing the environmental cause, but as a rule they do not have authority to attack the problem of energy crises at their roots and to press ahead immediately with the necessary shift in resources. One of the few exceptions is Germany's Environment Ministry, which was authorized to deal with renewable energy in 2002. This led to tensions inside the Ministry, whose classic assignment was to alleviate the consequences of resource consumption, meaning that it was attacking the problem at the end of the resource chain rather than at the beginning. This inevitably leads to sideshow battles. The more environmental policy deals with pollutant particles instead of the sources of pollution, the more extensive is the growth in the number and scope of environmental laws accompanying the number of recog-nized particle dangers — rather like that well-known criticism of criminal law practice whereby the little guys go to the gallows and the big fish get off scot-free. Particle-oriented environmen-tal protection is also directed against renewable energy. When the environmental authorities cannot find a single hair in the renewable energy soup, they shake their heads until a hair falls in.

In this way, along an administrative path, we come full circle to the nature conservation purists described above. Holistic analyses overtax the limited authority held by environmental policy making; as a result, such analyses of the big picture are requested by environmental scientists only on rare occasions. Corporations, too, prefer to commission environmental science studies that are particularistic (affecting their immediate interests). By contrast, environmental institutes that insist on a universalistic perspective put their economic existence at risk for lack of any demand for their services from political and economic clients. To some extent environmental science was drawn into this mire, and to some extent it sank down and lost sight of the holistic gestalt, even though registering that integrated picture ought to have been its real job. Not least of all for this reason, expert knowledge about renewable energy is underdeveloped in the field of environmental science – which can be seen by looking at many of the studies presented here. The conference books of scientific and technical conferences on renewable energy, some of which include up to 2000 participants with hundreds of scholarly contributions offering insights as broad as they are deep into the state of things, remain completely ignored in countless studies. This makes it even easier for authors to deliver assessments that are highly restrictive and based on only fragmentary knowledge.

Weakening through integration: Environmental NGOs

Whenever international NGOs are discussed, what is often meant are *all* non-governmental organizations, idealist organizations lumped together with private sector business interest groups. Yet normally one thinks only of the idealistic organizations that are committed to environmental protection, development aid or human rights and that finance their work from membership contributions and donations. Most of these are financially weak, with only a small, poorly paid staff along with some comrades-in-arms who work in an honorary capacity and can muster a capacity for self-exploitation. Their strength lies in their ability to shed light on secret or concealed problems, to expose the causes and identify those responsible, and to specify alternatives that get to the root of the problems. In order for them to exercise this role, their most important capital is independence from governments and from powerful established interests as well as a willingness to engage in confrontation. These are the features that gain them public attention and influence.

By now the art of 'modern governance' has learned to add the tactic of gently ensnaring NGOs to its arsenal of co-optative techniques. NGOs in the environmental field have always exercised a role of spokesperson for the movement. If they were still being viewed as annoying troublemakers in the early years, these NGOs have now become regular team players on the advisory boards of environmental policy making. While they agitated for many years to create public pressure, today they have been integrated into decision-making processes – and thereby into the making of political compromises. The strategy of the fatal embrace has changed the NGO spectrum more than it has altered political institutions. Not a few NGOs now have favoured access to governments. The EU Commission alone currently pays a billion euros to NGOs of all shades, either in the form of direct organizational subsidies or by allocating project funds.[26] The funds are not allocated simply out of sympathy for the aims of the NGOs. Frequently the organizations take care of business that governments themselves are not in any position to handle. But that is not the sole motive on the government side; just as interest groups practise 'landscape conservation' in political institutions, governments and other public institutions do the same within the NGO spectrum. NGOs that have become overwhelmingly and permanently dependent on government money to finance their activities, and that would no longer be able to work without these funds, lose their independence this way. They become quasi-NGOs or 'quangos' (in the jargon of the UK civil service). And even if an NGO does not necessarily become a propaganda arm of its public donor, the upshot is that it loses its capacity for confrontation – while its adversaries lose their fear of confrontation.

Why NGO representatives are susceptible to this mechanism of soft co-optation can be easily explained. The larger their public role becomes, and the more deeply they are integrated into decision-making processes, the more they have to professionalize themselves. When public funds become accessible to them, there are obvious reasons for drawing on this money. This facilitates their work; they get to transform unpaid work in an honorary capacity or badly paid work into normal paid work, and they can hire staff. At the same time, however, many NGOs overstep the invisible boundary at which opportunity changes suddenly into opportunism and a self-imposed restriction on issues to raise. The disputatious public discourses they once instigated turn into consensus-oriented discourses that take place in committees. The result is harmonious cooperation. It also becomes standard practice to implement projects for the World Bank and receive commissions for this from the Bank's credit allocation. The Swiss sociology professor Jean Ziegler has observed that speeches addressed to the World Bank have 'suddenly [turned] milder', 'these NGOs ultimately behave like cheap whores',[27] and 'many of the leading personalities and cadres of the NGOs were later discreetly hoisted into the upper levels of the World Bank'. The Indian writer Arundhati Roy has observed that many are already 'accountable to their funders' and act as 'a sort of buffer' between institutions and the general population. The 'NGO-ization of resistance' is transforming that opposition into a 'well-mannered, reasonable, salaried, 9-to-5 job'.[28]

Such developments are not exactly surprising. NGO actors are also of this world. They want to put their work on a more solid financial basis. They neither can nor want to be cast forever in the role of opposition. If they make adjustments, this is no more worthy of criticism than is the case with politicians who once took radical positions and later dive into the mainstream of conventional political behaviour. Only there is no reason to grant NGO actors some kind of all-purpose halo and to overrate their constancy. At least there is no reason to turn whatever stance they are taking at the moment into the critical measure of all things, as if this were always the most that could be practically advocated or achieved if one wishes to remain 'realistic'. Instead of being 'sand in the machinery' of the energy system handed down to us, parts of the environmental movement have become 'oil in the transmission' of government policy and UN organizations, as Irm Pontenagel put it in a recent article.[29] The great defiance of yesteryear has turned into the tiny reformist ambition.

These kinds of transformations match, almost down to the last detail, the communications strategy of big corporations, whose methods were described by Judith Richter in a briefing given to the US NGO Corner House.[30] The first rule is to 'depoliticize' debate by declaring that every political question is really one that can only be solved technocratically. The next step is to 'divert' criticism of the main issue by organizing discourses about side issues, discussions to which NGO representatives are invited and where the impression is created that they are going to be heard from now on. Criticism that is all too intense, however, is warded off. Then a careful distinction is drawn between actors who are willing to strike a consensus and those incapable of doing so, between participants who are 'rational' and those 'incorrigible radicals' who are 'confrontational' for the sake of it'. The invited guests then imagine that they are on the way to achieving their goals. The collective designation for this method is 'proactive neutralization'. It is meant to seem as if no fundamental differences exist any longer, only untoward circumstances for which understanding is solicited and that should be overcome in a cooperative spirit. In the arsenal of NGO advocates who have been integrated in this fashion, the arrows remain in their quiver, and even the quiver ultimately has to disappear, since it no longer fits the new suit these NGO advocates are now wearing.

'Between government advising and rebelliousness: what kind of NGOs does the environment need?' was the question posed at the 2005 Environmental Conference held by the parliamentary caucus of the Greens in the German Bundestag. Here NGO representatives attempted to describe their altered role. 'The simple, straightforward adversary is missing', a conference statement read – this at a time when there was one ongoing campaign by Germany's electricity companies promoting a 'renaissance of nuclear energy', a second on behalf of building a major new 40,000-megawatt power plant, and a third was that assault on the Renewable Energy Sources Act. A few days later the Raw

Materials Convention of the Federation of German Industry (Bund der Deutschen Industrie) took place, where one speaker after another denounced the 'excesses' of ecological policy as a threat to the economy overall. With all these attempts at roll-back, can it really be said that there are no 'straightforward' adversaries any longer? 'The neoliberal discourse is dominant', the Green party conference statement goes on to say, by way of explaining why the environmental movement has been put on the defensive. But why, then, can't environmentalists at least see the high priesthood of this neoliberalism as an adversary? As a result of this absence of an adversary (the statement goes on to say) environmental politics can 'no longer be done with simple demands; it has become a highly complicated policy field'. And yet, as arduous as it may be to make a fundamental shift to renewable energy, the goal is crystal clear and 'easily' formulated; it can be substantiated in a variety of ways.

Another statement to emerge from the Green party caucus talked about an 'inner reflectiveness' that has set in because the environmental movement has become caught up in a discrepancy: 'Inefficacy with respect to the fundamental questions of growth and consumption' may be contrasted with the movement's 'success [in] having practically arrived at the centre of society by virtue of being at the seat of government'. But how can it be the goal of an NGO to have arrived at the seat of government without achieving any success in what it regards as 'fundamental questions'? Isn't the success story of individual persons with government connections being confused with the movement's success – just as many politicians who have landed a government office by playing down or abandoning their original programmatic goals confuse their individual success with their party's programmatic triumph? At most, 'arriving' in a government can be in accord with a movement's self-image when that government has actually adopted the movement's goals and implemented them in practice. But in that case the movement would have experienced such a sweeping triumph that it would have transcended itself and could now just dissolve. The 'secret of success' in any movement is being free of the institutional restrictions on action that go along with governing and of the deference any political party must show towards the different values and interests of its voters. A movement does not have to campaign for office, but in exchange it does enjoy greater freedom to describe problems without whitewashing and to articulate aims without compromise so that it can change public opinion. Only in this way can it be a driving force for the changes it seeks.

The environmental question, it goes on to say in the conference statement, has 'become more complicated' for the environmental movement. Whereas 'earlier it had been clear' that:

> individual materials are 'evil', the eco-balance sheet now displays a bewildering picture of arguments pro and con. There are specific interests in the differentiated NGO scene: the water pollution controller becomes an adversary of the friends of hydropower, the landscape preserver an enemy of the friend of wind.

For this reason the environmental movement needs to 'assume a moderator function, so that they don't appear to the outside world as if they are reciprocally stabbing each other in the back'. Yet can an environmental movement be an ever-shifting conciliation committee between contradictory goals, with compromise formulas and without fundamentally clarifying the hierarchy of problems and threats? Would it not become congealed and end up standing in its own way? Political parties can also become congealed and shapeless when they ban controversial questions from their internal discussions in order present a picture of unanimity and avoid endangering their chances at the next election. For this they have at least a tactical reason, one that can decide in the short run whether they might be able to gain power or hold onto office. A movement does not have this rationale, and certainly not if it believes that it has 'no adversary' any longer. An NGO is pursuing self-neutralization when it allows itself to be talked out of politicizing the debate, of countering diversionary manoeuvres, pointing out who's in charge, and attaining intellectual hegemony (along with conceptual sovereignty) in the public debate. An NGO that lets itself be talked out of these things becomes a doormat for the status quo, even if it had started out acting like a tiger jumping at that status quo.

It is no accident that the environmental movement, as it emerged from the 1970s, was by no means the driving force behind whatever breakthroughs there were to renewable energy. It certainly did prepare the ground by creating a critical awareness in society about the environmental dangers created by nuclear and fossil energy. But it was organizations dedicated specifically to renewable energy, including many local solar initiatives, that sowed the seeds and nurtured the growth of renewables. And it was technicians who thought up and worked out the facilities and applications. Only certain sections of environmental organizations made a contribution, while others even put the brakes on the development of renewables.

There are, not least of all, psychological reasons for this, having to do with the genesis of the environmental movement. Originally the movement was focused on preventive actions meant to counter the destructive impact of unchecked growth: preventing the construction of nuclear power plants, coal-fired power plants or new superhighways. Strategies for energy avoidance fit into this pattern. There is nothing wrong with consuming less nuclear and fossil energy. One need not be afraid of doing the wrong thing. Taking a clear stand that says 'yes' to renewable energy, however, requires a change in mentality that is psychologically overtaxing for many people – even when their attitude of rejection turns them into accomplices for structural conservatives in the energy business.

It is also no accident that, in the meantime, a new spectrum of NGOs has crystallized: the so-called anti-globalization movement, which is aimed against *Gleichschaltung* (against enforced conformity) among all economic systems in line with the principle of global freedom for markets without any consideration for social welfare, ecological consequences and fundamental principles of democratic self-determination in the polity. Organizations such as attac, which holds the World Social Forum every year, have little to do with the NGOs that disport themselves at international and national government conferences and inside their committees – and only a few of the 'old' NGOs are part of the new movement. That is the normal course of things, an outcome of the contradictions, integration and normalization of the environmental movement.

The environmental movement is only seemingly a 'societal unit'. For quite some time now, very different plans for environmental policy have been followed within the same movement. The environmental movement gave birth not only to advocates for renewable energy, but also to appeasers and to actors opposed to any shift towards renewables. If one desperately maintains the fiction of common ground, this means putting up with excessive restrictions on the introduction of renewable energy in the name of environmental protection. Individual environmental organizations themselves stand at a fork in the road. If they stick to their ambivalent attitude about renewable energy, their ecological credibility will have to be called into question. If they want to overcome this ambivalence, they need to bring about an internal and inevitably conflict-rife process of clarification. This will certainly cost them some members, but it will also allow them to gain new ones. A clear positioning on behalf of renewable energy does not mean dispensing with making it ecologically optimal. There is no indissoluble contradiction about advocating the installation of wind power plants that alter the landscape while also advocating mixed cultivation and regional nutrient cycles for bio-energy or hydropower plants adapted to nature – but with the fundamental attitude of wanting to use this potential everywhere.

At issue is the creation of new alliances between the advocates of renewable energy and sections of society overall who might be won over (and who need to be won over) to the shift towards renewable energy. This new alliance cannot come into being, however, if every small-minded misgiving has to be taken into account. There cannot be a successful debate about the shift to renewable energy, a debate in which the traditional nuclear and fossil energy powerhouse will try to pull out all the stops in its register of settling scores and distracting from real problems, if environmentalists adopt an attitude of 'pleasing everyone and hurting no one'. The new environmental movement needs to be a movement for renewable energy if it is going to do justice to its holistic aspirations.

Activation or nihilism? The world energy crisis and values polarization

Democratic industrial societies – with their scientific elites, high level of technology and broad information base – claim that they overwhelmingly follow reason-oriented and pragmatic standards of behaviour and are free of fundamentalist or irrational inclinations. If that were really the case, there would not be so many protracted crises in the developed world, and certainly no global ecological crisis. It is more than self-evident that society's reorientation towards a more efficiency-driven approach to energy and towards renewable energy would have been rung in on a large scale three decades ago. Yet instead, more and more people do not even want to hear anyone so much as hint that such a reorientation is the only way to avoid the apocalyptic consequences of nuclear and fossil energy use. In the meantime, there is even a Pentagon study on 'an abrupt climate change' that discusses how 'imagining the unthinkable' has indeed become practically imaginable.[31] Yet the logical conclusion is not drawn by this study's authors either – although it is actually not hard to grasp that a radical shift to renewable energy can ward off this danger and other energy crises of catastrophic proportions. Here the stakes are nothing less than making the world 'incapable of self-destruction' again, as the contemporary philosopher Peter Sloterdijk has put it.

The denial of this logical conclusion does not just come from lack of information. It is by no means simply the result of a discrepancy between knowledge and interest, a discrepancy that, in the case of the energy business, would at least represent a kind of rationality that is interest-based and calculable. There is a more deep-seated problem, which is the denial practised by many people who are not entangled in the web of energy business interests, a denial of renewable energy's potential as a solution, even if this refusal is accompanied by an awareness of the dangers that come from nuclear and fossil energy use. Many people want neither to hear nor know the truth, and if they do hear it, they do not want to believe it. If they believe it, it is either forgotten or repressed again – or they do not let the knowledge penetrate their consciousness. This mentality is more likely to be encountered among members of the social 'elites' than in the general population. It has to do with psychological barriers that cannot simply be explained away by the way people subjugate themselves to those marvels of highly complex technology without which modern life has become unthinkable. The photovoltaic transformation of sunlight into electricity – a technology without moving parts, without any noise, without any kind of emission – is an even greater marvel than nuclear technology. Nobody has to submit to this solar technology, but everyone can take shelter under it.

A 'political neurosis' is how the writer Arthur Koestler described the discrepancy between those unimaginable dangers than have become imaginable and human conduct, which is guided by our emotional life: 'Since Hiroshima, humanity as a whole has had to live with the prospect of its annihilation as a biological species'; since that time, mankind has had a 'time bomb around its neck' and has been 'living on borrowed time'. A 'psychoactive fallout' has occurred, an 'intellectual assimilation' to this condition, whose potential truth 'is too awful for one to stare it openly in the face'. Getting accustomed to this condition weakens the symptoms, and people accommodate themselves to 'pseudo-normal conditions'. They accept only the 'pleasant outcomes', and all the other 'indigestible' results are shoved aside. This built-in 'inner censor' works 'more thoroughly than the state censor of a totalitarian country' and causes people 'to act doggedly against their own welfare'.[32]

The philosopher Peter Sloterdijk also talks about an 'Internationale of Soldiering On'; the most powerful social groups have 'invested so much entrepreneurially, politically, vitally, and ideologically in fatal practices so that accidents, no matter how large-scale, are denied from the very outset the right to cause doubts in principle about the procedures'. But even among the less powerful, 'feelings of powerlessness and lack of competence coalesce into a mental constitution that is indolent and incapable of experience'. For these reasons there are 'masses of irreversibly formed mentalities that are catastrophe-proof and that, in the bunker of their conviction, are a match for any shock'.[33]

Following Chernobyl in 1986, the mechanism of ignoring nuclear technology no longer worked, in spite of tireless attempts by the incorrigibles to portray this catastrophe as a one-off exception. The longer we go on without another atomic worst-case scenario materializing, however, the sooner this psychological mechanism will take hold again. It is only possible to speak of a learning process, however, when the danger has not only been seen but when, in addition, the obvious and compelling conclusions have been drawn.

Environmental catastrophes and 'no future' mentalities

Everyone who has warned about environmental catastrophes expects (or at least hopes) that collective learning processes do really exist. Yet these warnings – just like some of the catastrophes that actually materialized as forewarned – have an ambivalent effect. On the one hand, they prompt people to advocate warding off dangers. Yet on the other hand, other people react in exactly the opposite way: the greater and more complex the danger, the less they believe that one might still be able to undertake any action against it. This feeling is intensified, and even takes on the character of a certitude, when politics is also not pursuing any convincing strategy to overcome real environmental dangers, and when no such strategy appears to be within sight. Environmental literature and reporting is full of catastrophic warnings that are never accompanied by convincing counter-measures. All too frequently these suggested counter-measures are either formulated in such a general way that nobody can do anything with them, or they are so restricted to some partial aspect so that the remedies seem silly in relation to the enormity of the danger, or they are conceived in such a long-term perspective that they are bound to be perceived as coming much too late.

What should people think when the world's problems are supposed to be solved at mammoth conferences and then the mountain only gives birth to a pair of tiny mice; when the Kyoto Protocol is cheered and it is simultaneously noted that it is wholly inadequate; when political and business elites discussing gigantic problems always declare that only the most minimal action is feasible because more would be 'unrealistic' or even dangerous? One cannot expect that people will massively commit to a particular prospect when political, economic and scientific authorities tell them that this prospect actually no longer exists or is unattainably remote. That leads to the spread of apathy, lethargy and a 'no future' mentality. So far only a few people have described the dangers comprehensively and, in the same breath, pointed the way towards an equally comprehensive solution, as did the German television journalist Franz Alt in such exemplary fashion for a mass public (for example, in his spectacular broadcast 'Escape Route from the Greenhouse').

There are many ways in which the 'no future' mentality expresses itself. These include the complaining and cynicism (or nihilism) of those who are informed about the dangers but see attempts at averting dangers as a pointless and burdensome waste of time. Some talk in a continuous complaining tone about the dangers, as if they could not live without them. Their behaviour calls to mind the poet Friedrich Hebbel when he said: 'There are people who would rejoice about the end of the world if only they had predicted it.' One rather nihilistic way of expressing the 'no future' mentality is to greet those who have failed to give up with just a tired smile, if not with outright aggression.

Prototypical for such attitudes are the persistent spiteful words printed by Germany's weekly news magazine *Der Spiegel* regarding renewable energy. Lack of information is not something one can impute to the magazine, nor can it be accused of commercial dependence on advertising customers from the energy business. Nor is it (yet?) propagating the fashionable renaissance of nuclear energy, especially since this magazine once made a significant contribution towards enlightening the public about nuclear power's risks. *Der Spiegel* is also not in denial about climate dangers and the wars over oil. But some of its recently published articles about renewable energy betray obvious emotions of anger and resentment, especially against wind energy, that seem inexplicable to many readers. 'The big flop' was the magazine's title cover in April 2004. Wind energy, it said, was a 'bad economic investment devouring billions'. The 'rank growth' of wind power facilities was leading to 'a blight on entire landscapes'. Wind power's contribution to easing the strain on the environment was deemed not worth mentioning. The magazine reprints essays that are presumptuous enough to make statements like the following: 'Never before has any phase of industrialization caused a more brutal destruction of the landscape.' This was penned by the writer Botho Strauss, who, looking out from his country house onto the heaths and forests of the Uckermark region in Brandenburg, is more disturbed by the wind turbines in his field of vision than by the not too distant lunar landscapes of the region's lignite coal production. The efforts of plant operators to find more appropriate sites for wind turbines and of local governments to share in their profits are denounced as 'threats, corruption or simply an unusually contested deal'. In another article, the magazine labels the Renewable Energy Sources Act's promotion of photovoltaic cells an economic 'trip on the wrong side of the road'.[34]

In a number of countries, a feeling of hopelessness has also induced many former environmental activists to capitulate, a trend for which declining membership in environmental organizations is one indication. Some react in the way just described. Others become radical renegades fighting against what they previously advocated but now brand as an illusion. One example is Ben-Alexander Bohnke, a former member of Germany's largest environmental organization BUND, who in 1997 published a book entitled *Farewell to Nature*. Nature, the book says, is 'incurably ill' and 'should not even be saved'. According to Bohke, the rescue attempt undertaken by 'romantics weary of civilization' was even 'dangerous'. The alternative would be a 'total technology' – for which people would have to emancipate themselves both from 'external nature' and from their 'inner nature'. Humanism and ecology would have to be abandoned and replaced by 'hominism' – if need by way of 'techno-psychotherapy' using electronic brain prostheses and psychopharmacological drugs that facilitate people's adjustment to the technological environment – and by a 'life liberated from nature'.[35] Dirk Maxeiner, the former editor-in-chief of the journal *natur*, and his co-author Michael Miersch have also been generally bad-mouthing the ecological movement in a series of books and articles, from the *Lexicon of Eco-Errors* to the *Mephisto Principle*. Here and there they confront those who warn about environmental destruction with environmental improvements that have already been achieved – all the while failing to mention that most of these improvements were initiated by the very movement they are now chiding. If only they were taking aim at those who hysterically turn every encroachment on nature into a global danger, their analysis would at least be accurate. But in the meantime all they do is condemn each and every critique of technology as 'pessimism about progress'. By contrast, they praise 'self-interest' as something that does good even if it intends to do evil, and they earn the applause of audiences who are grateful for anything that eases the burden of their conscience. The 'do-gooder' is turned into a contemptible figure who does nothing more than hinder society. *Der Spiegel* praised these authors by saying: 'Brilliantly formulated in part, often polemic, at times loutish, they attack the politically correct blind faith of dizzy, starry-eyed idealists.'[36] Also much in demand on the rostrums of industrial lobbyists is the Danish statistics professor Bjørn Lomborg ever since his book *The Skeptical Environmentalist: Measuring the Real State of the World* came out, a book that flatly denies climate change due to traditional energy consumption.[37]

Political neuroses and divided values

In the 1970s, George F. Kennan had this to say about the nuclear arms race: 'We have done this helplessly, almost involuntarily: like the victims of some sort of hypnotism, like men in a dream, like lemmings heading for the sea, like the children of Hamlin marching blindly along behind their Pied Piper.'[38] The strategy of a 'balance of terror' seemed like a highly rational construct – an attempt to ban the danger, defuse the destructive potential, and yet continue upgrading. A comparable attempt is now afoot once more with respect to the destructive potentials of fossil and nuclear energy. Instead of using every available means to replace these destructive energy forms, people cling to them and take their consequences into account as a 'residual risk' (to use sociologist Ulrich Beck's term).

The energy corporations, in turn, are only too happy to exploit this one-dimensional, uniform, neurotic discussion so long it can be turned against renewable energy – even if the motives and opinions in each case are mutually exclusive. The promotion of growth is propagated, even at the price of additional environmental destruction – in order to have economic power to compensate for the consequences. Investment security for large power plants and liberalized energy markets are promoted. Anything goes: indiscriminate competition and nature conservation; climate protection and plenty of cheap flights, as well as a vast increase in traffic flows for world trade; cheap energy at the same time as energy conservation; boundless technological optimism in relation to traditional energy technologies but technological pessimism so long as it is directed against renewable energy. In this spirit of 'anything goes', nuclear and fossil energy is privileged at the same time that renewable energy gets promoted.

Existential anxieties about energy security are channelled against renewable energy, although none of renewable energy's advocates has ever called for shutting down all conventional energy facilities as an initial step to test how energy needs can be met. So where is the risk? Anxieties about economic subsistence are projected onto the costs of renewable energy – although the largest and fastest-growing cost risk for society is demonstrably the perpetuation of nuclear and fossil energy use. 'Why choose the greater – why choose, in fact, the greatest – of all risks in the hopes of avoiding the lesser ones?'[39] This question, posed by Kennan to the nuclear weapons strategists, may also be addressed to those who, for reasons that are incomprehensible rationally, want to prevent, arrest and postpone the shift to renewable energy and who, as a result, inevitably and continuously increase the risks of traditional energy provision.

One may observe a diffuse 'movement' whose individual elements are united only in what they jointly, though for different reasons, wish to thwart. Their ideological and journalistic spokespersons strike a tone that betrays the reactionary character of their struggle against renewable energy. It is no coincidence – owing to the rapid breakthrough to renewable energy that has been taking place in the Federal Republic – that Germany is the scene of the crime. 'On the verge of the awakening' was the headline of an article from the conservative

Frankfurter Allgemeine Zeitung (FAZ), meant to instigate resistance against renewable energy. The article put the price for 130,000 new jobs in the wind and solar energy branches at 'many lost jobs', whose number remained in the dark. Even before the magazine *Spiegel* published its signal article about 'The big flop' of wind power, there appeared in the FAZ an article entitled 'Flops with wind wheels' in which the paper was incensed about this 'money-devouring branch' – whereby the FAZ was appealing to the same 'envy complex' it otherwise mocks in debates about excessive income differences. The promotion of renewable energy is scandalized as a danger for 'Germany as a business site'. The extra cost of renewable energy, according to the paper, amounts to an annual 1.5 billion euros to the detriment of electricity customers. The FAZ did not waste a single critical word, by contrast, about how the four electricity corporations that control transmission lines in Germany have pocketed profits well in excess of this amount for electricity transport. On the very day Germany's Chancellor delivered his speech to the Renewables 2004 conference, the FAZ pronounced in its lead editorial that the entire programme for promoting solar electricity was physical nonsense – using the whopping lie that the production of solar cells devours more energy than they could ever create.[40] The fact that this 'energy amortization period' amounts to less than two years, and that conventional energy plants (whose job, after all, is to consume energy constantly) can never win back their energy – these facts are simply overlooked. A comparable statement might be an accusation against the car industry saying that the five-litre cars they are trying to sell are really 100-litre cars.

'Windy accounting' was the title of another article, in this case in *Spiegel* again.[41] It announced, ominously, what a previously published study had determined: that, for the expansion of wind power over the next ten years, 845 kilometres of new transmission networks would have to be built at a cost of 1.1 billion euros so that the share of wind power in 2015 might climb to over 10 per cent of electricity supplies as a whole. Yet this supposedly horrendous figure – which elicited from then Economics Minister Wolfgang Clement the startled remark, 'who is supposed to pay for this?' – is a comparatively low sum.

It is less than half of what the electricity business invests annually in its transmission network. In order for this report to sound even more startling, the electricity transmission lines to be built for wind energy are labelled 'gigantic' – as if those for traditional large power plants were more like webs of delicate filigree. The business magazine *Capital* warns against promoting solar electricity facilities by unceremoniously redefining the private investments of 11 billion euros expected for solar's growth by 2010 on the basis of the Renewable Energy Sources Act as governmental 'investment subsidies' and thereby making it seem as if the electricity they produce and the jobs they create are worthless.[42] In numerous business commentaries, the tax write-offs that every business enterprise is allowed to take for any investment it wants are denounced as a business-hostile 'subsidy' when they are used for investments in renewable energy. Following this abstruse logic, the entire economy would have to be regarded as subsidized and therefore 'business-hostile', since all businesses can write off investments from their taxes.

These obsessive tirades presented under the cover of serious economic competence are meant to confuse the public and put renewable energy in its place. Public sympathy for renewable energy is the greatest thorn in the side of these campaign leaders. Their campaign will only work out if the advocates of renewable energy let themselves be intimidated and become meek – or if they underestimate the possible effect of this campaign because its statements are so obviously untenable or because the renewable energy side falls short of taking the offensive in confronting such a negative campaign. The upshot would be that renewable energy would gradually lose public support. Conflicts are affected by opinions, and some unfounded opinions, no matter how grotesque they may be, are often more effective than facts. In the increasingly virtual world of mass communications, it is becoming easier rather than harder to make water look like liquid manure and liquid manure like water. Precisely because renewable energy is confronted by so many one-dimensional prejudices and reservations, the phalanx of preventers (with their psychological games of deliberate deception) plays a role that should not be underestimated. The impression should be solidified that it is not worth the money and effort to champion renewable energy. If the advocates of renewable energy neglect the struggle for opinion instead of focusing their arguments even more on this struggle, they run the danger of losing their most important leverage: support from the general public.

A 'movement' forged together out of so many hair-raising assertions and differently motivated resentments is ultimately bound to fall apart. Only no one knows just when – and how much additional valuable time will have been lost by then. What matters is publicly encapsulating whatever is hiding behind all the noise: the conflict between holding fast to the traditional energy system and using energy that is produced on a renewable foundation – a conflict between two different energy structures and cultures. The more clearly the problem is labelled, the sooner every individual, but also every political organization and every business, is forced to decide what goal each wants to stand for.

The conflict about renewable energy is culminating in a conflict of values. How are today's elites, in their old age, going to tell their grandchildren that they unfortunately had to hazard the consequences of every predictable energy debacle because the shift to renewable energy was too arduous, the sight of wind turbines too unbearable, and a few temporary cents' worth of higher energy costs too unreasonable? How can they claim generational solidarity in order to finance their retirement funds if today they are behaving egoistically as a generation and fending off, delaying or simply acting indifferently towards initiatives to give society a new energy foundation?

How stable a society's value system is, and how many people still orient themselves towards humane values, first becomes apparent in an existential crisis. It is in a crisis that opinions part ways, and lambs can become beasts of prey, though beasts of prey hardly ever turn into lambs. The later it becomes apparent how great the crisis potential of today's energy system is, the smaller are the opportunities to forestall the crises. The time for an energy shift is now. Today's generation needs to introduce this shift irreversibly. To this end it will have rethink its old one-dimensional notions.

References

1 Herbert Marcuse, *One-Dimensional Man* (London: Routledge & Kegan Paul, 1964), p182 et seq

2 Uwe Pörksen, *Plastikwörter: Die Sprache einer internationalen Diktatur* (Stuttgart: Klett-Cotta, 1988), p13 et seq

3 Jean-Marie Harribey, 'Das Gerede von der Nachhaltigkeit' in *Le Monde Diplomatique*, German edition (*die tageszeitung, WOZ DIE WOCHENZEITUNG*), 10 July 2004

4 Eike Schwarz, 'Dezentrale Energieversorgung und Versorgungssicherheit im neuen Energiewirtschaftsgesetz', *Solarzeitalter* 1/2005, p12

5 A. de Moor, 'Towards a grand deal in subsidies and climate change', *Journal of the Natural Resource Forum*, May 2001

6 Donald Losman, 'Economic security: A national security folly?', *Policy Analysis* 401/2001, available at www.cato.org/pubs/pas/pa409.pdf

7 Council of the European Union, *A Secure Europe in a Better World: European Security Strategy* (Brussels, 12 December 2003, available at http://ue.eu.int/uedocs/cmsUpload/78367.pdf)

8 Timothy J. Brennan, *A Shock to the System: Restructuring America's Electricity Industry* (Washington, DC: Resources for the Future, 1996)

9 Sharon Beder, *Power Play: The Fight to Control the World's Electricity* (New York: New Press, 2003), p325 et seq

10 Paul Krugman, 'In broad daylight', *New York Times*, 27 September 2002; Woodrow W. Clarke and Ted Bradshaw, *Agile Energy Systems: Global Lessons from the California Energy Crisis* (Amsterdam: Elsevier, 2004)

11 Franz Oppenheimer, *Theorie reiner und politischen Ökonomie*, 4th ed. (Berlin: de Gruyter, 1919), p558 et seq

12 Wilhelm Röpke, *Jenseits von Angebot und Nachfrage*, 3rd ed. (Zurich: E. Rentsch, 1961), p145 et seq; English edition *A Humane Economy* (Wilmington, DE: ISI Books, 1998), p90 et seq

13 Robert Kagan, *Macht und Ohnmacht: Amerika und Europa in der neuen Weltordnung* (Berlin: Siedler, 2003), p45

14 George F. Kennan, *The Nuclear Delusion* (New York: Pantheon Books, 1982), p180

15 United Nations, *Johannesburg Declaration on Sustainable Development*, adopted by the World Summit on Sustainable Development, 2–4 September 2002, available at www.un.org/esa/sustdev/documents/ WSSD_POI_PD/English/POI_PD.htm

16 David Hales (facilitator), 'Conclusions of the multi-stakehodler dialogue', Renewables 2004 conference, Bonn, 1–4 June 2004, available at www.renewables2004.de/pdf/msd_en.pdf

17 International Parliamentary Forum on Renewable Energies, 'The challenge of the 21st century', Bonn, 2 June 2004 (Berlin, Deutscher Bundestag)

18 Hans-Joachim Luhmann, 'Absehbares Ergebnis der Kyoto-Periode: Die Industrienationen werden mit ihren Emissionen bis 2010 um 10 Prozent zulegen, die Welt um 50 Prozent' (jochen.luhmann@wuppertalinst.org); Sekretariat der Klimarahmenkonvention (Secretariat of Framework Convention on Climate Change), Cf. FCCC/CPI 2004/INF. 2, from 19 October 2004; see, too, Fritz Vorholz, 'Das Symbol von Kyoto', *Die Zeit* 7/2005

19 Sharon Beder, *Global Spin: The Corporate Assault on Environmentalism* (White River Junction, Vermont, 2002), p91 et seq

20 Wilhelm Röpke (see Ref. 12)

21 Umweltbundesamt (ed.), *Umweltverträglichkeit kleiner Wasserkraftwerke. Zielkonflikte zwischen Klima- und Gewässerschutz: Texte* 13/98, January 2005, p139 et seq

22 Amitai Etzioni, *The Active Society* (London/New York: Collier/Macmillan, 1968), p120

23 Hans-Christoph Binswanger, 'Die verlorene Unschuld der Windenergie' in *Blätter für deutsche und internationale Politik* 10/1997, p1272 et seq

24 Klaus Bosselmann, *Im Namen der Natur* (Bern: Scherz, 1992), p374

25 Thomas S. Kuhn, *Die Struktur wissenschaftlicher Revolutionen* (Frankfurt: Suhrkamp Verlag, 1967), p209

26 'NGO im Förderbiotop', *Wirtschaftswoche* 6/2004

27 Jean Ziegler, *Die neuen Herrscher der Welt und ihre globalen Widersacher* (Munich: Bertelsmann, 2002), p170

28 Arundhati Roy, 'Tide? Or ivory snow? Public power in the age of empire', transcript of full speech by Arundhati Roy in San Francisco, California on 16 August 2004, www.democracynow.org/static/Arundhati_Trans.shtml

29 Irm Pontenagel, 'Sand oder Öl im Getriebe?', *Solarzeitalter* 2/2004, p32 et seq

30 Judith Richter, 'Engineering of consent: Uncovering corporate PR strategies', *Corner House Briefing No. 6*, (August 2002)

31 Peter Schwartz and Doug Randall, *An Abrupt Climate Change Scenario and its Implications for United States National Security* (Washington DC, Pentagon, 2003)

32 Arthur Koestler, *Die Armut der Psychologie* (Bern: Scherz Verlag, 1980), p313 et seq and 47 et seq

33 Peter Sloterdijk in *Wieviel Katastrophe braucht der Mensch?* Ed. by editorial staff of *Psychologie heute* (Weinheim: Beltz, 1987), p51 et seq

34 'Die große Luftnummer', *Der Spiegel*, 29 March 2004

35 Ben-Alexander Bohnke, *Abschied von der Natur* (Düsseldorf: Metropolitan, 1997)

36 Dirk Maxeiner and Michael Miersch, *Lexikon der Öko-Irrtümer* (Munich: Piper, 2000); idem, *Das Mephisto-Prinzip: Warum es besser ist, nicht gut zu sein* (Munich: Heyne, 2003); idem, *Die Zukunft und ihre Feinde: Wie Fortschrittspessimisten unsere Gesellschaft lähmen* (Frankfurt: Eichborn, 2002)

37 Bjørn Lomborg, *The Skeptical Environmentalist: Measuring the Real State of the World* (Cambridge: Cambridge University Press, 2001)

38 George F. Kennan (see Ref. 14), p17

39 George F. Kennan (see Ref. 14), p180

40 Stefan Dietrich, 'Vor dem Erwachen', *FAZ*, 17 September 2004, Wienand von Petersdorff, 'Luftnummern mit Windrädern', *FAZ*, 7 March 2004 and 4 June 2005

41 *Der Spiegel*, 24 January 2005

42 *Capital*, 2 September 2004

Part III

Energy Autonomy: The Archimedean Point of the Breakthrough to Renewable Energy

It is impossible to achieve a comprehensive and timely break-through to renewable energy with the one-dimensional conceptual approaches described above, with the plans derived from them, and with supporters who calibrate their every move based on this kind of thinking. The established system is keeping renewable energy detained in a prison, with a bit of freewheeling activity allowed if need be. The mere fact that these plans are endorsed by a dazzling majority of actors from the economic and energy policy fields, including players from the energy and environmental science policy-advising business, is no reason to be impressed by them. The only majorities that should command respect are practical decisions arrived at democratically, and even these do not constitute a definitive 'popular will' that one dare not call into question in order to bring about other decisions. To turn majority opinions into the standard for analysing problems and developing strategies is just opportunistic herd behaviour. To let oneself be guided this way is naive and unimaginative. To expect anything more substantial in the future from the complacent advocates of one-dimensional approaches is to indulge in an act of blind faith. These narrow-minded cheer-leaders render homage to a superficial realism that never thinks beyond given constellations, a realism that is going to have the foundation pulled out from under it by future energy crises. In order to achieve a breakthrough to renewable energy, it is imperative not to let oneself be shut in any longer by these 'prison wardens' of the current system, these jailors who have put all of society under 'thought arrest'.

Yet all too many people are afraid of leaving this prison. The one-dimensional 'schools of thought' guiding the conduct of energy policy and the energy business impart a superficial sense of safety to their disciples. Whoever breaks away has to deal with his freedom. In her book *Critique Abandoned*, the US journalist Marcia Pally discusses the conflict people experience between their self that is 'incapable of breaking away' and their 'integrated self'. They need 'to establish a balance between breaking away and integration in order to keep neurotic anxieties in check'.[1] Who is it, then, whose job can and must be making the breakthrough to renewable energy? Who will do this, given that the number of actors thus far has been too small, and given that too many people have been shifting their own responsibility for this onto others? This is a situation captured nicely in that little story about 'Everybody', 'Somebody', and 'Nobody':

> *There is an important job to be done,*
> *and Everybody expects that Somebody would do it.*
> *Anybody could do it, but Nobody did it.*
> *Somebody gets angry about that because it is Everybody's job.*
> *Everybody thinks that Anybody should do it,*
> *but Nobody realizes that Everybody would not do it.*
> *It ends up that Everybody blames Somebody*
> *when Nobody does what Anybody has to do.*

What are the values and interests, and what are the material and intangible incentives that might motivate people to undertake initiatives on behalf of renewable energy – within whatever range for manoeuvre they have (or might be able to develop)? What pathways are open, and which roads are hopelessly booby-trapped with landmines or blocked by highwaymen lying in wait? Which initiatives can the different actors seize on their own, and which are dependent on others? These are questions addressed to a societal potential, a potential that needs to be activated. In his work *Community and Society*, the sociologist Ferdinand Tönnies identified some conditions and maxims for taking action this way:

> *The acquired knowledge of how a thing has to be done is thus the decisive condition, and it is presupposed that everybody can easily and automatically carry out the actions which are the application of such knowledge. The general human facilities are adequate: Nothing is required but what a human being can do provided he wants to.*[2]

The opportunities afforded by renewable energy are so multi-faceted that there is no single master plan allowing all the steps to be coordinated, and the number of sponsors is certainly not limited to just a manageable few, as is the case with the traditional energy system. And yet not just any approach among the many that are available will do. Not all roads lead to Rome. Imprudent steps can lead, in spite of the greatest possible exertions, into a labyrinth of dead ends. A rapid and broad-based breakthrough to renewable energy can only take place if its multi-faceted technological potential can be utilized without restrictions by a growing number of sponsors throughout society. The upshot will be a 'spring tide' of practical initiatives that is bound to upset all the energy plans and scenarios previously concocted by the major players.

'Thoughts without content are empty, intuitions without concepts are blind.' This statement by the philosopher Immanuel Kant says that concepts do more than just describe actual content; they are also meant to function as a guide to thought. The guiding concept of energy autonomy means that the goal must be to make energy available in a way that is self-determined, not heteronomous; energy must be free and independent of external constraints, free of opportunities for blackmail and outside intervention, used according to decision-making criteria of one's own. In the long run, all these dimensions of energy autonomy are possible only if renewable energy is used. The autonomous acquisition of renewable energy by a variety of actors is the only method promising success, the only way to make sure that the energy shift we need is carried out in a timely and irreversible fashion against the functional logic of the traditional energy system. This path to a breakthrough for renewable energy leads to a uniformly new structure of energy usage, which can only come into being alongside the current structure – and which replaces the latter, step by step, until it finally makes the old system superfluous. Energy autonomy should not be understood in some dogmatically narrow way; instead, it describes a variety of multi-layered plans, many of them individual or social, political or economic, local or national. It is all about setting in motion a process of constantly intensifying the degree of autonomy in the provision of energy, a process leading from partial to outright autonomy, depending on prevailing opportunities and needs.

The counter-plan to energy autonomy would be to integrate renewable energy into the existing energy supply system in order to contain it and keep it under control. This kind of integration corresponds to what the Italian political thinker Antonio Gramsci called 'passive revolution': an existing system confesses to its lapses in dealing with some generally relevant problem, accepts criticism, and thanks those who pointed out the error and took umbrage, but then the establishment declares itself to be the only entity competent to implement things from now on; then it interprets the problem according to its own rules and implements only non-essential changes.

'Give me a place to stand, and I will move the Earth.' This statement by Archimedes, the brilliant ancient Greek mathematician, does not refer to some superior mover of the globe who has masterminded all the world's skills. Rather, it is way of saying that the most important thing about any reorientation is always to recognize where its linchpin is located. There are many such Archimedean points for renewable energy. Orientation towards the leitmotif of energy autonomy is not just some ideal, not an ideological concept that ignores the imperatives of economic action.

Energy autonomy's unique economic opportunities ensue from the techno-logic of renewable energy demonstrated above. By linking energy production and usage locally or regionally, it is possible to avoid the complex technical, organizational, administrative and political (including military) costs that both nuclear and fossil energy make unavoidable as they take their lengthy trip from production to final consumption. Unique opportunities for motivating society result from the socio-logic of renewable energy. Renewable energy facilitates an independent way of life that corresponds best to human needs for individual and social self-determination and, thereby, to the 'programme' of liberal democratic societies. Realistic opportunities for implementation ensue from the structural logic of processes of change. The less each new approach is integrated into existing structures, the better its chances for rapid implementation. But above all, and more than anything else, energy autonomy serves the goal of maintaining and regaining a self-determined and secure livelihood both for the individual and for entire societies.

Active evolution

Today the world is teeming with 'revolutions' that are constantly being proclaimed to the point where they are indistinguishable from sensational product marketing, and every little change in the law is quickly pronounced a 'reform'. Both of these 'r' words have been worn out so much by overuse that they are hardly suited any longer to describe methods for achieving a truly fundamental transformation. The concept 'revolution' originally means an overthrow of prevailing conditions within a short period of time. 'Reform', by contrast, is the step-by-step alteration of a system.

The call for a 'solar revolution' adorns many a book title, and 'energy reforms' are constantly being urged. But both concepts, in their original meanings, are not suited to describing the historically imperative process of transformation leading to renewable energy. Modern society is so closely interwoven with the structures of the conventional energy system that it has become incapable of revolution against that system. No society can risk letting all the wheels grind to a halt, even for a moment. But the reform concept is also misleading because it rests on the assumption that the conventional energy system is reformable in principle. But that system is incapable of reform with respect to renewable energy – at least if we are serious about introducing renewable energy in more than a sluggish and fragmentary way. The system is capable only of blocking a thoroughgoing orientation to renewable energy, because such a reorientation would be tantamount to instigating its own self-dissolution. But above all, even today, the old system is no longer needed for many different uses of renewable energy. As these different uses and their technological optimization are broadened – especially by including energy storage technologies – the old system will be needed less and less, and ultimately it will even become completely superfluous.

Thus, the shift to renewable energy cannot take place along a revolutionary path, nor will this transformation happen through attempts at reforming the existing energy system. The established energy system will only lose its all-encompassing role for energy supply when there is an autonomous mobilization of renewable energy from a variety of starting points. We are dealing with an evolutionary process of vital growth in new forms of energy production, a process that accompanies the withering away of nuclear and fossil energy. However, we dare not count on any kind of 'natural' evolution that will only catch on once today's energy business has exhausted itself. This process would take too long and prove extremely perilous. What is needed is an active evolution that is deliberately propelled forward – with plans that dare not be subordinated, ancillary or ceded to conventional energy supply. Only for sub-areas of renewable energy is a specialized energy business needed. Specialization is required least of all for heating and cooling needs in buildings, because the trend for this kind of energy is to make demand capable of being satisfied completely without commercial energy delivery. Electricity consumption will take place partly through self-production, and partly through supply structures in predominantly regionalized feedback cycles. The fuel economy for transport operators will become decentralized and, proceeding from a variety of appropriate renewable energies, diversified in its resource base.

This process of conventional energy's structural displacement inevitably means a situation of sustained conflict. To attempt to achieve this displacement by seeking a consensus with the power centres of the energy business would mean leaving the potential of renewable energy unfulfilled; it would also mean holding up developments artificially. Any advocates of renewable energy who are betting on being integrated into the energy business can count on 'having the hand they hold out to shake be cut off', as an Arab proverb goes (with, at best, a little finger left).

The consensus negotiated in Germany between the Red–Green coalition government (1998–2005) and the electricity corporations to end nuclear energy only *seems* to contradict this assertion. That agreement conceded lengthy residual run-times to the electricity corporations so that they might be able to continue operating their atomic power plants well beyond the write-off periods for their investments. Their existence is not endangered in any way by this compromise, especially since they were tacitly offered compensation: government held off from putting a stop to the process of concentration in the energy business. From the outset, furthermore, the electricity corporations were counting on a change of government well in advance of their deadline for shutting down most of their nuclear power plants; a new government, they reasoned, would abrogate the withdrawal from nuclear energy.

For decades on end, the established energy business was able to make its decisions without adversaries or business competitors. Opposition first appeared in the form of an environmentally critical public – although that opposition was initially unable to relate the implementation of its demands to other economic sponsors. The only options left open to opponents of the established energy business were to block particularly problematic decisions, to demand stronger controls, and to restrict the energy business's room for manoeuvre. Only when investment decisions for renewable energy are made independently of the energy business will there be serious economic competition that can facilitate disengagement from the existing energy juggernaut. Autonomous investors in renewable energy should not have to ask if their investments are compatible with long-term contractual relations for the production and delivery of fossil raw materials and with investment plans for power plants, refineries and transport infrastructure. The more investment there is in renewable energy (and the more direct these investments are), the sooner the role of the conventional energy business will shrink.

The energy business will find it rather easy to get over the first five percentage points of market share that renewable energy takes away from it. Should the share rise to 10 or 20 per cent, the energy business will get caught in the maelstrom of simultaneous volume degression and cost progression. Panic will erupt – as is already the case in Germany – leading to different reactions: pressure on governments to end the 'irresponsible' goings-on; public campaigns blaming the growing cost of conventional energy supply on renewable energy; entrepreneurial diversification into other branches of the economy, but also (albeit it hardly as the option with the highest priority) getting into renewable energy on the part of the conventional energy business itself. If major energy corporations try the latter, they will logically tend to opt for forms of supply with which they can continue using their infrastructure to capacity and salvage their existing supply monopoly.

Instead of buckling under, governments and parliaments need to press ahead all the more forcefully with renewable energy and abandon their traditional deference to the energy business for the sake of society's overall welfare. Instead of entrusting society's basic provision of energy in highly negligent fashion to the internationalized 'energy market', the supply of energy can and must be delivered over to society, and to society's countless sponsors who can be activated to this end. It is a matter of society 'regaining power over power', as the philosopher Lothar Schäfer has put it in his book about the 'Bacon Project'.[3]

In the course of this process, sales will drop and the established energy corporations will fall below their threshold of profitability. Through major mergers creating mammoth conglomerates, they will try to postpone this day of reckoning for their bottom line. For soon after there begins a descent driving them either towards new strategies or into bankruptcy. Many local and municipal energy corporations, by contrast, will blossom if they convert to renewable energy using a decentralized supply. If it initially takes perhaps 15 years until renewable energy covers 10 per cent of energy needs, in the following 15 years it will be perhaps as much as 30 per cent and then already

90 per cent over the ensuing period. With each increase in the share of renewable energy, the pace of its spread will also be growing. Since the established energy business can now hardly afford to avoid renewable energy in any fundamental way, it must at least try everything within its power to prevent renewable energy from developing in a way that it cannot control. It might try taking over businesses that produce renewable energy technology. Or it might try using political connections to ensure that the only kind of new measures allowed will be ones facilitating the introduction of renewable energy (including decentralized combined heat and power still using fossil energy) in small portions that can be coordinated with the energy business. Following years of denial, this would be an attempt at integrating renewable energy into the structures of the energy business in small doses.

Autonomy instead of integration

Successful programmes for introducing renewable energy can be attributed either to autonomously initiated political strategies or to those strategies that have created a platform for autonomous action by investors. By contrast, all plans oriented towards integration into the energy business have either remained unsuccessful or are just marking time after they first get started; they amount to a de facto recognition of precedence for energy supply structures tailored to traditional energy.

The evidence proving the success of those strategies that exploit political autonomy and promote autonomous economic initiatives is striking. The handful of countries that have set out on the road to renewable energy independently of trends in international negotiations have accomplished more, both qualitatively and quantitatively, than all those efforts at political action that were integrated into international approaches. And it is no accident that most cities decided on their own to start the first path-breaking initiatives, since cities are not as tightly integrated into the 'political–energy business complex' as national governments are. It is noteworthy that there is a large number of small towns or even counties – for example, in Germany or Austria –

that have either been aiming at 100 per cent energy autonomy for the areas served by their local and municipal governments or that have already reached this goal. Without the practice of 'cost-covering reimbursement' for feeding solar electricity into the network — a financial arrangement, initiated by the city of Aachen and kicked off by the local Solar Promotion Association (Solarförderverein) and the Association's driving force, Wolf von Fabeck, that had been introduced into more than 30 German cities during the 1990s — there would have been no industrial foundation for the federal government's 1999 '100,000 Roofs Programme' and the associated massive increase in statutory reimbursement for solar electricity by the Renewable Energy Sources Act in 2000. Local government initiatives can, therefore, clear a pathway for more general legislation. If the cities and towns that are at the forefront of this solar transformation had earlier sought advice from scientific consultants who would have examined the projects according to their comparative costs as related to theoretical projects elsewhere, it is unlikely that a single one of these initiatives would have come about. Perhaps these local government projects were not always 'cost-efficient', but in exchange they certainly improved the quality of life and the social atmosphere in these municipalities, and they also created local or regional jobs.

The real entrepreneurial pioneers in the production of renewable energy technologies are, as a rule, newcomers and not traditional energy technology corporations, whose business relations with regular customers do not permit going it alone in any way out of the ordinary. Among operators of renewable energy facilities one finds a similar picture. Since the Renewable Energy Sources Act went into effect in Germany, over 95 per cent of investment was undertaken by private operators or municipal and local government energy companies. Although the electricity corporations constantly complain that the law guarantees risk-free investments with respectable profits for their renewable energy competitors, why haven't the traditional electricity companies jumped on this bandwagon themselves? Of all the wind power capacity installed worldwide in 2004, just 23 per cent (9750 of 42,400 megawatts) is in the hands of the larger electricity supply corporations.

The strategist looking for a breakthrough to renewable energy should therefore direct her or his attention towards three points:

- towards energy availability that is widely dispersed and independent, instead of concentration on particularly 'economical' international sites, for example, in the Earth's 'sun belt';
- towards political decentralization, instead of towards international institutions and 'market harmonization';
- towards stimulating autonomous investments, instead of towards investment planning by government and the energy business.

Independent availability instead of dependence

A precondition for independent energy availability is having the greatest possible proximity between where renewable energy is technically 'harvested' and where it is used. In other words, the orientation must be towards whatever natural potential is spatially closest. Renewable energy's technological development must therefore focus its priorities on those technical applications and utilization structures that work as independently as possible from the networked structures of traditional energy supply. Using renewable energy from remote sources is hardly possible without integration into the established supply system; it creates dependence. Integration means subordination to the decision-making criteria of third parties and abandoning the flexible advantages of renewable energy used in a decentralized way.

A significant example showing how quickly an autonomous technical system can be up and operating is road traffic, as contrasted with track-bound traffic. The car has a wider action radius and can be used more spontaneously than a track-bound vehicle dependent on a schedule. Hence the demand for cars grew rapidly along with sinking costs, technical refinements and improvements in travel comfort. This stimulated mass production and triggered a strong mutual reinforcement effect that was then reinforced further when government encouraged the use of cars by building public roads. The issue at hand here is not what the ecological or economic trade-off between road and rail traffic is or ought to be; rather, the point is to illustrate the conditions that facilitate rapid technological breakthrough. With the car, as a rule, the equipment operator and the user are identical. With rail traffic, the vehicle operator and the user are separate, and both have less flexibility because the track network is and cannot be as widely branched out as the street network. With network-bound electricity supply in industrial countries, there is admittedly an almost ubiquitous opportunity for utilization because the electri-city network is even more widely branched out than the street network. There is, however, significantly less flexibility for the operators of electricity production equipment. The production equipment operators need to subordinate themselves to the interests of the electricity network's operators; indeed, their subordination increases with the amount of electricity that is supposed to be transported and distributed through the network. Consequently, the dynamic whereby renewable energy might catch on in the field of electricity production is stronger the less that electricity production is dependent on these kinds of restrictions.

An even more significant example of the dynamic whereby new technological systems can be more easily introduced when they are unencumbered by network restrictions is that of information providers who are independent of a fixed-line (or 'land line') phone network. In contrast to wireless telecommunication, solar and wind power utilization operating with electricity storage batteries is even possible without using directional radio devices and technical satellites. For electricity using renewable energy, it is more important to orient plans for its technical development and market penetration around this model than to fixate on the functional and calculation criteria typical of traditional energy supply. It is because of this fixation that fantasy-like futuristic visions of the kind initially projected for information technologies — visions that were disseminated in countless books and periodicals, and which (to a large extent) were even fulfilled within surprisingly short time spans — have not (so far) cropped up in discussions about the future of energy.

The 'network-conservative' imbalance in these discussions has led to ignoring or neglecting those technological and political approaches with which network restrictions might be overcome. Technological instruments to this end are either electricity production plants capable of being operated autonomously, and in which the producer is simultaneously the user, or facilities that can adjust their production to network requirements. This way plants can become independent of the need to coordinate their own production with other producers (as well as with customers at any given time) in a way they cannot control – to become independent of the 'network management'.

The political instrument to be used here is establishing a priority – limited neither by time nor by quantity – for purchasing electricity from renewable energy through network operators at reimbursements that cover production costs and facilitate an adequate entrepreneurial profit. The technical limit for such a priority principle is only reached when more electricity is produced from renewable energy than is in demand. Such political priority regulations impose an imperative on the electricity supply system to orient (in other words, to adjust) its operating capacity around renewable energy. Instead of continuing to shackle renewable energy to the economic past, the electricity business is compelled to adjust to renewable energy. Then it will no longer be the case that renewable energy is regarded as an 'additive energy'. Instead, that designation will apply to conventional energy – for as long as it is still needed and used.

This process of detachment becomes technically easier the greater the diversity in the supply of renewable energy types that reciprocally complement each other, and the more that it becomes possible for renewable energy to make independent adjustments in electricity production from solar radiation and wind power in line with demand fluctuations and using renewable energy's own storage capacities. This will reduce those conflicts over renewable energy that are based on actual technical difficulties. The smaller the technically determined need for integration, the larger the political room for manoeuvre at the level of local and national government – and the greater the leeway for autonomous investment decisions. But the fundamental economic conflict of interest between potentially countless suppliers and users of renewable energy, on the one hand, and today's major energy suppliers, on the other hand, will not be abolished thereby. It is, however, a conflict that is more easily carried out the more technological autonomy there is. The larger this is, the more attractive and unassailable renewable energy's breakthrough becomes.

Political decentralization instead of globalization

At best, integration means participation, though by no means is it the same as self-determination. That also applies to the role of political institutions in the current energy system. This system is – with the exception of a few countries that have their own fossil energy or uranium deposits and major water power capabilities – dependent on properly functioning international cooperation in order to import primary energy. The energy business needs government in order to secure these imports, and governments needs the energy business, so long as the resource base remains conventional, in order to provide society with energy – a relationship of mutual dependence and participation (or co-determination). The autonomously available potential of renewable energy, by contrast, can be activated without having to consult primary energy suppliers. It is a potential that promotes independence from the need to cooperate with other states, who are also not damaged thereby – except, perhaps, for those states that have made themselves dependent, for better or worse, on the export of fossil energy resources. For the community of states as a whole, it is helpful every time renewable energy is introduced into any single country, because this helps defuse those global nuclear/fossil crises that ultimately affect everyone. That is why exploiting and expanding every country's role in support of renewable energy give us a philosophy of action that is generally desirable. The political integration approach, by contrast, offers the forces of retardation opportunities for participation where self-determination, not co-determination, is really in everyone's interest. The principle of political energy autonomy, therefore, is this: as much international regulation as necessary, as much decentralized politics as possible.

Applied to energy policy, this means strategies for local and regional government are needed that do not require waiting and settling for national strategies involving all levels of government; also needed are single-state strategies that do not require waiting for international agreements, leaving everything to the fulfilment of painstakingly negotiated objectives, and depriving one's own country of the freedom to choose strategic tools of action. The international approach is, as outlined earlier, inevitably 'paraplegic' because it needs to integrate governments that are obliging along with those that try to block initiatives, and because it needs to include too many different interests (both justified and unjustified). It cannot be expected that traditional one-sided thinking about energy and the tight-knit network of interests linked to the conventional energy business will be discarded and cut through everywhere and at the same time. Even with the best of intentions on the part of all involved, it is impossible to integrate into a single international set of roles either the motives for reorientation to renewable energy or the variety of approaches to action that are possible and necessary (each related to the specific conditions of a city, region, or state). 'Global environmental policy', according to Udo Ernst Simonis, is necessary, but not in the form of a single 'global governance' that replaces or truncates varied action by individual states. International laws, once they have been passed after lengthy and compromise-laden efforts, are like concrete. It requires just as much time and willingness for compromise to change them once they have proven to be misleading. To this end, 51 per cent majorities are insufficient. In his book *Demokratie im Zeitalter der Globalisierung* (Democracy in the Age of Globalization), philosopher Otfried Höffe admonished those looking at the whole process of political internationalization:

> to watch strictly that what has already been achieved is not put at risk anywhere. Democracy in any single country should not be jeopardized during the construction of a supra-regional union, nor should that union's democratic standards be jeopardized during the creation of a world republic.[4]

Political institutions, as a rule, have two roles relating to what they are meant to uphold. One role consists in using government's organizational power to undertake initiatives through public investments, aid programmes from its budget, research financing or training measures. The other consists in its function as a legislator, either restricting societal activities or expanding and privileging the scope for developing such activities. From the standpoint of realistic politics, the constructive contribution that international political institutions and conferences of treaty states can make towards the shift to renewable energy should reside in:

- carrying out initiatives on their own whenever they have an organizational capacity of their own; and
- abolishing existing international forms of discrimination against renewable energy in order to expand governments' autonomous scope for implementing policy and dismantle international barriers against renewable energy and energy efficiency technologies.

The constructive contribution of international institutions cannot and should not consist of taking the place of legislation by individual states, for example through attempts at international 'harmonizing' of policy tools. Internationally, it should be possible to agree on minimum goals in order to put pressure on the community of states, but implementation should be left up to individual states. When governments call for some kind of international consonance fixed by treaty, what they are really doing, as previously shown, is shirking their own practical responsibility.

The constructive tasks of international institutions

Admonishing international political institutions in a very specific way about taking their own official duties seriously, while openly reclaiming self-reliance, helps lead public discussion out of the billowy fog in which people typically just engage in finger-pointing about how other people should take charge. If it should emerge, however, that existing institutions cannot pull themselves together to do the job, then new problem-conscious groups of states will have to take charge and launch new international organizations on behalf of initiatives that each one of these states, acting on its own, cannot adequately manage. One high-priority job for UN organizations and the European Union – each in its capacity as an institution with some non-delegable responsibility for the shift to renewable energy – must be to overcome the flagrant disparities described in Part II: while international government organizations like the IAEA, EURATOM and the IEA act de facto as agents for the world-wide nuclear business and fossil energy business, there is no International Agency for Renewable Energy. The optimal approach would be for the different UN organizations and institutions – United Nations Educational, Scientifc and Cultural Organization (UNESCO), Food and Agricultural Organization of the United Nations (FAO), United Nations Industrial Development Organization (UNIDO), United Nations Development Programme (UNDP), United Nations Environment Programme (UNEP), World Health Organization (WHO) – to jointly establish such an agency, which would coordinate relevant activities and simultaneously render 'help for self-help'. Since UN organizations have let this disparity rest, however, it is urgent that a group of states take the initiative on behalf of such an agency. In the absence of such an initiative, voting for international action programmes on renewable energy remains nothing more than shallow chatter.

The World Bank and other inter-governmental development banks must ultimately be confronted with the demand to expand their energy credit portfolios and concentrate on the shift to renewable energy, just as the World Bank itself demanded in its 2004 'Industries Extractive Report' under the direction of former Indonesian Environment Minister Emil Salim – a report that has yet to have any follow-up. Since there is hardly any likelihood, however, that the World Bank would comply with such a request, it may be necessary to establish an 'International Bank for Renewable Energy and Energy Efficiency' like the one that Michael Eckart, president of the American Council on Renewable Energy (ACORE), proposed as part of his 'Solar Bank' programme. This could be established by a group of states or by a group of national development banks. Its main job would be the global organization of micro-credits for renewable energy, as has been practised in an exemplary and successful way by such institutions as the Grameen Shakti-Bank in Bangladesh, a subsidiary of the Grameen Bank.

The FAO at the UN had already thought about a 'Global Afforestation Action Programme' in the 1990s, although this programme never got beyond isolated activities. Large-scale afforestation would facilitate much greater 'CO_2 reductions' than are envisioned in the Kyoto Protocol – and at extremely low costs. This way, CO_2 could be retrieved from the atmosphere on a large scale and absorbed into biomass.[5] Collateral assistance for building agricultural forest economies could establish numerous new businesses in developing countries. The biomass potential cultivated worldwide would thereby be significantly amplified, which would ease the replacement of fossil fuels. Such an afforestation programme, including efforts to re-green semi-arid expanses, can potentially encompass several million square kilometres. The FAO is also the world organization that is best suited to carrying out the necessary certification of energetically utilized biomass, so as to guarantee that no more natural resources are extracted than are re-cultivated and that no tropical woods are deforested in order to build bio-energy plantations. The organization would have to spread the word about plans for cultivating and utilizing the wide variety of plant life that comes into question (vegetation that goes well beyond foodstuff plants) to agricultural schools and federations worldwide, and it would also have to implement training programmes.

The International Organization for Standardization (ISO), perhaps together with UNIDO, is as good as predestined to develop industrial norms and standards for renewable energy and efficiency technologies in order to overcome obstacles to technological transfer. The opportunities are even greater when it comes to technologies that are still young, before large competing industrial interests operating within different systems of standards and norms have had the chance to line up and get in the way.

UNESCO is likewise cut out for worldwide training campaigns about the use, exploration and advancement of renewable energy. The knowledge deficit about renewable energy at universities is dramatically large worldwide. Without a rapidly growing reservoir of trained technicians, this energy potential cannot be exploited, especially because of the large number of facilities that renewable energy requires. UNESCO would be the most suitable sponsor for the Open University for Renewable Energies (OPURE) that was proposed by EUROSOLAR and the World Council for Renewable Energy as a university network. So far, admittedly, UNESCO has not done an adequate job promoting scientific scholarship and education for renewable energy.

The UNDP, the world community's development organization, is virtually predestined to have its own projects assume a leading role for the three most important focal points of development – renewable energy, water and rural space – and to do this in a context that is comprehensive. It is still a long way from setting these priorities – further away than it already was during the tenure of its energy director Thomas Johannson between 1993 and 2001. UNEP has been pursuing these three emphases under its executive director Klaus Töpfer, but he lacks the institutional capacity for the practical implementation of these kinds of programmes.

Still, and in spite of everything, the critical importance of renewable energy for taking care of these responsibilities has not been sufficiently recognized in most of these organizations. Somehow, all the institutions are preoccupied with these tasks, and yet – with the exception of UNEP (which, however, is not an independent organization, in contrast to the others named here) – it is not a priority for any single institution; for most, it is incidental. These organizations need to be publicly challenged about this. And if they have thought of a programme, as the FAO did with its proposal for global afforestation, they lack the financial means to realize it. To give these organizations the funds they need to achieve their aims should be the task of governments and (equally important) of treaty conferences.

Dismantling the privileges for nuclear and fossil energy
in the international legal system

There are three treaty state conferences in particular that, along
with the EU, exert influence on initiatives for renewable energy
– the world climate conferences, the WTO conferences and the
verification conferences for the Nuclear Non-Proliferation
Treaty. What needs to be attempted at each one of these international levels is the systematic dismantling of the ways nuclear
and fossil energy are promoted; these forms of promotion
continually consolidate and extend the standing of nuclear and
fossil energy vis-à-vis renewable energy, and indirectly they block
the development of renewable energy. The fact that the issues
associated with these privileges have not even been broached by
the apologists of liberalized energy markets reveals either a lack
of knowledge about current market distortions or sanctimo-
niousness about the way they are discussed. But it also reveals
what consequences ensue from the absence of an international
institution for renewable energy.

A new task for world climate conferences

For the treaty state conference on global climate protection, this
means completely changing its agenda; instead of continuing to
haggle over improvements-for-the-worse in complicated worldwide accounting plans for dealing with climate-threatening
emissions, the conference should leave such plans to those states
that want to abide by them until they recognize their narrow
marginal utility. The attempt to broaden these accounting plans
in a 'Kyoto II' Protocol, which would turn the treaty into a kind
of 'Energy WTO', should be shelved before it fails after endless
years of negotiation or before it results in a dismal outcome –
while the current Protocol, in the interim, is being misused in
many countries as a way of containing dissenting initiatives to
implement renewable energy.

Thus far the treaty state conference on global climate protection has woefully neglected the most important factor among
growing climate dangers, the transportation sector. But this is
precisely where the conference faces a challenge, albeit a
challenge to come up with a truly effective political approach.

Its new focus has to be on ending the unspeakable worldwide practice of tax exemption for fossil aircraft fuels. This tax exemption contributes substantially towards the rapid growth of air traffic – from cheap flights to the shipping of fruit from New Zealand – which has especially grave consequences for the climate. Worldwide tax-exemption for fossil fuels used in ships should also be on the table, and not just because of growing ocean pollution, but also because of direct and – via the impact on oceanic ecology – indirect climate effects that are negative. In this way, a new climate protocol would focus on international greenhouse gas emissions.

An approach like this is bound to run up against massive resistance. While some interests behind this resistance are unjustified, other concerns are legitimate. With respect to the latter, the plan for international taxation of fossil aircraft and ship fuels does open up some opportunities for flexible design, such as differentiating between transnational and domestic air and ship traffic; exceptions to taxing domestic traffic should be allowed if individual countries so choose. Such opportunities for exceptions would then mostly apply to large territorial lands or island states that are more dependent than other countries on air and ship transportation services. Developing countries whose economies are highly dependent on air tourism might also expect to be granted exemptions and special transitional regulations. Above all, though, it needs to be agreed that tax revenue for transnational transportation services should be directed, mostly or completely, into a global climate protection fund that could be administered by the Secretariat of the Climate Framework Convention.

Simply having aircraft fuel for transnational traffic taxed at the average level used for fuel taxes in the industrial countries would result in revenues of well over US$50 billion annually. If just half of this sum were to flow into the climate protection fund, this would solve the financing problems of UN organizations for the aforementioned tasks, such as the global afforestation programme of the FAO or for the credit portfolios of renewable energy investments. An international R&D programme to create new aircraft and ship transmission systems no longer driven by fossil fuels could also be financed this way.

Developing countries dependent on airline tourism could be provided with financial assistance to diversify their economies by developing other sectors.

A shift in strategy conceived this way would at least be the logical implication of the negative prognosis articulated here concerning the Kyoto Protocol (should that prediction be confirmed in practice). After all, in its guidelines on the application of this Protocol (effective 13 October 2003), the EU declared that emissions trading should be part of a comprehensive and coherent package of policies and measures accompanying 'regulatory, fiscal or other policies' of the member states 'that pursue the same objectives'. Any future 'review of the Directive should consider the extent to which these objectives have been attained'. This also means that the Kyoto Protocol would have to be measured by its outcomes in comparison with other measures. To avoid such a comparison (not least of all), these guidelines proclaim that these other measures have to be withdrawn from circulation.

An appropriate energy agenda for the WTO

Thus far, the WTO and the negotiations among its signatory states to continue developing the WTO treaties have aroused the impression that they have nothing to do with the global energy problem; by extension, this means that the WTO process is also failing to protect the very foundation for all future economic management. So far the WTO has done nothing to counter the absurd imbalance between the duty-free status enjoyed by primary fossil energy trading and the sometimes high tariffs imposed on trade in renewable energy and energy efficiency technologies. It should have seized the initiative to correct this discrepancy a long time ago, at least in order to implement duty-free status for the latter. This way, the WTO could contribute towards dismantling the preferential treatment that fossil energy now enjoys within the global economic system. At the very least, there would be a chance to overcome the Janus-headed nature of the world energy system, a duplicity that has thus far been allowed to stand unopposed.

In many countries, subsidizing nuclear and fossil energy,

which has led to the privileging of entire economic sectors, is something the WTO treats as an unalterable fact. By contrast, the WTO treaty would allow the organization to intervene against national programmes promoting bio-fuels if these are only applied to the country in question. This 'WTO cudgel' is constantly being swung, at least at the national level, in order to prevent such initiatives, independently of whether the WTO actually wants to wield it. Thus, the WTO treaties restrict the cultivation of oilseed in EU countries, even if they are not used for the food market but instead for fuel needs and climate protection. The WTO may even prohibit trade restrictions on agricultural products from cultivation methods that are extremely dangerous ecologically, which means that it can also ban limitations on those bio-energy forms that are based on ruthless deforestation. This kind of WTO intervention would reduce the ecological advantage of these kinds of energy to absurdity.

These absurd barriers within the WTO system need to be removed. The trade barriers frequently applied to energy technologies are just as anachronistic as the principle of unrestricted freedom of trade for energy. Both privilege the traditional energy system in spite of the deadly dangers to the world economy that are brewing inside that system, and both prevent pragmatic solutions in the interests of all involved. This is shown by the persistent conflict between industrial and developing countries over agricultural markets, for example, over sugar markets. The aim is a general opening of agricultural markets in the industrial countries, who in exchange would have to accept restrictions on their own agricultural production. But the latter clearly contradicts the urgent need to replace fossil with biogenic fuels. The conflict could be immediately solved in a completely different way; the industrial countries could stop their agricultural exports and the developing countries could dispense with their call for market liberalization if they were offered a technical assistance programme and interest-free credits to build up their own production of bio-ethanol or other bio-fuels — so that they could quickly replace their petroleum imports with fuels produced on their own. With a strategy to replace petroleum with bio-fuels, there would no longer be a problem of agricultural production surpluses. Above all, the macroeconomic advantage of this kind of domestic fuel production (and of the petroleum import substitution that goes along with it) is considerably greater for the developing countries than the agricultural exports increased thereby.

Stopping the privileging of nuclear energy in international law

Article IV of the Nuclear Non-Proliferation Treaty guarantees technical assistance for the utilization of nuclear energy to countries that renounce the production, acquisition and dissemination of atomic weapons. This makes nuclear energy the only energy option that the international legal system has an obligation to promote. This privilege is duplicated at the EU level through the EURATOM Treaty, which even goes hand in hand with billions of euros to promote and subsidize technologies for nuclear power plants, a subsidy regime to which the EU's internal market regulations have never applied. Article IV of the Non-Proliferation Treaty not only privileges nuclear energy; it also (de facto) indirectly facilitates clandestine preparations for nuclear weapons production. Hence there is an urgent need for corrective measures. Such counter-measures might happen – as in a plan already drafted by EUROSOLAR and the World Council for Renewable Energy – by seeing to it that Article IV's obligation to provide nuclear technology assistance is met instead by substituting technical assistance to build domestic facilities that produce renewable energy.

Within the EU, the EURATOM Treaty is clearly ripe for dissolution. It is a relic that mocks the EU's goals of dismantling subsidies and promoting a democratic order. Since not even the EU's Constitutional Convention has so much as touched EURATOM's special status, revoking memberships in the EURATOM Treaty is surely the only way to work towards its dissolution – though this is a step that not even Germany's Red–Green government dared to take during its two terms in office (1998–2005).

Open investment instead of investment controls

There are three political plans for introducing renewable energy, which may be distinguished from each other in terms of their impact:

- price regulation in the form of guaranteed purchase prices, tax increases for nuclear and fossil energy, or tax reductions for renewable energy that constitute an economic incentive for investments;
- volume regulations that – even if they contain economic incentives – only facilitate introducing renewable energy as allocated by quota;
- obligations to introduce renewable energy requiring either no incentives or just supplementary economic incentives. As a political plan of action, these should be considered at the very latest when utilizing renewable energy is reasonable for the obligated parties and when it seems socially warranted.

The mobilization of autonomous electricity production by way of price regulation: The example of the Renewable Energy Sources Act

The international prototype for strategies of price regulation in the sector activating network-linked electricity from renewable energy is Germany's Renewable Energy Sources Act (Erneuerbare-Energien-Gesetz). Its two core elements are, on the one hand, priority network access to electricity from renewable energy for every plant operator and, on the other hand, a legally established reimbursement for every kilowatt hour fed into the electricity grid. Reimbursements vary according to whether the electricity comes from the conversion of solar radiation energy, from wind or water power, from biomass, or from geothermal energy. And then there is a further differentiation of these reimbursements: for electricity from wind power plants, according to whether the current originates in regions with strong or weak winds, something that can be read from the output of the facilities employed; for solar and biomass electricity production, according to the size of the facility; and then, in the latter category, there is yet another differentiation, according to whether home-grown vegetable raw materials or simply organic waste products are employed. Already existing water power plants with a capacity of over 5 megawatts are excluded. Reimbursements are calculated according to the state of technology and the costs of individual options, and these reimbursements are guaranteed for a period of 20 years after going into operation (for water power plants with a capacity of up to 5 megawatts, the guarantee is 30 years long). There is a built-in automatic reimbursement degression for new facilities that are installed in whatever is the next year, and this initial reimbursement always applies to the next 20-year period. The reimbursement is paid by the network operators into whose network the electricity has been fed; the ensuing costs are offset among all the network operators, which means that electricity price increases are distributed evenly for all electricity customers in the entire territory.

In this way, no network operator is at a disadvantage if more electricity from renewable energy is fed into its network than is the case with other grids. The law creates a separate market framework for electricity production from renewable energy; it is a law that simultaneously authorizes technological, industrial and agricultural assistance, favours a broad-based income distribution, and serves the cause of climate protection. Above all, this law creates room for numerous new sponsors. It is true that the plans for introducing renewable energy using a price-regulated market employed by countries like Spain or (until 1989) Denmark have been different in detail from Germany's Renewable Energy Sources Act, but these other countries' plans build on comparable principles.

Volume regulation as a defensive instrument against renewable energy

In volume regulation plans, especially as they are practised in the UK, Italy or the US — also called quota and certificate trading, ROC (Renewable Obligation Certificate) or RPS (Renewable Energy Portfolio Standard) plans — governments define a certain share of renewable energy that every electricity supplier has to include in its electricity supply. Implementing the required volume happens either by way of bids, which private investors can compete for with their own production or through the purchase of certificates. In order to give investors greater security, they are now guaranteed a specific reimbursement in some countries. This is based on the experience that, for many years, there were not enough investors, or on the experience of suppliers being allocated premiums that, for the most part, they did not even come close to implementing – as in the UK, where the non-implementation rate came to two-thirds of the premiums. The advocates of these volume-regulated concepts assume that these plans, in contrast to laws like the EEG, would lead to an 'efficient allocation of resources', that they would give plant operators incentives for technical improvements and cost reductions, that the plans would be 'in conformity with the market' (especially for a transnational market), and that they would facilitate integration into international emissions rights trading. The most prominent case of a volume-regulated plan is the Kyoto Protocol itself. The critique of Kyoto expressed in Part II of this book has been decisively confirmed on the basis of experiences with a volume-regulated promotion of renewable energy: not one of the volume-regulated approach's advantages, as asserted in numerous scientific studies over and against the price-regulated strategy, has been confirmed in practice.

The German share of total installed wind capacity in the EU was 49 per cent in 2004, and the Spanish share 26 per cent. Average reimbursements in Germany are between 6.6 and 8.8 euro-cents per kilowatt hour, and in Spain 6.4 euro-cents. By contrast, the UK and Italy, both using volume regulation, have shares of only 2.2 and 1.9 per cent respectively in the EU, and the reimbursements paid are 9.6 and 13 euro-cents. In Germany, accordingly, installed wind power capacity is 20 times greater than in the UK, and this makes electricity on average two cents per kilowatt hour cheaper to produce, although wind conditions are comparatively more favourable in the UK! There is no indication that volume-regulated plans make for higher efficiency and productivity, or that they guarantee fulfilment of target volumes.

Fulfilling the quota inevitably takes place only by way of the financially most attractive options, preferably with wind power. Accordingly, power plants conglomerate at a few particularly windy sites. There is then hardly any opportunity to establish a spatial link between electricity production and demand, one of renewable energy's most important socio-cultural advantages. If one were to attempt abandoning this one-sided fixation within the framework of a quota-based implementation, however, one would have to undertake a volume-based division into wind, biomass, water power or photovoltaic portions, which bureaucratizes the system and increases certification costs. For every future increase in the total or partial volume to be integrated into the electricity market, an arduous tug-of-war with the suppliers of conventional energy may be expected. If certificate trading is conducted with prices fixed across the board, then either the reimbursements will be so low that hardly anyone will invest – or they will be so high that operators producing more cost-effectively will make high 'windfall' profits. If the authorized volume is reached through competition between tenders of renewable energy supplies made according to the most favourable price tenders, however, this would contravene the principle of equal market opportunities for the electricity suppliers who are obligated to deliver. For in that case there are electricity suppliers who have to pay more than others to meet the same volume commitment because they are only able to draw on production from less windy or less sunny sites. In brief, volume regulation is not a sustainable concept for implementing renewable energy in the future. It is not even more 'market-oriented'. Whoever favours volume over price regulation, in spite of the demonstrable drawbacks, is only interested in expanding renewable energy in small portions, drip by drip. To sum up, admittedly, not every advocate of these quota-based concepts is an opponent of renewable energy, but all those who do want to put the brakes on renewable energy are advocates of quotas – if they are not altogether opposed to a political strategy for promoting the introduction of renewable energy.

By contrast, price-regulated plans like the EEG have some clear-cut advantages: they create a major incentive for technical competition among different kinds of facilities and, thereby, for productivity increases, because the more efficient a plant is within the framework of a fixed reimbursement for feeding power, the higher the operator's profit. Price regulation makes for a broader geographic distribution of facilities as well as greater diversity among owners, no bureaucratic outlay, and no certification costs. It gives an impetus to the entire spectrum of renewable energy. Price-regulated plans promote energy auton- omy in and for society.

The future of the Renewable Energy Sources Act

Price-regulating breakthrough strategies must therefore be kept going. In addition, they need to be continually updated. This is necessary because of developments that are triggered by the strategies themselves. Where the future of the Renewable Energy Sources Act (the EEG) is concerned, above all, this means intro- ducing an additional economic incentive for investments in plant-related electricity storage batteries or in hybrid facilities as described in Part I – by introducing a 'storage bonus' into the reimbursement system. According to current EEG regula- tions, every plant operator can feed his electricity into the network in volumes of any size and then leave network expan- sion and supply management to the network operators. This facilitates the operator's investments, but the consequence is growing friction with network operators, and the argument made by the electricity corporations that renewable energy is not possible without fossil energy keeps gaining public support. If each plant has a reserve capacity of its own, not only does renew- able energy become independent of the reserve postures of anonymous electricity producers. An added benefit is cost trans- parency in favour of renewable energy, and one of the central arguments in the campaign against Germany's EEG falls apart. Extensive network expansion costs can be avoided. It is not the expansion of supra-regional transmission networks that is then on the agenda, but rather the regionalization of network systems by local and regional electricity companies. Not least of all, this further development opens up for plant operators the prospect of shaping their own future for the period after reimbursement guaranteed by law runs out. Plant-related electricity storage and hybrid electric power plants allow plant operators to gain a stronger market position or become self-suppliers and full-time suppliers for electricity customers. If they are accustomed to obtaining a market price for electricity fed into the network, that price turns out higher the more they can deliver to this market specifically at times of peak demand. When they turn into full-fledged self-suppliers, their costs remain well below the market price for electricity from the network. If, in addition, they become suppliers for others, they can probably offer electricity below market price. In that a trend towards plant-related storage and continuous service by hybrid facilities is introduced and develops a technological profile, producers at plants for solar and wind electricity also round out their techni-cal profile. These solar and wind electricity facilities are then able to expand their markets into countries where there are no legislative regulations making renewable energy a priority.

Another step towards further development would be to transform the current method of reimbursement for renewable energy electricity, which is not dependent on the time of day, into a method based on time periods – such as a period between 6 and 10am, 10am to 2pm, 2 to 6pm, 6 to 10pm, and 10pm until 6am the following day. For every period there would be different fixed reimbursement rates, depending on how strong or weak the demand is in these periods. The time periods with the highest reimbursement would then (at least under Central European climatic and cultural conditions) be between 10am and 2pm and between 6 and 10pm, the lowest would be from 10pm to 6am the next day. The earlier high-reimbursement period would be to the benefit of solar electricity, which has optimal production conditions at those times, while the later periods would redound on average to the benefit of wind power, which tends to be produced in the evening; the actual economic value of both becomes apparent for all to see.

Price privileging for renewable fuels

The most effective instrument for the goal of replacing fossil energy in the fuels sector is tax exemption for renewable fuels. Legislation has been passed introducing these exemptions into several EU countries, including Germany, Spain, Austria and Sweden. Even today, complete tax exemption would make it possible for bio-fuels to be supplied more cheaply than taxed fossil fuels in every industrial country. At the local and regional

level, this would open up a market space for new fuel production and for direct marketing, which helps avoid long-range fuel
transport. In addition, tax exemption exerts effective market
pressure on the petroleum corporations to offer bio-fuels
themselves so as not to lose market share.

The higher the share of bio-fuels employed, the more
favourably does the tax advantage show up in the books. Not
only would this promote the trend among car drivers to drive
exclusively with renewable fuels. It also promotes the development and training of new fuels producers who concentrate
exclusively on supplying bio-fuels. Bio-fuels give independent
oil dealers and 'independent petrol stations' undreamt-of development opportunities.

By contrast, a mere volume regulation using a quota-based
admixture of bio-fuels means that the petroleum companies
retain their supply monopoly. In this case, agriculture and
forestry as suppliers of energy raw materials remain just as
exposed to the price dictate of a few large buyers, as is currently
the case in their relationship to the foodstuffs industry and to
their wholesale marketers. This would reduce opportunities for
regionalized fuels production. And the permanent political
conflicts one might expect about higher future admixture
volumes would act as a brake on long-term investments and
make farmers hesitate to enter into the production of energy
crops.

In contrast to the electricity corporations, far-sighted petroleum companies would even be more interested in price than in
volume regulation. With price regulation, these companies adjust
more flexibly. Their structural opportunities for reorienting
towards bio-fuels are relatively greater than those of the electricity business because a forward-looking oil company is not tied
to a fixed network and can use its distribution structure to reorient itself. Blockades to action among the petroleum companies
are more likely to be found in the so-called 'upstream' portion
of their business (from petroleum production to refining), and
less in the 'downstream' stretch (from refineries to filling
stations).

Tax exemption for bio-fuels

Many people doubt whether the plan to exempt bio-fuels from taxation can be permanently sustained. For the more that people shift to these new fuels, the higher are the revenue losses incurred by the state. Yet this fear of revenue shortfalls originates from a perspective that is much too static. The tax losses that come from constantly lower fuel taxes are compensated by other tax receipts and savings in social welfare spending that come from the numerous new jobs created by bio-fuel production. This compensation only happens, however, when bio-fuels production takes place within one's own national economy. Making sure this happens is a central element of any long-range strategy.

This is not the only reason why plans to make bio-fuels tax-exempt need to be developed further. Different kinds of bio-energy do not have the same average production costs. In order to avoid utilizing biomass in a one-sided manner, the next logical step is differentiated taxation. To facilitate a continuous shift to renewable energy, the only decisive thing is making sure that all bio-fuels can always be offered on the fuels market at more affordable prices than fossil fuels. This guarantees society a smooth, interruption-free transition.

Another essential differentiation criterion is the balance sheet on energy from bio-fuels production. If renewable energy is used to produce even more renewable energy, the full effect of tax exemption is felt. But if, for example, half a ton of fossil energy is consumed in order to produce a ton of bio-fuels, the tax exemption would be reduced by 50 per cent. This would provide an additional impetus for a general reorientation in energy, and ecological doubts about bio-fuels could be dispelled.

For society to introduce bio-fuels on a broad basis, certificates of origin for primary resources are required, meaning certificates from producers that enjoy the widest possible international recognition. There are specific sites of origin and certain primary resources that need to be excluded from any tax privilege at the very outset. There obviously can be no legitimacy for biomass that was taken from forests chopped down rampantly or from palm oil or sugar cane plantations where tropical forests had previously been cleared.

Diversity instead of market harmonization

The polluter-pays principle in environmental protection implies that those obliged to compensate for damages are the same parties who caused the damage. This principle legitimizes price-regulating market intervention by government in favour of renewable energy. To reject such intervention as a violation of market principles is equivalent to a denial of ecological and social welfare responsibility. So long as discussion about an environmentally sound energy supply is restricted to fossil energy, the only possible option is price regulation using higher energy taxation as an instrument to make people save more energy. In order to achieve a truly broad impact, however, this energy taxation – whereby depleted fossil energy obtains its ecological price – needs to be set so high that the general threshold of toleration would quickly be exceeded. An example of this was the early demand of the Greens to tax a litre of fuel so that the price would be driven up to 2.50 euros. This brought about massive protests, which showed that this kind of measure had no chance at all politically. With renewable energy, by contrast, it is possible to have a price regulation that is capable of gaining social acceptance, no longer by taxing fossil energy at higher rates, but instead by privileging the price for renewable energy in the manner described. This is the form that is most true to scale from a social welfare standpoint when it comes to generally applying the polluter-pays principle. It serves to balance out the old and current subsidies and monopoly privileges lurking in the energy system, which makes it the best political instrument for establishing a market balance. Everyone who views giving priority to this kind of price regulation favouring renewable energy as merely provisional – and who is working politically to replace this priority, if possible, with an ostensibly international market model – either has not understood this key point or does not want to understand it.

In order to exhaust the natural, technical and societal potential of renewable energy as we head down the road towards completely dismantling nuclear and fossil energy, it is essential that we do not limit ourselves to those spaces that are particularly suited to producing renewable energy and are therefore regarded as cost-efficient. If our location criteria were that restrictive, wind power plants inside Europe would be sited almost exclusively along the Atlantic coast of Europe, biomass would be overwhelmingly produced in Sweden or Finland, and photovoltaic facilities would be installed in Sicily, Greece or southern Spain. All other aspects of renewable energy use, such as regional policy goals or the re-establishment of agriculture through energetic biomass production, would fall flat.

This kind of fallacy is even found in the revised version of the Renewable Energy Sources Act that went into effect in 2004. The updated law excludes wind power plants whose production, as a result of wind conditions, amounts to less than 60 per cent of the fictitious 'reference plant' described in the law. The restriction is justified with reference to the insufficient 'macro-economic efficiency' that comes from the energy feeding and reimbursement guarantee. This revision gave the Renewable Energy Sources Act a lopsidedness with which (in a way favour-ing a cost mentality conceived exclusively in energy business terms) the opportunity to create new energy businesses using renewable energy was rebuffed.

If the criterion behind this regulation were to be transferred to photovoltaics, the Renewable Energy Sources Act would only apply to plants in areas with above-average solar radiation. Since the operators of renewable energy plants at less favourable sites do not by any means receive a higher reimbursement per kilowatt hour, they obviously have other motives than merely realizing the highest possible profit. They want to be active about avoid-ing emissions even when the 'pay-off' is worse there than elsewhere. To ignore this motive is absurd, however, and indirectly it even imposes the proviso of a one-sided profit-maximizing mentality on individuals who want to implement the polluter-pays principle voluntarily.

Market harmonization as a snare for renewable energy

Political attempts at revoking price regulations that have either proven successful or promise success are, nevertheless, constantly being tried. This happened the first time in Denmark in 1999, and it was even done under the direction of

Environment Minister Svend Auken, who was committed to renewable energy. At that time he was actually the driving force behind the Kyoto Protocol among the EU's environment ministers. Convinced of the effectiveness of certificate trading for emissions-reducing investment, he wanted to lead the way with a good example and start orienting the Danish push for renewable energy around this pattern from the outset. For the Danish electricity corporations, this was a heaven-sent opportunity. This unholy alliance between 'eco-efficient' market competition and electricity companies led to the quota plan, which nearly brought the expansion of wind power in Denmark to a complete standstill. Without Germany's price-regulated market, the Danish wind power plant industry would probably have been swept away. Owing to the unsuitability of quota plans, ten EU member states have already decided to orient themselves around the EEG. This has made the energy business all the more persistent in its attempts to topple the law again.

Even German electricity corporations are attempting a similar attack, disguised under the label of a 'bonus model'. In an internal position paper they have revealed what bothers them about the EEG: the 'priority, when it comes to hooking up, purchasing, and transmitting' energy, for 'not allowing any taxation of renewable energy's expansion', and the prospect that the law's official minimum goals – 12.5 per cent share of electricity supply by 2010 and 20 per cent by 2020 – are 'expected [to be] overfulfilled'. They are calling instead for electricity from renewable energy to be self-marketed by producers. They want reimbursement to be added up using a 'market price' ultimately determined by the electricity companies plus a 'bonus'. In order to conceal from the public that their plan is to interrupt the further expansion of renewable energy, they hold out the 'initial' prospect of a partly higher reimbursement than what the EEG currently provides. We know that this is an attempt to catch mice with poisoned bacon because this 'bonus plan' is supposed to lead to Europe-wide certificate-trading with renewable energy on the basis of a quota regulation. The plan is meant to 'be employed as a transitional model on the way to a free market'. If the 'bonus model' were to be introduced, the electricity corporations could, in the interim, reduce reimbursement by lowering the market price or refusing to feed renewable energy into the electricity grid, ostensibly on grounds of network stability. The energy companies' position paper provides a foretaste of how far they could go in lowering the market price. According to the paper, the price for electricity from the smallest facilities should be zero cents.

This proposal is connected with the strategy of EURELEC-TRIC, the association of European electricity companies. As early as November 2004, in a declaration issued jointly with the organization RECS (Renewable Energy Certification System), this association had called for moving 'as soon as possible' to a completely harmonized Europe-wide system of certificate trading. This would offer 'clear incentives to the most cost-efficient solutions'. A 'pan-European market' for renewable energy should be created, according to a position paper from the organization early in 2005: 'Market players need clear rules for importing and exporting.' This market already exists, so there is no longer any way to neglect it. 'In the end, the renewable energy market is a demand-oriented market with all the features of a domestic market. On the supply side, all subsidies will ultimately be forbidden. EU policy needs to move in the direction of this kind of market.' The 'market harmonizers' act as if electricity production from renewable energy would be overflowing in individual countries, so that (in their view) the national market is already too narrow.

There are deliberately obstructive reasons behind the push for a pan-European harmonization of ways to introduce renewable energy. This harmonization could even be seen as a downright violation of the subsidiarity principle inscribed in the various EU treaties. In no way can a Europe-wide system of certificate trading prove that it is a 'better' way to promote renewable energy, as all 'laboratory experiments' in individual countries show. The kind of certificate trading practised in Sweden is lauded as a model – both by RECS and EURELEC-TRIC. There, out of an investment total of 70 million euros in wind power during 2003, 24 million alone were for certificate costs.

Volume regulation banishes renewable energy into a market niche

These forays would ultimately lead into the niche for an 'eco-energy market'. Separate eco-energy suppliers are banking on people who are willing, on grounds of ethical responsibility, to pay more for 'green electricity' than for 'black' fossil or 'yellow-black' nuclear energy. This is analogous to the 'bio-market' for foodstuffs, a market that satisfies the need for ecologically culti-vated, poison-free foods. Another analogy would be environmental ethics funds, in which people provide money for ecological investments in spite of lower profit expectations; solar funds for developing countries are also in this category. Such initiatives facilitate practical projects that would not exist other-wise. They cultivate behaviour in line with business ethics.

'Eco-energy' market plans, however, are no substitute for general political regulations. Rather, they need to be understood as publicity campaigns, as demonstrative initiatives, or as acts of resistance against ossified structures. But they run up against a psychological barrier whenever (and so long as) they need to operate on the basis of higher prices for green energy, in other words, when they are handicapped by price discrimination rather than advantaged by price privileging. In contrast to the market for biological foodstuffs, where customers exchange the disad-vantage of higher costs for the individual advantage of healthier and tastier food, customers of green electricity only have the individual disadvantage of higher costs. The customer finds himself in a world that is the reverse of the world of the polluter-pays principle: to get green electricity, which helps avoid environmental damage, he ends up paying more than all those people who just keep on adding to pollution with their energy choices. This is an upside-down world and not sustainable as a general social principle. Faced with this kind of bonus awarded to egoistic behaviour, the individual who decides to engage in altruistic behaviour doesn't stand a chance. To banish renewable energy into this self-abnegating market niche for eco-electricity is the pipe dream of the traditional energy business and of free market dogmatists.

There have long been offers from electricity companies to take cost-effectively produced electricity from their own, already amortized hydropower plants out of their previous energy supply mix and sell it at above-average cost as 'green electricity' — as a side business, without changing anything else about traditional production structures — a cynical exploitation of the good will of those people who fall for these kinds of tricks.

In order to prevent this de facto betrayal of well-intentioned electricity customers, EUROSOLAR and the major German environmental groups award the 'Green Electricity Label' only to those eco-electricity providers who plough their earnings from electricity purchases back into new investment in renewable energy — and who politically champion the general promotion of renewable energy.

Ecological responsibility instead of indifference

Yet economic incentives, even if they are attractive, do not tell the whole story. Legally mandated reimbursement for electricity fed into the network from photovoltaic facilities has been designed by Germany's Renewable Energy Sources Act in such a way that everyone who has the appropriate kind of installation space in his house could control such an installation without economic risk. The credit and module costs can be refinanced from the revenues they bring within 15 years on average, and the reimbursement will be paid annually for 20 years in order to cover the risk of breakdowns and overcome mistrust about the novelty of renewable energy. Measured against these starting-out conditions, there would have to be more than the approximately 30,000 investors in small and larger facilities newly installed in Germany in 2004; the number of investors would have to be, instead, a figure ten times that. In this way, bio-diesel, already tax-exempt in Germany for ten years, will be supplied more cheaply than fossil diesel fuel; in esterified form, bio-diesel is already employable in almost all diesel vehicles. But in spite of the many complaints about high petrol prices, demand remains relatively small; every taxi, bus or transport business could save considerably on operating costs, and yet so far only a relatively few have seized this opportunity. The 'pure solar house', which can already be built in an architectonically ambitious manner without additional costs, tends nonetheless to have a scarcity value; even in sun-drenched countries one searches in vain for such buildings. There is more than a problem of insufficient information lurking behind this absence of applications building on renewable energy. Even if information were available, a majority of people are prevented from wanting to take the initiative because of habit, inertia and indifference; this is true even when they are sympathetic to renewable energy.

Legally imposed duties to practise environmental protection are, therefore, also a strategically necessary component of any shift to renewable energy. These kinds of duties already exist in a wide variety of situations: from heat insulation standards in new buildings to emission protection regulations, from government-imposed requirements for fuel quality to the ban on environmentally damaging substances. In Japan there is a so-called 'top runner' programme, according to which the energy standard achieved by a manufacturer of energy-saving devices becomes the requirement for all manufacturers of similar devices within three years – a legal regulation whose introduction into Germany has been taken up as a cause by Bundestag member of parliament Ulrich Kelber.[6] The 'eco-tax' also represents an 'environmental purchase obligation', as does the Renewable Energy Sources Act, since the additional costs that occur are paid by electricity customers. The normality of such obligations is one of the most important legal arguments for the Renewable Energy Sources Act, as the environmental lawyer Gert Apfelstedt has convincingly elaborated.[7] The only reason the eco-tax is not more conspicuous is that it is integrated into the price of electricity and is therefore 'invisible'.

There is no reason why we should do without 'visible' purchase obligations in order to mobilize renewable energy. On the contrary, the more transparency there is (coupled with that pertinent argument that explains both the individual utility of continual energy cost reduction and its social utility), the greater the opportunities for widespread public acceptance. The fact that people shrink back from this when it comes to renewable energy is merely an expression of insufficient political courage to go on the offensive in countering the prejudices against renewable energy cultivated by the energy business.

The most important approach would be to make the utilization of renewable energy obligatory for construction in buildings that are new or about to be renovated. Everywhere that governments have made decisions of this kind, these policies have met with broad public acceptance. Berlin's city parliament even passed a resolution like this unanimously in 1997; it was, however, never implemented by the city government. While there was public acceptance for these measures, they were not accepted by the energy and construction industries, to whom the city administration catered in spite of what Berlin's city council had decided. With broad public backing, small German cities like Schalkham and Vellmar passed and implemented legislation anchoring measures mandating renewable energy in the development plans these towns are required to approve, something also done by several Spanish cities. The obligation to use renewable energy should also long ago have been envisioned for the operation of motorized ships and boats on inland lakes, on grounds of water protection as well, and the same goes for the use of vegetable-based lubricating oils – and in the foreseeable future, when the right kind of potential is available, this should also include renewable fuels. The requirement should also be extended on a step-by-step basis to devices with integrated solar electricity production.

There are also many committed advocates of renewable energy who talk most of the time in categories of cost and price or let themselves be drawn into a one-sided discussion this way. This is a psychological trap that overlooks the variety of motives people act upon and voluntarily constricts strategic opportunities for renewable energy. Every human being is more than an 'economic man' who only thinks from one day to the next. Individual economic utility here and now is not the only instinct driving human behaviour. There are long-term as well as short-term economic interests, interests in security and quality of life, in one's hometown, one's native country, in the world. That is why, if society is going to be motivated on behalf of renewable energy, people need to be addressed in the breadth of their motives. How can we increase the number of volunteers, and how can those who are not so willing (and who need not be deemed mean-spirited on that account) be moved to make an 'obligatory contribution' in a democratic and reasonable way that is in everyone's interest? What moves society and its politicians towards the shift to renewable energy?

Activating society

Every activation of society requires a driving force. If the goals propagated by these driving forces have an igniting effect, they lead (in the words of Amitai Etzioni, cited earlier) to a 'mutual reinforcement of overall societal and personal activation', to a chain reaction. This chain reaction can, however, turn out to be a flash in the pan if the idea, however seductive, proves on closer examination to be dubious or dangerous – or if the necessary staying power cannot be summoned up. By contrast, the chain reaction will continue to spread if the idea corresponds to the values that sustain society and if there are persuasive reasons to vouch for it.

The idea of a system change to renewable energy meets all the requirements of a concept that can motivate a growing number of people, since it is an idea endowed with reasonableness and values that speak to ethical needs and different interests. The presence of political neuroses shows that appealing to reason alone does not suffice to activate society on behalf of renewable energy – in spite of the basic sympathy that is there. Moreover, since it cannot be assumed that everyone who is not committed to renewable energy lacks reason, renewable energy's protagonists should not simply address people based on their economic motives. The protagonists' strategy needs to do more than educate about opportunities; it also has to illuminate what the prospects are. Ideal values are at stake as much as different social interests and currents. Values and interests can be supported by emotional as well as by rational motives, or by both simultaneously. Often each type of motive is in conflict not only with the other kind, but sometimes also with 'pure reason', as we know (at the latest) since Kant.

From sympathy to activation

Sympathy for renewable energy is easy to arouse. It corresponds to natural sentiments and every person's realm of experience, especially in everyone's relationship to the sun. Sympathy turns into practical commitment when people become aware that renewable energy is more than something capable of evoking our sympathy, when they also see that it should be taken seriously and is capable of completely replacing fossil and nuclear energy.

Renewable energy's champions should therefore get to work developing scenarios for concrete opportunities in the places where they live, in their regions and national governments, showing the public that (and how) it is possible to meet energy needs with technologies that have already been tested and are available for exploiting the potential of renewable energy in each specific context. The only thing that the protagonists of renewable energy might learn from the defenders of nuclear energy is how to present a large-scale, all-encompassing perspective, as the nuclear industry did from the 1950s through to the 1970s, when it was able to cast its spell over an entire generation. One need not go so far as to promise society that switching to renewable energy will bring us to a land overflowing with milk and honey. The disenchantment that followed waking up from the nuclear dream has helped exhaust society's willingness to accept positive utopias, a disillusionment that has also been reflected in scepticism about the solar vision. In order to pick up steam socially, it should be enough to communicate the message that renewable energy is opening up a definitive opportunity for people to overcome existential energy crises.

In order for a cultural movement in favour of this energy shift to emerge, every effort must be resisted that downplays the economic and social value of renewable energy and blurs the fundamental differences between renewable and nuclear or fossil energy. These differences compel a clear affirmation of renewable energy against any notorious attempt at relativizing or devaluing it. The reasons for a shift to renewable energy are so compelling that this transformation would have to be undertaken even if all the horror stories and statistics about its cost turned out to be true.

The conflict between these two basic options – fossil/nuclear or renewable energy – is being fought out with an extreme disparity between the opportunities available to each side. But it is only seemingly a fight between Goliath and David. The role of the giant in the current energy supply scene is played by fossil energy, but its role is dwarf-sized compared to renewable energy's natural potential. Conventional energy's greater strength in the public mind derives from its long-standing anchoring in people's memory and from their energy habits; its greatest weakness is its lack of legitimacy, a shortcoming that will inevitably become larger. Manoeuvres to distract from the causes of energy crises may therefore be expected to increase – as will the exploitation of people's egoistic motives against the 'economic burdens' of renewable energy. On the renewable energy side of the battle, the greatest weaknesses are its novelty and a widespread underestimation of renewable energy's potential. Its potentially greatest strength comes from its unique power of legitimacy, which can only be shown to advantage when the possibility of a comprehensive energy shift is there for all to see. The energy debate needs to be conducted in a way that highlights fundamental contrasts – and not just as a discussion about energy, but as a societal debate. The contrasts need to be made clear: energy that is ready for the future versus energy imprisoned by the past, common good versus egoism.

The values-based legitimacy empowering renewable energy

Since the first societies were formed, the tension between individual liberties and social responsibility, between the principle of the individual and the principle of social welfare, has been a major theme of political philosophy and the development of legal systems. Discussions about this tension revolve around the different characteristics of these values: which should receive priority, how one can guard against the extreme forms of total social ruthlessness practised by some individuals or against a freedom-killing collectivism, and how one can simultaneously do justice to both values. Without lived liberal values, every society turns rigid; without a social welfare ethic – which includes not just a sense of social obligation but also, as the legal scholar Klaus Bosselmann has put it, 'property's ecological obligation' – society goes to ruin, and its vital resources erode.

It is probably not possible to bring values like individual freedom and the common good into any kind of permanent balance. Both correspond to fundamental human needs. Each, when given a one-sided interpretation, is incompatible with the other. In his *Theory of Justice*, the philosopher John Rawls wrote that the individual utility principle:

> *seems [to be] incompatible with the connection of social cooperation among equals for mutual advantage. It appears to be inconsistent with the idea of reciprocity implicit in the notion of a well ordered society... [Without] strong and lasting benevolent impulses, a rational man would not accept a basic structure merely because it maximized the algebraic sum of advantages irrespective of its permanent effects on his own basic rights and interests.*[8]

Individual freedom needs to be protected from the whole, and the whole from excessive individual liberties. Individual freedom is not the only elementary human need; another one is the 'bonum commune', the 'Good Society' as in the title of a book co-authored by the Berkeley sociologist Robert N. Bellah. These needs impart a unique legitimizing power to renewable energy. Not only does renewable energy satisfy material energy needs, but it also makes it possible to use energy in a way that is individually free and unhindered without thereby doing harm to other people and society as a whole. The use of renewable energy facilitates harmony between individual freedom and orientation towards the common good.

Political efforts to protect people against emissions merely by establishing 'threshold values', by contrast, do not get to the root of the problem, namely the energy source itself. In this respect societies throughout the world are still in a pre-civilized stage. To tolerate avoidable emissions is like explicitly allowing every individual to simply dump his garbage onto the street or in front of his neighbour's door (or hold it under strangers' noses). It legitimizes unsociable behaviour, which is not considered unsociable only because almost everyone does the same thing – and because there is nothing else to do in the absence of readily available emissions-free energy. If waste disposal legislation were to be abolished and garbage collection stopped, everyone would find this intolerable. Then society (along with its garbage) would be thrown back into the same condition in which it finds itself with respect to energy emissions. We view it as self-evident that every household has to pay for garbage collection. Avoiding energy emissions, by contrast, is deemed infeasible, although it would cost less than garbage collection, and it has not even been made obligatory yet in places where it would not create any additional cost.

To burden other people with pollutants, moreover, violates basic human rights. In Article 2 of Germany's constitution (the Basic Law) it says: 'Every person shall have the right to life and physical integrity.' In her jurisprudential analysis, *The Priority of Personal Value over Material Value*, Nina Scheer concludes, on the basis of the demonstrably serious effects of energy emissions on human health, that the German state 'violates [its] safeguarding obligation derived' from Article 2 of the Basic Law 'when it refrains from setting a direction for energy policy that removes these impairments, although it would be in a position to do so, because emissions-reducing alternatives do exist'.[9] The argument that the higher cost of pollutant-free energy utilization stands in the way of this fundamental right does not hold water. A basic right may not be subject to the proviso that it is valid only if it 'pays' to follow it.

A broadly informed and motivated public is the most important ally an ambitious breakthrough strategy can have. This we know from every successful political action ever undertaken against the recalcitrant supporters of the traditional energy system. All social organizations that claim to represent the values underpinning society must therefore be confronted with the energy question and take a stand if they do not wish to lose their public legitimacy.

This is especially true for political parties if they are interested in being more than organizations helping professional politicians compete for office and power. Social democratic parties can no longer credibly stake the claim justifying their existence as the party working towards a free society rooted in justice and solidarity if they do not undertake everything within their power to avoid the social welfare and ecological costs of nuclear and fossil energy use. Their credibility is damaged if, instead (and in defiance of the principle of inter-generational solidarity), they pass this responsibility on to the next generation, which threatens to fall apart as a result. Conservative parties who want to be more than the embodiment of established privileges and vested interests dare not accept how the continued depletion of natural resources driven by the use of fossil and nuclear energy leads to the erosion of traditional values and to people being uprooted. Liberal parties who have made themselves the standard bearers of individual liberties above all else forfeit this claim when they understand liberty primarily as the freedom to produce pollutants that constrict other people's freedom to live well – or when they place global economic freedom above a conception of political liberalization that also includes the possibility of limiting freedom to destroy the environment. And even Green parties face the question of whether their concept of the ecological market economy still places the ecological principle ahead of the market principle as a matter of priority.

Even the churches, in light of the world's nuclear and fossil crises, can only sustain the credibility and soundness of religious values if they draw upon these values and derive a commandment to use renewable energy. The Christian journalist Franz Alt has articulated this by saying that religion can no longer get by without an ecological ethic, just as the fundamental ecological decision in favour of renewable energy cannot be achieved without ethical motives. The preservation of 'Creation' and 'faith' in that Creation are only possible if the Big Bang's gift of energy from the sun, which is the trigger of all life, becomes once more the exclusive source of energy for human beings.[10] In his book *Global Exit* about the relationship of the churches to the 'total market', the Christian journalist and church critic Carl Amery was just as urgent in emphasizing that the churches, for the sake of their very raison d'être, need to oppose every attempt at giving the market priority over Christian-humanitarian values and the protection of the ecosphere.[11]

Fracturing and refounding the economy

Since the traditional energy business does not want to be a sponsor of the shift to renewable energy, and could only be supportive in a limited way, and since (in any event) there cannot and should not be any more waiting, the question arises: which social groups do have an original interest in pressing ahead with the shift to renewable energy? In the more than 200-year-old history of economic systems in modern times, a seemingly indissoluble division of labour has been practised: the energy business provides the energy, business provides the devices for utilizing energy, and the consumer uses both. What is made out to be an alien element within the energy system then appears as a foreign body inside the economic system as well. What the energy business sees as an affront against 'energetical correctness' is, accordingly, an affront against 'economic correctness' as far as 'the economy' is concerned. Only by way of this psychologism can it be explained why renewable energy businesses are still seen as illegitimate children of 'the economy' – and not as the nucleus of its refoundation.

For decades, the energy business was able to shore itself up by relying on the economy's organized interests, from business lobbies to the trade unions; a tight-knit trio of interests. That it is possible, nonetheless, to unravel this trio has been shown by developments in Germany, where a fast-growing new entrepreneurial sector independent of the old troika has grown up as a result of legislation to promote renewable energy. When the president of the Federation of German Industries (the Bundesverband der Deutschen Industrie or BDI) nonetheless persists in crusading against the EEG in the name of the 'economy', he is no longer speaking for all the organizations and businesses under his umbrella. The German Engineering Federation (Verband der Deutschen Maschinen- und Anlagenindustrie, VDMA), one of the largest members of the BDI, has come around to supporting these laws openly; it has recognized the kind of future opportunities its businesses derive from the shift to renewable energy. Among Germany's trade unions, in the meantime, all except the Mining, Chemical and Energy Industrial Union are now supporting the EEG. German unions, in contrast to most of their counterparts in other countries, have recognized the opportunities that renewable energy provides for the electronic, metal, construction and foodstuffs industries. The same holds true for craft unions and agricultural interest groups.

This opens the way for a split in 'the economy', a fracture in the business community that is a necessary precondition for any breakthrough to renewable energy. It is a fracture between those business interests that are or feel themselves to be dependent (for better or worse) on the traditional energy business and those that recognize and pursue their future opportunities in the shift to renewable energy; between short- and long-term interest orientations, and (increasingly) between business in general and the energy business in particular, and even within the latter itself. These interest conflicts come to light through the creation of a 'critical mass', in other words, through a growing number of renewable energy businesses inside Germany that are already earning annual sales of more than 10 billion euros. But even earnings of this magnitude are not enough to make most business interests reorient themselves towards renewable energy. It is also necessary to make businesses on the whole see the dangers of holding fast to the traditional energy system, and especially to make them see the opportunities that a shift in energy will bring to numerous branches of the economy – and to make them recognize the contribution they can make in their own interest.

This also holds true for businesses in the field of renewable energy technology, companies that previously focused on technologies promoted by government-sponsored aid programmes. Because of that focus they were largely orienting their production towards distinct individual facilities, and so they have got into the habit of making additions to their product palette depend on government expanding its aid programmes. These businesses have therefore cropped up almost exclusively in countries where government has sponsored aid programmes that permit business investment on a larger scale.

Yet it is in their own interest for these renewable energy entrepreneurs to go beyond the products they have been offering based on government assistance. For these programmes' continuation and expansion – and, as a result, the very existence of renewable energy companies – are in jeopardy so long as they do not command a broad and irrevocable consensus within the political system. Companies that produce (for example) wind power or photovoltaic facilities for the German market (a market stimulated by the Renewable Energy Sources Act) should therefore not become dependent on this law continuing to exist unamended and on other countries introducing comparable legislation. These companies also need to make themselves capable of operating under other market conditions by offering systems solutions, such as complete household supply systems using renewable energy or the complete provision of developing country villages with the entire palette of individual facilities needed to supply them with energy. They need, in other words, to develop 'systems solutions' that facilitate the independent availability of renewable energy. How large a market there is for such systems solutions is demonstrated by a single case: the Indian government's 2005 decision to no longer connect (as had long been the plan) its country's 84,000 villages – in which alone there reside 250 million inhabitants – to an electricity network, and instead to bank on an autonomous energy supply system using renewable energy – a plan that is currently getting a trial run in 100 villages courtesy of Decentralized Energy Systems India (DESI Power).[12] And these companies also need to get organized into their own business associations so that they can lobby intensively for common quality standards, which they can use to create a social foundation for establishing confidence in renewable energy technologies and to counteract the widespread mistrust deliberately fomented by their rivals. This kind of organizing and lobbying for confidence-building standard-setting has already been done in the area of photovoltaics by the PV-GAP (Photovoltaic Global Accreditation Programme), under the direction of the US photovoltaic expert Peter Varadi.

Existing renewable energy companies have an added special responsibility. To the extent that they are stand-alone enterprises independent of energy corporations, they need to try maintaining this independence. If they merge with other businesses or broaden the circle of their shareholders, they should do this with shareholders who are outside the spectrum of the energy corporations. Every merger with a conventional energy company harbours the danger of a 'backlash' against renewable energy that could annul overnight the years of hard work that went into building up this business sector.

The spectrum of potential winners from a shift in energy, however, goes well beyond the producers of renewable energy technologies. It also encompasses the vast majority of all other businesses, only a few of whom (admittedly) have recognized that they have a self-interest of their own in achieving independence from the energy business. There are many companies that would appear to be substantially more predestined for a role of their own as renewable energy technology producers than are the big corporations of the energy business.

Thus, it is in the interest of the car industry to abandon its 100-year alliance with the petroleum industry. Cars and, by extension, their manufacturers are regarded as an environmental danger largely because of the fossil fuels used to drive them. When it comes to bottlenecks and price explosions as a result of scarce petroleum in the foreseeable future, this will affect the car industry immediately – in contrast to the petroleum companies, which have profited from every price increase so far. In the interest of securing their long-term existence, therefore, the car companies need to become a driving force pushing for the use of renewable energy. In their hand they hold a trump card they can use to facilitate this reorientation, namely by producing and marketing energy-saving cars that can be driven with bio-fuels and/or electricity. This trump can help the car companies clear the way for society to undertake the shift to renewable energy. To do this they would initially have to focus on drive technologies that make it possible for vehicle operators to shift fluidly from fossil to bio-fuels without having to buy a new car first. They need to use their economic weight to create political parameters that will facilitate introducing bio-fuels into the market.

Even more, the car industry might even be predestined to become a producer of stationary motor power plants, whether we are dealing with communal heating plants, motors operated using fuel cells, or with Stirling or compressed air motors. Not only can the car industry contribute its experience in motor development; it can also bring in its experience marketing decentralized installations using a wide-reaching network of dealers and workshops. For this reason, too, the car industry should no longer leave the design of energy laws exclusively to legislators in the electricity companies' sphere of influence. The more that energy laws favour the introduction of decentralized facilities for producing electricity, the greater are the market opportunities for motor manufacturers, including on the small power station market.

The electrical and information technology industry should not have to wait for government to pass laws promoting its participation in renewable energy. It is already within its power to optimize electricity storage battery technologies, to develop new ones and put them up for sale. It is not just the market for existing renewable energy plants (a market that grows faster as storage technologies become better and less expensive) that awaits these new products; they are also anticipated by the market for improvements in the way today's electricity supply systems are serviced. Small devices that produce electricity on their own are especially attractive for the younger generation. Extra costs that might be incurred will hardly play a role in this group's purchasing decisions. Such additional costs can only be small, and it is easy to convey to the users of these devices that savings in electricity costs make up for the added expense. So what is the industry waiting for?

It is in the interest of the railway companies and the rail vehicle industry to make a commitment to developing locomotives operated with fuel cells. This opens up the possibility for powering locomotives with electricity produced on board, so that overhead train wires would no longer be needed. This would help save substantially on infrastructure and maintenance costs in railway operations.

It would be in the interest of airline companies and the aircraft industry to prepare intensively for the time when fossil aircraft fuels will be subject to taxation or perhaps no longer even be available. Aircraft also need a foundation in renewable fuels. Air travel is a potential sector for using hydrogen, because hydrogen can be produced at airports and supplied without additional infrastructure expense. In light of the importance of freight transport by air, moreover, it is incomprehensible why neither the air travel industry nor the airline companies have shown any interest in reviving the dirigible. Plans for a 'Cargo-Lifter', the product of a private initiative financed by numerous small stockholders, were filed away in 2002. The plan envisioned lifting freight goods above the firms manufacturing them into dirigibles and then delivering them immediately to their destination. The world's largest production hall is located in the environs of Berlin. This Cargo-Lifter, which can be driven with bio-fuels, could make freight transport faster, more flexible and more environmentally friendly without major infrastructure expense.

It is also in the self-interest of the shipbuilding industry and of ocean shipping companies to convert to renewable energy. Many seagoing shipping companies would have already introduced bio-fuels to operate their ship motors if fossil fuels had not been available to them tax-free. Large passenger and transport ships can also avail themselves of special opportunities to produce renewable energy on board, whether it be from wind power, which can also be used for electricity production without free-standing rotors, or from solar electricity devices integrated into ship roofs or into walls on board. Hydrogen electrolysis on board is also a technical option.

Agriculture also has a unique opportunity to revive and turn itself into the economy's most important resource base. Farming has this chance for a revival (something once deemed inconceivable) through the integrated cultivation of plants for foodstuffs, energy and raw materials – a 'three-field economy' as Christiane Grefe, a reporter for the liberal German weekly *Die Zeit*, calls it.[13] The many different points of departure for this new direction in agriculture were pointed out at the European Conferences on Biomass for Agriculture, Energy and Industry, the two biomass world conferences in 2000 and 2004 in Seville and Rome, as well as at the annual EUROSOLAR conference, The Farmer and Forest Ranger as Energy and Raw Materials Steward. In the cultivation of plants for raw materials there lies a chance to 'ecologize' the chemical industry for a fundamental 'metabolism', as this has been described by the plant chemist

Hermann Fischer: plants will replace petroleum as the diverse basic material of the future.[14] In my book *The Solar Economy* (under the heading 'Forwards: Towards the primary economy'[15]) I described the fundamental importance of this development as a reorientation whereby agriculture's marginalization since the Industrial Revolution will be permanently ended and a sociological decentralization (in place of further centralization) will be introduced into our mega-cities. Opportunities for a natural second line of business and for increased productivity will also open up for the foodstuffs industry if it proceeds systematically and vigorously to commercialize its biological residues and waste – to produce electricity on its own or to produce and market bio-fuels.

Next to agriculture, it is the construction business, including the building materials industry, that will experience the largest upswing if it seizes the opportunities provided by solar construction. Numerous new building materials and construction methods – from glass that insulates as it produces electricity to energy-saving wood constructions – could be employed. If every building is going to be capable of using cost-free solar energy optimally for heating and cooling purposes, it needs to adapt these new materials and methods to the conditions of the local topography and bio-climate – each with its own special solar plan. Solar retrofitting of the existing building stock plus new solar buildings are a 'gold mine' for the construction trades, architecture and building engineers.

And, finally, there is the municipal (or local government) and regional energy business, which is taking electricity production back into its own hands and, as a partner for regional agriculture, is discovering the production and marketing of bio-fuels as a new line of work. The same holds true for the 'energetic' marketing of organic waste in cities and local governments. On the basis of local government marketing of all energetically useful biomass and waste material, as well as on the basis of direct utilization of the local potential for solar radiation energy, wind, water, terrestrial and atmospheric heat, it is possible to come up with integrated utilization plans that have short routes from production to consumption, plans with which a centrally organized energy business (with all the expensive outlays for its wide-ranging infrastructure) cannot compete. In these local schemes, the public's energy outlays remain in circulation inside municipal and regional economic channels.

Even large energy corporations might be able to reach conciliation with renewable energy by transforming themselves into holding companies for independently operating enterprises at the local and regional level; this way, they would also be able, in the words of Joseph A. Schumpeter, 'to avoid ... coming down with a crash' and instead 'turn a rout ... into orderly retreat'.[16] As matters stand, however, they will probably be the last to attempt this.

In short, not only will new industrial enterprises emerge when renewable energy prevails, renewable energy will also open up opportunities for old branches of industry. The more autonomous investments flow into renewable energy, the faster old plant and equipment will be replaced by a new generation of decentralized energy facilities – and the better it will be for the industrial economy. What the energy business experiences as the destruction of capital breathes new life into industry and reinforces the economy at large.

The renewable energy of politics

Mobilizing renewable energy with the aim of reclaiming energy autonomy should also make it possible to renew the political energy of society, its politicians and its political institutions. Motivating political actors requires more than recognizing the potential extent of these crises; it also requires imagination informed by insights from economic sociology, imagination about how renewable energy technologies that are relatively small and still few in number point the way towards a wholly different and pervasive new system. And it requires the political foresight to appreciate that decisions about a society's energy foundation are also decisions about whether constitutional democracies are going to endure or be replaced by a transnational 'energy state'.

Political self-assertion in place of the transnational energy state

The central political motive for a renewable energy strategy leading to energy autonomy is the possibility of guaranteeing or restoring the right of self-determination for states and civil societies and, within these political civil societies, maintaining democracy and general economic freedom. The development of the electricity industry into a transnational great power shows that this argument is not based on exaggerated fears. That industry's next strategic move – massive entry into hydrogen production – would mean that the electric power business would also assume the role of fuel producer after it has already largely taken over gas supplies. That would either be tantamount to displacing the petroleum multinationals or to an international merger of the electricity with the petroleum cartel – and thereby equivalent to the establishment of an energy superpower whose political influence would overshadow all previous positions of power in the energy business.

Energy scientist Cesare Marchetti, the most frequently cited promulgator of a super-centrally organized Hydrogen Age, is one of the few who has openly sketched out the consequences of this futuristic vision for politics (and therefore for civilization). He proceeds analytically in much the same way as this book has, only under the omen of hyper-centralized electricity and hydrogen production rather than under the more auspicious sign of widespread decentralized energy production. Marchetti adopts a techno-sociological perspective. He describes – with hymn-like praise – an energy supply system that he defines as 'horizontal'. It is a system supported by transnational enterprises that arches over 'vertically' organized states. These enterprises would become 'the strongest forces in the struggle with political power'. They would be the nucleus of a 'world government'. This 'grand design ... is developing itself' as a direct consequence of 'very large energy centers' operating worldwide that Marchetti sees above all as a result of nuclear fusion technology. As an optimal site for these centres he discerns (simply because of the gigantic need for cooling water) islands (say, in the Pacific Ocean) from which hydrogen could be transported to every region of the globe.[17]

A similar vision of the future is described by the US constitutional scholar and historian Philip Bobbitt in his 2002 book *The Shield of Achilles*, though without looking at the key role of a new kind of great power: the energy imperium. The global trend towards transnationally organized world corporations, according to Bobbitt, is driving unstoppably towards the dissolution of the nation state, which will be replaced in a new historical stage by the 'market state'. The nation state is thereby losing not only its cultural boundaries and the cultural values underlying its foundation, but it is also losing its capacity to use legislation that can shape society, balance social forces and pursue independent strategies. Social values would become fragmentary, the population would increasingly view political institutions as 'a kind of enemy of its people', as an institution of bureaucratic paternalism.[18] The residual function of the state would no longer consist in accommodating and balancing different group interests in social welfare, but rather in satisfying individuals' interests in personal development and in securing freedom of movement for transnational enterprises.

Such a development, however, is most probably coterminous with decaying and therefore violence-filled societies in which, on the one hand, cultural monotony and social lethargy dominate while, on the other hand, social revolt, religious fundamentalism and new nationalistic excesses run riot against intolerable but seemingly inalterable conditions. It represents a departure from the values of security in life and the notion of 'bonum commune', the very opposite of all the values worth striving for in civilization. It is not a new historical stage, but rather a plunge into civilization's dungeon. It means that transnational enterprises appear as the incarnation of a global interest, while states and civil societies embody 'special interests'! The 'market state' degrades political institutions into territorial administrations serving global conglomerates. Although there is no reason at all to paint this trend in rosy colours, it is entirely conceivable. Unlike Bobbitt, Marchetti describes which power centre would inevitably be dominant under this scenario. Ultimately everything would be dependent on a centralized energy power. The 'horizontal' energy supply structures he describes in an act of deliberate rhetorical confusion would actually be the most vertical power conceivable, the ultimate in entire societies' dependence on inter-state energy oligarchies, on a transnational 'energy state'.

As a rule, a network is put together so that its participants can expand their room for manoeuvre through 'horizontal' cooperation. Yet the network becomes a fetter when those participating can no longer work independently of it. A network implies equality, but equality of a kind that cannot exist if it contains some key factor on which all other network participants depend. So long as a state has sufficient fossil energy reserves of its own at its disposal, governments can still wrest themselves out from under the control of private energy oligarchs – as Russian President Putin recently did vis-à-vis the petroleum company Yuko, analogous to President Theodore Roosevelt's (ultimately failed) attempt at the beginning of the 20th century to wrest US power from that of Rockefeller's Standard Oil Trust. (The analogy suggests itself in spite of the serious differences between the two leaders' ways of thinking about economics and the public purpose.)

When a society becomes completely dependent on energy suppliers and monopoly structures that lie outside their range of influence, its loss of power becomes definitive. That is why, for decades, democratic governments felt compelled to make an undignified pilgrimage to the Saudi capital in order to keep the oligarchs there in a good mood and even help maintain them in power. That great global power, the United States of America, trembles in fear of unrest in Saudi Arabia. And however political conditions in the countries of the former Soviet empire turn out, democratically elected politicians there, in order to get enough of the 'devil's tears' (as oil magnate Rockefeller called petroleum), may actually find it necessary to strike deals with political devils.

Every political actor should be aware that he degrades himself into becoming a servile teaching assistant for a transnational energy-state-in-the-making if he makes no attempt to stop this trend. This would cast him once and for all in the most ungrateful role that the energy business has to dispense, namely that of a helpless lightning rod for the legacy of fateful consequences energy oligarchs are bequeathing to the world. Under those circumstances it would be more consistent (and more lucrative) to get out of politics altogether and move over into the management of the energy oligarchy. There are already numerous role models for this kind of career change. But this kind of subordination to a developing transnational energy state no longer has anything to do with politics in the sense of action oriented towards the common good.

Maxims of the energy shift

Above and beyond the set of political tools (just described) for stimulating society's renewable energy potential, there are ten maxims of political action that can be used to achieve a break-through to renewable energy within the span of a few decades and to render that breakthrough irreversible.

First maxim: Reclaiming intellectual autonomy

The most important step is reclaiming intellectual and mental autonomy in the energy question. In the first instance, this means facing reality and ending the self-deception that the tradi-tional way of supplying energy has any kind of sustainable future or can be made to have one. And it means shunting aside the psychological barrier that obstructs the vision of a thorough-going energy shift.

Second maxim: A new economic development model

The global fossil/nuclear energy system has, in spite of its dominance, proven incapable of supplying the world's population with energy. One-third of humanity has continued to be excluded from what that system supplied. The number of those excluded is bound to increase, not decline, and so will the glaring disparities in global economic development. There is also a disparity within the industrial countries, between its economic centres and the rural areas that depend on these centres for surpluses. Sooner or later, this means that every society loses its footing.

Neither the kind of growing structural unemployment that affects most industrial countries nor impoverishment in the developing world can be overcome if no new net value is added in the agricultural sector, and this agricultural growth can only come from a shift to the renewable resource of biomass – from a natural resource economy that will become the physical foundation for the industry of tomorrow.

We now understand that copying the development pattern of industrial societies is the wrong way for development policy to proceed. One of the critical reasons why the consequences of this insight were not sufficiently heeded is that two different economic development models cannot be pursued in a global economy that is becoming more integrated. By reorienting both industrial and developing countries towards renewable energy, this contradiction can be overcome.

That this approach might contain a kind of social insurance policy against serious employment crises is something that only one leading politician from the 20th century understood, President Franklin D. Roosevelt (1933–1945). One element of his New Deal was economic incentives for the urban unemployed to start a new livelihood as farmers. The programme did not have any long-range impact because it lacked the dimension of a general switch from fossil to renewable resources, especially since the Tennessee Valley Authority, another component of the New Deal, spurred the centralization of electricity production. The Brazilian government under President Lula, who promised the Landless Worker's Movement a new foundation for agricultural livelihood, will only be able to fulfil this promise if the government bases its economic strategy on a shift in resources instead of (once again) on centralized energy provision.

That industrial countries as well as developing countries need this kind of new energy and new economic paradigm is something that can be seen inside the EU by the situation in eastern Germany or southern Italy, the Mezzogiorno. In the latter, decades of political effort have not been able to create a sustainable economic foundation, in spite of billions in subsidies. For eastern Germany, as we can see a decade and a half after the two German states were united, something similar must be feared. As a result of productivity gains in the industrial and service sectors, the times are gone in which as many jobs can be created in the traditional way as are lost through the development of technological labour productivity. The new east and south European member states of the EU, with their large share of employment programmes in agriculture, confront the same problem. By switching to an economy based on their own natural resources, these countries can create new, permanently viable economic structures that counteract the creeping disengagement of entire regions from the rest of the country.

In order to make the historically imperative switch to renewable energy succeed, the world energy map needs to be redrawn. This requires asking what will become of today's oil- and gas-producing countries. The question must be posed right now so that these countries do not crash economically without forewarning or drown in their own chaos. The question cannot be answered without a new development model. The oil- and gas-producing countries have no choice but to build up an industry based on small- and medium-sized business.

Third maxim: Market priority for domestic resources as a matter of principle

Establishing a market priority for domestic resources in each country's pattern of resource consumption needs to become, as a matter of principle, a precondition for safeguarding the future. This priority could even be justified by the 1947 General Agreement on Tariffs and Trade (GATT), which has become an unamended component of the WTO treaties; more specifically, the rationale may be derived from Article XIX about 'Emergency Action on Imports of Particular Products' as well as from Article XX concerning 'General Exceptions'. In Article XIX it says that any contracting party shall be free:

> to suspend the obligation [incurred under this Agreement] in whole or in part [if] any product is being imported into the territory of that contracting party in such increased quantities and under such conditions as to cause or threaten serious injury to domestic producers in that territory of like or directly competitive products.

For any state, a threat to resource security means an absolute state of emergency, and this fact is becoming increasingly clear in light of supply crises. Once a supply crisis has definitively occurred, it is hardly possible for the crisis to be overcome in the short or medium term. Article XX of the GATT treaty says that:

> nothing in this Agreement shall be construed to prevent the adoption or enforcement by any contracting party of measures ... necessary to protect human ... life or health [or] relating to the conservation of exhaustible natural resources if such measures are made effective in conjunction with restrictions on domestic production or consumption.

Making domestic resources a market priority, something that leads directly to renewable energy, is sound crisis prevention. All societies have a right to this safeguard – and sooner or later all societies will have to lay claim to this priority. This makes it all the more important to establish the maxim's validity in principle right now.

Fourth maxim: A ranking order for replacing conventional energies

A political strategy committed to energy autonomy needs to be oriented around three criteria that yield a ranking order for replacing conventional energies. According to the criterion:

- of material availability, the priority should be on replacing those conventional energy forms that will be exhausted most quickly worldwide; accordingly, replacing petroleum and natural gas is most urgent;
- of energy security, conventional import energies need to be replaced first;
- of environmental relief with respect to combustion processes, at first glance (after the special case of nuclear energy) it should initially be coal, then petroleum, and finally natural gas that gets replaced. If, however, one takes into account the entire supply chain of these energy potentials, from production to final consumption, along with the

different high energy losses associated with each of these, the result is a more differentiated picture.

Applying these three criteria yields a different set of emphases for how to replace conventional energy in each country – and also conflicting goals, since the criteria produce conclusions that can contradict each other. The conflicts among these competing goals are not something that can be overcome by an energy market. They need to be solved politically.

Fifth maxim: The political transformation of renewable energy's macroeconomic advantages into microeconomic incentives

Since the macroeconomic advantages of mobilizing renewable energy described here do not automatically show up in the microeconomic costs for using renewable energy, it requires political skill to translate these advantages into microeconomic incentives. This fifth maxim not only gives us an explanation for the pricing privileges that renewable energy should enjoy, but also establishes the necessity of linking the mobilization of renewable energy to the promotion of a basic economic structure for producing renewable energy in individual national economies. One example is a programme to promote solar-thermal household installations at perhaps 20 per cent of the investment total that brings a return to the state coffers that is higher than this total. The labour cost share for these installations comes to around 60 per cent of the total investment, which leads to state revenues of 24 per cent of the investment (calculated simply on the basis of a social insurance contribution ratio of 40 per cent); in addition, there are revenues from value-added taxes that the state takes in. One precondition for this calculation is, in this case, that the manufacture of these solar installations takes place within one's own national economy.

Sixth maxim: Real decartelization in the energy business

The fundamental meaning of a market economy does not reside in the construction of market equality for dissimilar products; it lies instead in the prevention of monopolies, duopolies and oligopolies, that is to say, in their decartelization. Where the energy business is concerned, this would have to mean decartelizing the energy companies that produce raw materials from the companies that produce electricity; even more specifically, this means decartelizing the ownership structure. This would make it easier for electricity producers to get into the business of electricity production from renewable energy on their own – much like the process we can see at work in Spain. This would be more in conformity with a market economy than the current state of affairs. The same applies to the takeover of electricity and gas networks by the public sector. This does not necessarily mean a single gigantic state enterprise; instead, there could be national, regional and municipal network-operating companies running the high and medium tension networks as well as distribution networks so that these can become truly independent of the producers. How obvious this approach is can be seen from the 2004 takeover of the Danish transmission network and of the Dutch gas network by each one of these countries' respective governments.

In the fuels sector, keeping filling stations independent of the petroleum conglomerates is a minimum requirement politically. Filling stations need to have their freedom secured by law to buy and sell bio-fuels from independent producers.

Seventh maxim: The pioneering role of government as a user of renewable energy

In the shift to renewable energy, political institutions need to take on a pioneering role. Mostly this consists of converting public buildings to using renewable energy – much like what has already happened, at the initiative of EUROSOLAR, with the refurbished Reichstag parliament building in Berlin as well as with completely new government buildings in Germany's capital. Newly constructed public buildings need to be completely oriented towards renewable energy. This is 'state-of-the-art technology', and public authorities should be the first to calculate in macroeconomic terms.

They should also take on a pioneering role when it comes to mobilizing on behalf of bio-fuels. The extensive vehicle fleets maintained by public institutions should be generally converted to using these fuels. Any government or city administration that performs this kind of public service on its own is legitimizing political initiatives in a way that creates economic incentives for the rest of society; it is also enjoining obligations that can reasonably be imposed on everyone.

Eighth maxim: Orienting rural and urban planning to renewable energy

The broad dispersion of plants and facilities that is necessary to achieve energy autonomy makes it imperative to rethink rural and urban planning. A vast number of administrative rules was created during times when nobody was thinking about using renewable energy. One also cannot solve new conflicts about rural land use with old rules. A society that refuses to make room for decentralized use of renewable energy encourages the conservation of an old-fashioned, highly centralized system for supplying energy, delays the switch to renewable energy, and arbitrarily drives this switch, once it has become inevitable, into a kind of centralization that is unnecessary and 'suboptimal' as far as renewable energy is concerned, for example in the form of offshore wind parks owned by electricity conglomerates. Regions are thereby deprived of the advantages that naturally accrue to regional economies from renewable energy.

Renewable energy needs to become the beneficiary of a generalized planning privilege within the framework of local self-government and administration, with forms of owner participation tailored to each local population. This planning privilege means that renewable energy plants should not be generally excluded from open spaces in the rural landscape. Local self-government in this context means that specific siting approval decisions should be a matter of democratic personal responsibility at the local level – instead of being left up to bureaucratic institutions detached from the locality, to authorities who do not live in the region for which they grant or refuse a given site approval. Democratic local government site approval should even be allowed to go so far as to require operators to offer the local citizenry priority shareholding in wind power projects. Acceptance is enhanced when it is not some anonymous investment company laying claim to a scenic setting for construction of a wind park on behalf of the citizens, but when (instead) there is a municipally owned public utility or a citizens' cooperative acting as a shareholder in the project.

Paper regulations or anonymous public authorities are no substitute for local self-government and local citizen participation. Even if such participation occasionally results in arbitrary decisions against renewable energy, mistakes can be corrected democratically at the level that is immediately affected. The best opportunity for dismantling administrative obstacles and bureaucracy is when we take a chance on local democratic government as an advocate for renewable energy (when, as Willy Brandt might have said, we 'dare more local energy democracy') – up to and including the awarding of new water rights for small hydropower plants. Even then, nevertheless, there would have to be some possibility for appealing arbitrary negative decisions on a case-by-case basis. Owing to the importance that the shift to renewable energy has for society overall, arbitration offices need to be set up at the regional level that will conduct their hearings publicly.

In addition, at the level of national government, provision needs to be made for siting spaces for wind power use in which a general building permit will be valid, such as priority tracts alongside major highways and railroad lines. This will open up a major potential for installation spaces.

What applies to landscape use and design also applies to architecture and city planning – to the path from the 'Fossil City' to the 'Solar City'. This fossil-to-solar pathway means a lot more than installing solar roofs and facades. It is an opportunity to overcome the functional partitioning that has contributed to the disintegration of cities, because emissions-free energy production will make it so that residential, industrial and recreational areas no longer have to be sealed off from each other. It means basing land use and construction planning on the opportunities provided by each type of renewable energy in context, and thereby using nature's potential – for electricity production, heating and cooling, lighting and shade – more systematically in cities. In short, it means recognizing the sun and its immediate 'products' as 'cultural components' (Jürgen Claus) and, to this end, drawing lessons from the extensive instructional material provided by the cultural history of building. The impetus for this has already been elaborated by Sophia and Stefan Behling in their book *Sol Power* about the history of solar architecture, by Thomas Herzog in his 'European Charter' for *Solar Energy in Architecture and Urban Planning*, and by Peter Droege in *Renewable Energy and the City* – and some of the many and varied practical methods for solar urban design were demonstrated at the international conference, The City As Solar Power Station.[19]

Ninth maxim: Overcoming the knowledge deficit

Shortcomings in science and educational policy with respect to renewable energy need to be quickly remedied, especially in the agricultural, natural and technological sciences, in architecture and in economics, and in the fields of general and occupational education and public research. The problem is so urgent that we cannot wait until a new generation has grown up. The catchwords for initiatives like this include such things as the establishment of post-graduate studies in renewable energy, correspondence courses, continuing education and advanced training course offerings, teaching materials, and a great deal more. Renewable energy represents a new paradigm – and so it lays the foundation for a new school of thought.

To build this new foundation with the help of scholarly institutions is an endeavour in the best scientific tradition. New schools of thought require new scientific and research institutions; they do not take shape on the basis of established organizations. To date, Germany's major research centres have successfully defended the priority of nuclear research within the larger field of energy research, in spite of resolutions to the contrary from the legislature and the government that provide these centres with their funding. So long as there is no institutional breakthrough to renewable energy in public scientific organizations, nuclear energy will always try to stage a comeback.

This shift in priorities for research policy is long overdue. Although it does not come from conventional scientific authorities, this new direction in research can depend on support from a new, already motivated generation (as well as on yet another new generation that is coming along and capable of being motivated even more) – with R&D prospects like those described by Helmut Tributsch from Berlin's Hahn-Meitner-Institut.[20] The opportunities range from new solar cell materials, which are a thousand times thinner and can achieve a solar energy yield of up to 68 per cent, to completely new heat storage technologies that are copied from nature; from concentrator technologies to new wind power technologies that can also be employed in cities; and all the way to extensive research into natural plant material that is suitable to the demand for energy and raw materials. Not only is there no task more important for science and research; there is also none more fascinating. Any 'innovation policy' that ignores this simply looks old-fashioned.

Tenth maxim: The counter-remedy to the impending global depression – jump-starting the business cycle with renewable energy

The Russian economist Nikolai Kondratieff described how new technologies that quickly turn into mass products (like railways, cars, electronic devices, television) spawn a 'long wave' in the business cycle from which new industrial branches, together with new jobs, emerge. Only computer technology has not had a comparable impact, because its deployment had drastic consequences for jobs in the industrial and service sectors. This means that, for the first time, highly developed national economies confront a situation in which economic growth does not correspond any longer with job growth.

Mobilizing renewable energy could give rise to the world's first 'Super-Kondratieff', a long wave in the business cycle that would carry the economy into an entirely new structure. In contrast to conventional energy's inevitably rising costs, including its growing social welfare costs, renewable energy's continuously declining costs, including its falling social welfare costs, could lead to a sustainable economic upswing that mobilizes domestic markets and is not dependent on the behaviour of global corporations. An action programme built on Maxims Five and Seven could set so many different kinds of private investment in motion that the resulting economic upswing, in spite of the fiscal outlays that would be needed to fund incentives, would also redound to the benefit of the public purse. This kind of fundamental decision for a new economic strategy would not involve any 'imponderable risks, but only opportunities', as Olaf Preuss, the editor of *Financial Times Deutschland*, has emphasized in his book *Energie für die Zukunft* (Energy for the Future).[21] It is a matter of 'jump-starting the business cycle' by using renewable energy, as a counter-remedy to the impending global recession now looming because of the bottlenecks and price hikes in world oil supplies constantly characterized as portentous writing on the wall by global business journals like the *Financial Times*, *Wall Street Journal* and *The Economist*. In his latest publication *Winning the Oil Endgame*, Amory B. Lovins has also described this challenge,[22] for which no economic policy to date has been prepared.

Autonomy of action

Many will doubt that the renewability of politics described here is realistic. There are many empirical reasons for such doubts in light of the arduous tug-of-war over renewable energy. The strategies aiming at autonomous action, the approaches to activating society, and the maxims for political action outlined above represent the optimum that is conceivable and possible for a rapid acceleration in the shift to renewable energy. None of these approaches will be pursued everywhere and at the same time. But the more of them we adopt, the more we can expect to see amplification effects that mutually reinforce each other, and the faster renewable energy will actively evolve.

It is appropriate, moreover, to address a counter-question to the doubters: how much realism is there among those who imagine that we can keep providing our societies with energy if we do not undertake a rapid shift to the renewable kind? Those who say this are really advocating plans that are illusory. Under current circumstances they wield a lot of power, decisively more power than do the champions of renewable energy. But because of their unrealistic plans they no longer have any power over what matters: control over the conditions that produce energy crises in the first place.

Yet although the plans favoured by the traditional energy business are illusory, it is a sector that has a clarity of vision about its goal – regaining control over investments that are critical for the development of energy economics overall – as well as the tenacity, persistence and enormous organizational clout to sustain this conflict for control. In addition to the public organizational privilege enjoyed by nuclear energy because of agencies like IAEA and EURATOM, nuclear energy's champions are also organized more tightly than the diffuse spectrum of actors advocating renewable energy. This was documented by Brussels attorney Dörte Fouquet in her case study 'Nuclear renaissance'; the World Nuclear Association counts everyone involved in the nuclear technology industry worldwide, without exception, as one of its members, including public agencies for nuclear energy. FORATOM, the trade organization of the nuclear industry headquartered in Brussels, has 800 firms as members. The European Nuclear Society claims 20,000 members. In 2005 alone, it held 60 conferences. Its Nuclear Information Committee Europe (NICE) coaches the media quietly but intensively.[23]

The champions of renewable energy, by contrast, need to achieve greater clarity about their strategic goals, and to improve their organizational clout considerably. Awareness of how important this can be is less developed among the many organizations and businesses involved in renewable energy than it is in the established energy business. Without concentrating their forces, those on the side of renewable energy will hardly be able to stand the test of their conflict with the nuclear lobby – and this will be just as hard at the level of international institutions so long as international governmental organizations for nuclear and fossil energy confront little more than a ragtag bunch of international networks for renewable energy that are minimally funded by contributing governments. This is 'a policy without a network', as the German member of parliament Hans-Josef Fell put it; we are dealing with activities governments use as alibis to avoid the resoluteness they should apply to strengthening renewable energy internationally, including in an institutional capacity.[24]

Recent developments in Germany have shown what autonomy-conscious and autonomy-promoting action for renewable energy can achieve. The question posed so often all over the world as to what made this development possible can be answered in four sentences. First, the initiative to write laws making the breakthrough possible came not from the executive branch of government but from the parliament, where a majority was garnered for this legislation. Second, the right plan was pursued and defended against every attack, whether it came from Germany's Federal Constitutional Court or the European Court of Justice. Third, public backing was the most important kind of support; it emerged because the conflict was carried out in public, so that it aroused attention broadly, and because the fundamental and general value of renewable energy was accentuated by its champions. Fourth and finally, initial successes and the new economic opportunities that arose as a result made it possible to build new alliances – in a constellation that had never existed before. This constellation comprised not only renewable energy and environmental organizations, but also the Federal Association of Medium-Sized Business, the German Farmers' Association, and the Metalworkers' and Construction Workers' Unions.

The debates about renewable energy in Germany that exist because of this successful breakthrough have all the features of an international proxy war. There is no need and no political space for both things at the same time – for the perpetuation of conventional energy by building big new power plants and for the further expansion of renewable energy. It is ultimately a zero-sum game. The conflict has become more explosive because both poles of energy provision – the electricity corporations and the sponsors of renewable energy – emerged stronger from developments that took place in energy policy and the economy since 2000, and also because both developments were promoted by politics at the same time.

The conflict embedded here is bound to overshadow all previous conflicts over renewable energy. If the electricity corporations do not succeed soon in stopping the expansion of renewable energy at the level of political action, they will be forced to shelve their own plans for expansion. That it why today's conflict about the Renewable Energy Sources Act is already a conflict about a historical turning point, in spite of the relatively small share of renewable energy in Germany's electricity supply. How this conflict turns out will decide what strategies for renewable energy are adopted in other countries. Making renewable energy the foundation for a sustainable future is a priority for the human condition. This priority calls for a kind of renewable energy that is intellectual and spiritual – as a political condition.

References

1 Marcia Pally, *Lob der Kritik: Warum die Demokratie nicht auf ihren Kern verzichten darf* (Berlin: Berlin-Verl, 2003), p319

2 Ferdinand Tönnies, *Community and Society* (East Lansing, MI: Michigan State University Press, 1975), p145

3 Lothar Schäfer, *Bacon-Projekt: Von der Erkenntnis, Nutzung und Schonung der Natur* (Frankfurt: Suhrkamp Verlag, 1993), p126

4 Otfried Höffe, *Demokratie im Zeitalter der Globalisierung* (Munich: C. H. Beck, 1999), p139

5 Udo E.Simonis, *Energieoption und Waldoption – der technische und der natürliche Weg zum Klimaschutz* (October 2004, available at http://skylla.wz-berlin.de/pdf/2004/p04-008.pdf)

6 Ulrich Kelber, 'Das Top-Runner Programm', *Solarzeitalter* 1/2005, p32 et seq

7 Gert Apfelstedt, 'Ökoenergie-Pflichtbenutzung und Warenverkehrsrecht', *Zeitschrift für Neues Energierecht (ZNER)* 1/2001, p2 et seq

8 John Rawls, *A Theory of Justice* (Oxford: Oxford University Press, 1972), p14

9 Nina Scheer, 'Der Vorrang des Personenwerts vor dem Sachwert', in Joachim Bücheler (ed.), *Praktische Visionen* (Bochum: Ponte Press, 2004), p52

10 Franz Alt, *Der ökologische Jesus: Vertrauen in die Schöpfung* (Munich: Riemann, 1999), p29

11 Carl Amery, *Global Exit: Die Kirchen und die Totale Markt* (Munich: Luchterhand, 2002)

12 Hari Sharan, 'Implementing a new energy paradigm', lecture at United Nations High Level Panel 'Re-Thinking the Energy Paradigm', 21 April 2005, Geneva

13 Christiane Grefe, 'Die neue Dreifelderwirtschaft', *Die Zeit* 30/2002
14 Hermann Fischer, 'Land- und Forstwirte als Grundstoffproduzenten' in EUROSOLAR (ed.) *Der Landwirt als Energie- und Rohstoffwirt. Produktion – Ausbildung – Arbeitsplätze* (Bonn: EUROSOLAR, 2002), p57 et seq
15 Hermann Scheer, *The Solar Economy* (London: Earthscan, 2002), p316 et seq
16 Joseph A. Schumpeter, *Kapitalismus, Sozialismus und Demokratie* (Bern: Francke, 1950), p148
17 Cited by Peter Hoffmann, *Tomorrow's Energy* (Cambridge, MA: MIT Press, 2001), pp260 et seq and p281
18 Philip Bobbitt, *The Shield of Achilles: War, Peace and the Course of History* (New York: Knopf, 2002), p468 et seq
19 Jürgen Claus, *Kulturelement Sonne: Das solare Zeitalter* (Zurich: Edition Interfrom, 1997); Sophia Behling and Stefan Behling with Bruno Schindler, *Sol Power: The Evolution of Solar Architecture* (Munich and New York: Prestel, 1996); Thomas Herzog, Norbert Kaiser and Michael Volz, *Solar Energy in Architecture and Urban Planning* (Munich and New York: Prestel, 1996); Peter Droege, *Renewable Energy and the City* (2004, available at www.world-council-for-renewable-energy.org/downloads/WCRE-City_paper.pdf); EUROSOLAR (ed.), *The City – A Solar Power Station: The State of the Art of Solar Building and Ecological Urban Planning* (Bonn: EUROSOLAR, 6th European Conference, Solar Energy in Architecture and Urban Planning, 2000)
20 Helmut Tributsch, 'Der Kardinalfehler der vernachlässigten Solarenergieforschung', *Solarzeitalter* 4/2000, p15 et seq
21 Olaf Preuss, *Energie für die Zukunft* (Wiesbaden: Gabler Verlag/Financial Times Deutschland, 2005), p18
22 Amory B. Lovins, E. Kyle Datta, Odd-Even Bustnes, Jonathan G. Koomey and Nathan J. Glasgow, *Winning the Oil Endgame: Innovation for Profits, Jobs and Security* (Snowmass, CO: Rocky Mountain Institute, 2004)
23 Dörte Fouquet, 'Nuclear renaissance: Case study' (unpublished manuscript, Brussels, 2005)
24 Hans-Josef Fell, 'Politik ohne Netz. Das internationale Netzwerk für erneuerbare Energien', *Solarzeitalter* 1/2005, p35 et seq

Index